LATIN AMERICAN PHILOSOPHY
IN THE TWENTIETH CENTURY

Frontiers of Philosophy

Peter H. Hare, Series Editor

Advisory Board

LATIN AMERICAN PHILOSOPHY

IN THE TWENTIETH CENTURY

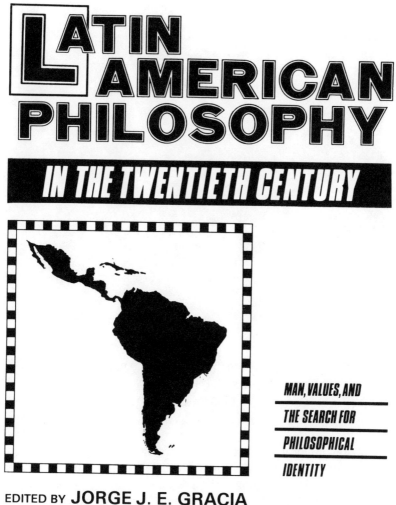

MAN, VALUES, AND
THE SEARCH FOR
PHILOSOPHICAL
IDENTITY

EDITED BY JORGE J. E. GRACIA

With translations by William Cooper, Francis M. Myers,
Iván Jaksić, Donald L. Schmidt, Charles Schofield, and Jorge J. E. Gracia

PROMETHEUS BOOKS
700 East Amherst St., Buffalo, New York 14215

Risieri Frondizi and Francis M. Myers,
in memoriam

Published 1986 by Prometheus Books
700 East Amherst Street, Buffalo, New York 14215
Copyright © 1986 by Jorge J. E. Gracia
All Rights Reserved

Library of Congress Cataloging-in-Publication Data

Latin American philosophy in the twentieth century.

(Frontiers of philosophy)
1. Philosophy. 2. Philosophy, Latin American.
I. Gracia, Jorge J. E. II. Series.
B29.L295 1986   199'.8   86-91551
ISBN 0-87975-333-1

Contents

6   Contents

PART THREE: THE SEARCH FOR PHILOSOPHICAL IDENTITY

Preface

A collection of philosophical readings is justified if it responds to a need. Its quality, however, depends on the authors and texts that it includes and on the help it may provide for better understanding the issues on which the collection is built.

That the English-speaking world needs a representative collection of readings from Latin American philosophers is beyond dispute: only two such collections exist. The first one, entitled *Contemporary Latin American Philosophy* (1954), is a translation of an anthology originally published by Aníbal Sánchez Reulet in 1949. Apart from the fact that the book has been out of print for almost thirty years, it should be clear from its year of publication that it is dated. The other collection is my recently published *Philosophical Analysis in Latin America* (1984), but this is a specialized text that deals only with the impact of the analytic movement in Latin America. Given the growing importance of Latin America in the world today, some account must be taken of the philosophic thought of the area. American scholars have already taken note of the so-called "boom" of the Latin American novel and of the flowering of other forms of literature, but they have for the most part neglected the development of philosophical thought in the region.

The preparation of a truly representative collection of readings from Latin American philosophers presents serious difficulties. Generally, Latin American thinkers have an extensive list of publications. In several cases, their collected works extend to more than twenty volumes. Other difficulties are the heterogeneity of the themes in their works, and the uneven quality of the writings. These characteristics stem largely from the variety of responsibilities these authors have assumed and the demands of the activities in which they have engaged. Furthermore, part of their writings is scattered in short-lived journals that are difficult to locate. The abundance, diversity, and difficult access of the material are bewildering to one who does not know where to begin. Perhaps this explains why Latin American authors are more often mentioned than read, and why we lack a representative collection of readings in English.

The present collection has been gathered from the works of only major Latin American thinkers and is meant as a guide in the study of their thought. It aims to be a point of departure rather than an end, encouraging careful study of the works from which the texts are taken, and supporting the efforts of those who wish to continue the study of its basic themes.

The selections included here are limited to twentieth-century authors. Such a restriction could be justified as conventional procedure, but there is a more important reason for it: the preceding centuries provide few authentic philosophical works. Indeed, pressured by more urgent needs, Latin America did not often confront the study of philosophy for its own sake until the beginning of this century.

In order to avoid a general and disconnected work, the collection has been focused on three fundamental and concrete problems, thereby maintaining a certain unity. This approach has the added advantage of making it possible to retain a general perspective while avoiding the risk of superficiality. The three themes in question were chosen not only because of the special attention they have received from Latin American thinkers, but also because these issues—the interpretations of man and value and the search for philosophical identity—often lay bare the root and intellectual orientation of Latin American culture. Owing to these thematic limitations, several thinkers of significant stature, such as Mariátegui, Ardao, Larroyo, and others, have been omitted, but this shortcoming seemed small if compared with the advantages of following the chosen procedure.

The authors' importance has been one of the fundamental basis for their inclusion. This importance was measured by the theoretical quality of their ideas and the influence they have had in Latin America. Space limitations, however, demanded the exclusion of many pages from each author, exclusions that were neither easy nor pleasant. The pages presented here were selected from thousands studied over a period of years. The choice, therefore, was neither hasty nor uninformed.

There were also other considerations that determined the inclusion of some authors and texts and the exclusion of others. For example, thinkers such as Octavio Paz, José Enrique Rodó, Jackson de Figuereido, and José Pereira de Graza Aranha were left out because of the purely philosophical nature of the collection and their more literary approach to ideas. None of the Spanish *trasterrados* (Xirau, Gaos, Nicol, García Bacca, Ferrater Mora, Recaséns Siches, and so many others) who have contributed so much to the development of philosophy in Latin America have been included. Members of the analytic movement, such as Carrió, Bunge, and Castañeda, have not been anthologized because their work is already known and available in the United States, either directly or through the collection of papers referred to earlier. Latin American Thomists like Derisi and Amoroso Lima have also been excluded because their philosophical position does not differ significantly from that of Thomists elsewhere. Finally, space restrictions have made it impossible to include selections from such important figures as Delgado, Vasallo, Pucciarelli, Rougés, Alberini, Llambías de Azevedo, García Maynez, Ferreira da Silva, Millas, Molina, Mayz Vallenilla, Schwartzmann, Dussel, and many others who have made important contributions to philosophical anthropology, axiology, and the issue of philosophical identity in Latin America.

This work is introduced by an essay on contemporary Latin American philosophy. Each of the three parts into which the book is divided is also introduced by an essay, the first on man, the second on value, and the third on the search for philosophical identity. Each essay summarizes the more prevalent approaches to its theme and introduces the thought of the philosophers whose writings have been included. A brief biographical sketch precedes each author's text. Added at the end is a select bibliography that is meant to provide helpful information and also to serve as a guide for future research; it should not be regarded as exhaustive.

The selections included in the first two parts were made in collaboration with Risieri Frondizi, who was the senior editor of a more extensive collection, published in Spanish and Portuguese, entitled *El hombre y los valores en la filosofía latinoamericana del siglo XX* (1975; reprint, México: Fondo de Cultura Económica, 1980). The introductory essays to those parts as well as the biographical sketches of the various authors contained therein have also been translated from that edition, although modifications were introduced in order to adapt them to the new context. The authors responsible for the introduction and sketches are identified at the end of each by their initials. The textual selections follow the order of the discussion in the introductory essays. Square brackets indicate additions made by the editor or the translators.

The institutions and persons who have provided assistance in the preparation of this work are numerous. To each of them I would like to express my profound appreciation, but limitations of space prevent me from doing so explicitly in every case. I am particularly grateful, however, to Mrs. Josefina Barbat de Frondizi for her permission to print Frondizi's introductory essays and for allowing me to edit them to fit the present context. I am also grateful to the translators of the texts, who spent long hours at their difficult task. It should be added here that William Cooper is responsible for all the translations, including those of the introductions and biographical sketches, except for those of the texts from Frondizi, Korn, Deústua, Reale, Zea, Roig, Bondy, the introduction to the third part, and the biographical sketches to Zea, Roig, and Bondy. The introduction and biographical sketches of the third part and the Frondizi selection in the first part were written in English by their respective authors. The texts from Korn and Deústua were translated by Francis Myers, the text from Zea by Iván

Jaksić, the text from Bondy by Donald L. Schmidt, the text from Roig by Charles Schofield, and the text from Reale by Jorge J. E. Gracia. Finally, I would also like to thank the authors and publishers who generously granted permission for the publication of the texts included here.

The Editor
1985

Introduction

Major trends in contemporary Latin American philosophy emerged from the reaction against positivism.

Excepting scholasticism, positivism is the most widespread and deeply rooted philosophical movement in Latin America. The depth of its impact was due to historical factors: it arrived at the proper time and it addressed the needs of that age. This positive philosophy, developed by the Frenchman Auguste Comte (1793–1857), attempted to develop a rigorous, systematic understanding of man both as an individual and as a social being. Comte sought to base his understanding on experience and reason and to let it serve as a means for solving social problems. To achieve this objective, he sought to impose upon the study of human affairs the methods, criteria of truth, and conceptual precision that had borne such excellent results in the natural sciences. He coined the term "sociology" to designate the new science of social phenomena and gave special attention to its development. He maintained that the sciences were characterized by an undeniable unity and could be arranged in hierarchical order, according to the degree of mathematization they would allow, with physics as the fundamental science and sociology the less scientific. Sociology, the newest and most complex of the sciences, required much empirical investigation before its discoveries could be reduced to mathematically formulated laws.

Comte was not moved by a mere desire to know. Knowledge was a servant of action and should lead to the solution of concrete problems. This practical aspect, perhaps, was one of the most captivating for Latin Americans, who desired to overcome anarchy, eradicate misery and disease, and place their own countries on the path of progress.

This, however, was not the only reason for the wide acceptance that positivism experienced. There were also reasons of a strictly cultural and theoretical nature. Latin America had been nurtured in scholasticism and consequently, the sciences of man were in a deplorable state. Conceptual and terminological vagueness, irresponsible speculation, as well as unfounded and archaic dogmatism were predominant characteristics. Positivism, however, brought principles based on experience and logical rigor, and offered

13

the assurance of constant progress, insisting that its claims rested on proved knowledge. There would be no more fruitless theories, idle speculations, and vain attempts. At last a sound procedure had been found that, although it required great effort, would lead to the gradual solution of Latin America's problems.

Furthermore, positivism benefited greatly from the prestige of science. It was then natural that scientific prestige should be transferred to positivism, since the latter proposed to limit its methods to those used by science. It was believed that a new era had begun in which scientific study would make it possible to find the causes of social evils and to eliminate them, just as medicine had begun to eradicate endemic diseases.

Comte's law of the three stages also captured the attention of many Latin Americans. This law claims that humanity passes through three stages, the theological, the metaphysical, and the scientific or positive. In the theological stage, the interpretation of reality is founded on prejudices and superstitions. The metaphysical stage is dominated by speculation in which facts are either ignored or are not given adequate attention. Finally, in the positive stage, speculation is replaced by the confirmation of facts and their rigorous interpretation, and knowledge is founded upon experience.

Latin American thinkers applied this law to the history of their own countries and believed the law was confirmed by experience. An example of this attitude is found in the *Civic Oration* that was delivered by the Mexican positivist Gabino Barreda in Guanajuato (1867), in which he refers to and applies the ideas of Comte. Having this oration in mind, President Benito Juárez named Barreda as a member of a committee to draft the law, approved on December 2, 1867, that gave birth to public education in Mexico. The fact that another great teacher, Justo Sierra, succeeded to Barreda's position and continued to apply positivist principles to educational policy, explains the strength that this perspective acquired and its predominance in Mexico until the fall of the dictator Porfirio Díaz in 1911. Positivism was the official philosophy during the twenty-seven years of the dictatorship of General Díaz, whose government was guided by Comte's slogan "Order and progress."

The chaos and backwardness that prevailed in some Latin American countries explain why positivist ideas captivated the minds of so many thinkers and politicians.

Positivism made a significant impact in Brazil, where the positivist slogan, "Order and progress," was incorporated into the Brazilian flag and into the attitude of its political leaders.

Positivism also exercised a strong influence on Argentine education, especially in the "School of Paraná," where Scalabrini, Ferreira, Herrera, and others provided leadership. This prestige was further enhanced by the tenaciousness of José Ingenieros and his works, by the *Revista de Filosofía,* and by the Cultura Argentina publishing house.

As is natural, positivism developed its own distinctive mode in each country. Ideas acquired new life in crossing the Atlantic, and they developed according to the sociocultural ecology of each country. One should also keep in mind that Latin American positivism was nurtured principally by two sources, Comte and Herbert Spencer (1820–1903). The latter, a proponent of evolutionism, was considered a positivist in Spanish America, as occurred also with John Stuart Mill. However, Comte and Spencer differed in their intellectual orientation, one being French and the other English, and the quality of the positivism in any given country was affected by the degree to which one or the other of these men exercised the predominant influence. Generally, the ideas of Comte had a greater weight in Brazil, Mexico, and Chile, whereas Spencer received greater attention in Argentina, Uruguay, and Cuba. On some occasions, due to political considerations, the influence within each country varied, as in the case of Cuba, where Enrique José Varona rejected Comte's ideas because they did not favor the emancipation of that country from Spanish rule and instead gave preference to Spencer and his idea of liberty.

In spite of these and many other national differences, one can speak of Latin American positivism as a unified, yet evolving trend in which the influence of Comte is greater toward the beginning, and that of Spencer predominates toward the end. John Stuart Mill's influence was a subsequent and minor development.

Due to the inflexibility of Comte's ideas, the reactionary attitude in the final period of his life when he founded the "religion of humanity," and his approval of the coup d'état of Napoleon III in 1851, Comte's thought was rejected more violently than was Spencer's.

The general decline of positivism stems from several factors. National distinctions, of course, must be taken into consideration since the predominance of any particular cause varies from country to country. Although there were causes common to all Latin America, the reaction against positivism in each country emerged from a complex national situation, rooted in cultural, political, and philosophical conditions that make it difficult to isolate specific factors. Thus it is best to speak of predominant influences.

The first general cause is the deception that Latin American intellectuals experienced when reality did not measure up to positivism's promises and aspirations. Immediate and assured results were promised and anxiously awaited, but progress was slow and uncertain. To uphold the general principles and criteria that should be used in the study of social problems is one thing, but it is quite a different matter to develop a specific form of knowing in which an effective scientific procedure is applied in order to solve the concrete problems of a country.

Stark reality shattered many illusions. It soon became evident that divesting oneself of traditional prejudices was not sufficient. The ideal of a scientific knowledge of social reality, which had been converted into an idol, began to crumble in the face of difficulties, and the initial, naive optimism gave way to corroding pessimism.

Comte himself did not satisfy the expectations he had awakened and, to make matters worse, no thinkers who measured up to his standards emerged in Latin America. The majority were content to repeat the ideas of the master without being able to apply them to the reality in which they lived. Philosophical theory cannot be converted into dogma; rather, it needs a continuing creative direction since its application to reality is not a routine, mechanical task. The complexity of the reality surpasses theoretical schemes.

Another general reason is the deterioration Comte's positivism suffered in his own country. With no outstanding disciples, since Littre and Laffite were not capable of building on the ideas of their master, positivism began to lose its nerve when Comte died in 1857. In time, new critical ideas, such as those of Boutroux and Bergson, appeared in France and eventually they were used to support Latin American revolt.

One of the issues about which the dissatisfaction was most profound was liberty. Opposition of different kinds united around this issue to repudiate positivism's empirical stance. Some of the opposition was philosophically bent, some was political, and some was aesthetically oriented.

The indiscriminate application of the principle of causality to every existing thing led positivism to deny freedom to man. Psychology was a biological science and the supposed freedom of choice or creation was felled by a scientific guillotine. The Argentine José Ingenieros carried this point of positivist doctrine to an extreme.

Theoretical objections to determinism acquire a great momentum in the moral realm. No one can be responsible for an act if it is determined, the critics of positivism claimed, influenced perhaps by their reading of Kant. Fires, hurricanes, and epidemics are not responsible for the deaths they cause. But men are indeed responsible because they have free choice; they are masters of their conduct and thus deserve punishment or praise. If the conduct of men were determined by causes or factors alien to their will, they would deserve neither praise nor punishment. Furthermore, suffering, disciplined effort, the struggle against sin, and other noble actions would lose their meaning. It was natural for the works of Henri Bergson to be received with great enthusiasm in Spanish America, on the basis of his refutation of determinism and his defense of liberty.

Another reason for the Latin American rejection of determinism was the implicit denial of aesthetic creation. Because they are gifted with a great aesthetic sensitivity and creative capacity, as is evident in the work of Rubén Darío and many other writers and artists, Latin Americans could not accept a mechanical explanation of the creative process. And many refuted positivism because it denied or was unable to explain creation in art, as is the case with Deústua.

However, the principal reason for the rejection of positivism with respect to freedom came from the political realm. In some instances, as in Mexico, positivism was associated with a dictatorship that had been overthrown; in others, Cuba, for example, it supported the colonial status quo over against the possibility of independence to which many aspired. In all the countries, suffering, first under Spanish oppression and then under a succession of dictators, had been too extensive for anyone to be ready to set freedom aside. Indeed, freedom had become the battle flag. If positivism did not make room for freedom, then positivism must be abandoned.

Alejandro Korn succinctly expresses the state of mind of the men of that time when he writes, "We cannot accept a philosophy which obliterates human personality, reduces its unity to a biological phenomenon, denies it a right to forge its own values and ideals and prohibits thought from transcending the limits of empirical existence."[1]

In addition to the reasons discussed above, a theoretical reason also influenced tendencies to reject positivism. The distinction, developed by Windelband, Dilthey, Rickert, and others, between the sciences of nature and those of the spirit became significant and influential and opened up the possibility of limiting positivism to its own forte, i.e., the physical and biological realm. In time, a new approach to the study of human problems emerged, which emphasized value, purpose, novelty, and creation over the natural realm. Thus, reality was divided in two and each part corresponded to a special type of knowledge. The establishment of these forms of knowledge, that of the subjective spirit and of the objective spirit or culture, was a major concern of the generation following the positivists, and the distinction between these two types of science persists even yet. Sciences of the spirit (*Geisteswissenschaften*) were thus separated from positivist domination and began to develop independently.

The dissatisfaction in Latin America and the ideas coming from Europe hastened the search for new approaches. In this search, appeal was made to political aspirations as well as to aesthetic and religious experience, although the spirit of religiosity, perhaps, played a more important role than religion. Metaphysical preoccupation, suppressed by positivism, experienced a rebirth. General dissatisfaction was encouraged by philosophers such as Boutroux, Bergson, and Croce, who had overcome positivism in Europe and were traveling new paths.

In each country, the reaction against positivism took on a characteristic expression, although the dissatisfaction itself was fairly uniform throughout Latin America. Mexico, however, gave first expression to the dissatisfaction and shaped it into a unique series of events. With the fall of the dictatorship of Porfirio Díaz in 1911, positivism also fell, for its foundations already had been undermined.

In 1909, a group of young men who later acquired well-deserved renown in the field of philosophy and letters founded the "Ateneo de la Juventud" (Atheneum of Youth). They studied the classics, especially Plato and Kant, and contemporary philosophers who had rejected positivism, such as Bergson and Croce. The influence of Nietzsche and Schopenhauer, who had thrown their weight against the narrow scientistic emphasis of positivism, was also felt. Following these studies lectures were given in which positivist doctrine was roundly criticized and new ideas were proposed. Of that group two men are especially well known as philosophers, Antonio Caso and José Vasconcelos. Selections from their writings are included in this book.

In Argentina the struggle against positivism was quite different. In the first place, positivism was not involved in any political movements. Furthermore, positivism had had an effective role in the development of educational institutions and, through José Ingenieros, had acquired renown in scientific and philosophical circles.

The two most distinguished figures in the struggle against positivism in Argentina were Alejandro Korn and Coriolano Alberini. Perhaps the latter, although less gifted in creative ability, had more influence than the former in casting it out of official teaching programs. A caustic spirit, Alberini allowed no truce with positivism in the University of Buenos Aires, an institution of which he was dean of the faculty of philosophy and letters on several occasions. Korn was less aggressive and fought positivism through his own sound, original philosophical position. In addition to his writings, his major contribution was encouraging the formation of a group of students whose philosophical orientation was foreign to positivism. Francisco Romero, who was introduced to philosophy through reading Spencer, felt the influence of the group that surrounded Korn. Thus in Argentina, positivism was overcome through the development of a different philosophical orientation rather than through sharp polemics.

Similar reactions are found in other Latin American countries. Metaphysics, heatedly attacked by Comte, returned to the fold. In some cases, this was due to the renewal of the classical concerns of Christian philosophy, and in others, to the rise of philosophical speculation in contemporary German thought.

PHILOSOPHICAL THOUGHT AFTER POSITIVISM

In the aftermath of positivism, four stages have emerged in the development of philosophical thought. The first is referred to as the stage of the "founders." These were the men who first rejected positivist thought although, in some cases, they are also included in the ranks of the positivists, since this was the philosophical position they first espoused. The "founders" were Deústua in Peru, Caso and Vasconcelos in Mexico, Korn in Argentina, Vaz

Ferreira in Uruguay, and Farias Brito in Brazil. Dependent first on French philosophers such as Boutroux and Bergson, and later on German philosophers—Nietzsche, Husserl, Dilthey, Heidegger, Scheler, Hartmann, Jaspers—as well as the Italian Croce, the "founders" developed a new orientation in Latin American philosophy. They did not form a school nor did they propose to do so, but they did formulate new approaches and develop new attitudes and methods of work.

The generation following the "founders" continued their thrust, but it was free from the polemic with positivism that had influenced the formation of that founding generation. Francisco Romero is the major figure here, and he, together with Ramos and Astrada, is included in the present work. This generation is characterized by an intense interest in the problem of man and by the influence of historicism, phenomenology, and existentialism.

The third stage emerges with the work of those born around the year 1910. In this group, the influence of German thought continues to be predominant, in some cases because of studies in that country—García Maynez and Llambías de Acevedo, for example—and in others, because of the influence of exiled Spanish philosophers such as José Gaos and Joaquín Xirau.

The prominent figures in the second stage were men whose professional preparation was not in philosophy but in law, medicine, or military science. In this third stage, however, almost all have pursued university studies in philosophy. The development of the discipline becomes more professional and technical, although less dramatic, but it is also more responsible and specialized. None attempts to elaborate a complete philosophical system, such as that of Vasconcelos with its metaphysics, ethics, and aesthetics. Instead of great encompassing works, specialized monographs were the rule. Indeed, a certain sparseness stemming from self-critical attitudes characterized their publications. At the same time, there was an increase in the number of those who studied philosophy, and interest in the field became broader as new departments were established in the universities that lacked them, such as those in Tucumán and Córdoba in Argentina, the Central University in Venezuela, as well as universities in Colombia and Panama. This tendency has continued to the present. The list of thinkers who belong to this generation is very long. Four of them are represented here: Reale, Zea, Miró Quesada, and Frondizi.

The fourth generation is the most active. Those from the first and second generations whose works appear in this collection have died. Those from the third generation [except for Frondizi who died in 1983] continue their intellectual labor, which has been clearly defined in their published work. Many of those in the fourth generation, however, are still developing their philosophical perspective and their principal works have not yet appeared. Hence, only selections from two authors have heen included here: Augusto Salazar Bondy and Arturo Roig.

At this point, the perspective becomes more complex due to the increasing number of persons who seriously pursue philosophical studies and the greater diversification in interests and currents of thought. To be sure, the traditional interest in German philosophy has remained; however, contemporary British and American influences, such as those of Alfred North Whitehead, Bertrand Russell, C. I. Lewis, R. B. Perry, and John Dewey, have had an increasingly significant impact since Frondizi began to introduce them after he returned in 1936 from his studies at Harvard. In more recent years, attention has been focused on logical positivism and analytic philosophy. Examples of this interest are the journal *Crítica,* published in Mexico, and the Argentine Society for Philosophical Analysis. Serious studies in the philosophy of science began under the contagious enthusiasm of Mario Bunge and continued with other scientists committed to philosophical study. This period also reflects a resurgent interest in Marxism, although no single person is outstanding as a leader of the group. The most significant influences of this period are Jean-Paul Sartre, in his existentialist as well as Marxist periods, Merleau-Ponty, and the analytical school.

These four stages overlap in many cases because they do not reflect movements but individuals who respond to their own interests. A man such as Deústua, who lived to be ninety-six years old, developed beyond his positivist orientations and made significant contributions in both the first and second stages. The work of others, such as Romero and Astrada, permits them to function in different stages also. Some of the philosophers, with the passage of time, changed and developed their views, as in the case of Astrada, who turned from existentialism, as found in Heidegger, to Marxism and thus is included in a more contemporary group.

It would be vain indeed to summarize the thought of those mentioned above. And, in any case, the more important figures in this book speak through selections from their own works, with each selection preceded by a brief introduction to aid in understanding the text.

Rather than summarize philosophical views, we would prefer to delineate the principal characteristics of Latin American philosophy of this century taken as a whole, recognizing, of course, that all of these characteristics cannot be applied in the same sense to each of the philosophers.

The first characteristic focuses on the background of the men under consideration. Most of them engaged in extensive studies in the humanities and even those who had formal training in biology are well grounded in literature, as reflected in their poetry and in their knowledge of contemporary and classical literary works, as is the case of Korn. This humanistic background proves to be an asset as well as a liability. The asset is the breadth of interest and the liability is a lack of empirical grounding, logical rigor, and conceptual and terminological precision. Generally, Latin American philosophers are competent writers. Korn, Caso, and Romero are good examples. At least they are concerned with the form of their expression,[2] a concern that occurs only exceptionally in North American philosophers. Along these lines, Latin Americans have followed the tradition of continental Europe, and in more recent times, that of Spain, with special reference to Unamuno and Ortega.

The second characteristic is a concern for social and political problems. Philosophy is not pursued as a disinterested form of knowledge, but as an orienting guide for individual and social conduct. Thus, its study is not neutral but passionate, because different philosophical views lead to different life styles. Man and his proper destiny are the issues to be decided and it is difficult to remain objective when the meaning of life is at stake. The excessive passion and polemic characteristic of Latin American philosophy is not due, as some would believe, to an overindulgence in emotion but to the type of problem with which it is concerned. The North American philosopher maintains his serenity because he studies technical problems, focusing on methodology and semantics where there is no significant play of emotions. Furthermore, the solutions to these issues do not significantly affect one's way of life, as is also the case in scientific fields. In Latin America, however, there are true conversions that change the personality of the philosopher when he alters his position with respect to the fundamental problems of life.

The concern for ethics, politics, and social philosophy explains the commitment the Latin American philosopher experiences. He does not seek to interpret reality through the mere desire to know; rather he is in search of a mode of conduct for himself and his fellow man. Thus, he becomes committed to a style of life for his country and the theory leads to action that often, unfortunately, weakens the theory and may reduce it to propaganda.

Theoretical aspects are of less concern than the practical consequences the theory may have, especially with respect to political, social, and educational reform. This tendency, present in many philosophical orientations, acquires a high degree of intensity in the case of positivism and Marxism. It is true that in more recent times philosophy has been pursued for its theoretical value, but it is no less true that the major concern has been with issues in human conduct.

The concern for the problems of national life and the commitment the Latin American philosopher makes explain the popularity that philosophy has in Latin America, in contrast to the esoteric attitude in the United States. The leading newspapers in Buenos Aires, Mexico City, Caracas, and other capitals frequently publish philosophical articles, and works in philosophy are sold in large quantities.

The interest of the philosopher as a philosopher in political problems has its counterpart in the interest of the politicians in philosophy. Eduardo Frei, who was a politician since his youth and the president of Chile from 1964 to

1970, was an eloquent example of this concern. In 1940 he published a book entitled *Politics and the Spirit*, in which he stated the philosophical justification of his political activities. The work lacks an original theoretical quality as it is based on the thought of someone else, namely, Jacques Maritain. It is important, however, that a politician should feel the need for developing a philosophical justification of his work. In his judgment, politics is an activity that proposes a style of life that finds its roots in philosophy. The same occurs with a former president of Chile, Salvador Allende, who, likewise, was concerned with the philosophical foundations of his social reform although his perspective was Marxist and, thus, different from that of Frei. This is a significant contrast to what happens in the United States. Here, politics as well as business are activities unrelated to philosophy. In all probability, neither Truman, Eisenhower, Johnson, Nixon, nor Reagan has given as much as an hour to searching for the philosophical foundations of his political activity or of his actions as president. To understand the significance of Latin American philosophy one must recognize the intimate link with the problems of the sociocultural milieu. Such a task is not isolated from reality, but it is the formulation of a theory in support of a praxis. Thus one can understand why people should become emotionally involved in the support of one view rather than another, since they lead to quite different modes of behavior.

With the exception of the traditional forms of neo-Thomism, Marxism, and to some degree neo-Kantianism and Mexican existentialism (Hyperion Group), one cannot speak of philosophical schools in Latin America. One is confronted rather with thinkers difficult to classify within the usual categories. Furthermore, they do not form schools and their students adhere more to a moral attitude than to the ideas of the teachers.

It is interesting that in Latin America, which is predominantly Catholic, there have been few thinkers of the first rank within that tradition. Those of a Christian orientation, Alberto Rougés and Antonio Caso, for example, do not fit into the traditional molds. Perhaps an explanation is to be found in that for Latin Americans, Thomism is not a strictly philosophical position; rather it is weighted with confessional and political purposes. Thus, new possibilities within that tradition are not explored. What is sought, rather, are arguments to defend a previously adopted position. Thus, the predominant writings in this tradition tend to attack or defend rather than pursue a theoretical investigation free from prejudice.

With a few exceptional cases, much the same is true of Marxism. Although it is the political philosophy that is more widespread, there are no exceptionally capable Marxist philosophers. For Latin American Marxists, doctrine is something that must be studied, proclaimed, and defended; critical investigation is a matter of secondary importance. In Thomism as well as in Marxism the proselytizing emphasis takes precedence over theoretical quality.

Neither Saint Thomas nor Marx, to be sure, would adopt such an attitude were they to appear on the scene. They would not reiterate philosophical positions with a lack of critical spirit and creative ability, as their followers do. Rather, they would elaborate a new theory, taking into consideration the significant historical events and scientific discoveries that have occurred since their deaths.

These two positions are the exaggeration of a characteristic that is frequent in Latin American thought. Theory is often converted into a dogma upon reaching these shores. When confronted by a theory one is forced to take sides and either defend or attack it. Thus, in philosophical writings, an affirming and often dogmatic attitude prevails, an attitude not concerned with giving reasons but one seeking to defend a position. One speaks of "being loyal" to the adopted doctrine. There is a lack, therefore, of a critical spirit, a creative capacity, and a desire to search. It would seem Latin Americans have inherited this dogmatic attitude from the Spaniards among whom one affirms one's personality by making shocking statements without regard for the facts. Good reasons and empirical evidence are of less importance than the assertive tone and the degree of intense personal conviction.

At present, Latin American philosophy is in a stage of normality. Philosophy is taught in most secondary schools and in the principal universities, and most of these institutions have centers for philosophical research. There is also significant interest in the history of philosophy as well as in systematic thought: specialized journals and reviews are published, national and international congresses are held on a regular basis, excellent translations, with scholarly commentaries, of classical as well as contemporary authors are published, as are original works of international significance. It should be understood however that the quality of philosophical studies is not the same in all countries. As outstanding examples one might point to Mexico and Argentina. Generally speaking, Central American countries, with the exception of Costa Rica, are those with the lowest level. In all, however, significant progress is evident, not primarily in the number of original thinkers, but because philosophical activity is found in many more institutions and receives broader support, and it has established roots in the culture and conscience of each nation. Since the "heroic" stage in which philosophy existed during the latter part of the last century and the early part of the present century has been definitely surpassed, one can hope that the best fruits will be those of the future.

R. F.

NOTES

1. Alejandro Korn, *Obras* (La Plata: Universidad Nacional de La Plata, 1938), 3:279–80.
2. This characteristic, together with their political awareness and pedagogical leanings, was pointed out by José Gaos in three articles. (See Bibliography.) These contain perceptive observations, but unfortunately they are not examples of good literature or clarity of expression.

Part One

Man

Introduction

Although Western philosophy has always struggled with the concept of man, it was only toward the latter part of the nineteenth century and the beginning of the twentieth that this issue came to a prominent position in philosophical thought. The latter part of this period, extending into the twentieth century, is the primary focus of Part One of this collection of readings, and it seeks to provide a general overview of the way the anthropological issue has been confronted by Latin American philosophers.

The most striking characteristic of the study of man as encountered in Latin American thought is the variety of the approaches to the issue. In contrast to the precision and the well-defined boundaries within which the problem of value is formulated (See Introduction to Part Two)—with focus on the conflict between axiological objectivism and subjectivism—the study of man is confronted in a multifaceted, complex manner. Positivists at the end of the nineteenth and the beginning of the twentieth centuries are concerned with the psychological description of man in order to resolve the mind-body problem; neo-scholastics concentrate their efforts in the investigation of man's universal and eternal essence; philosophers who were influenced by Bergson's vitalism (Caso, Vasconcelos, Farias Brito) and by new German ideas attempt to formulate a new interpretation of what is intrinsically human; at the same time, the existentialists deny any possibility of an essential definition, giving preference to an existential humanism. This pluralism is the reflection of the many facets this problem assumed in European anthropological discussion, and it also stems from the inherent ambiguity of the question that anthropological speculation seeks to answer, namely, 'What is man?'

The way this question and its context are interpreted seriously affects the nature of the answer, since there are at least four separate problems inherent in the question itself: the ontological problem of the status of man, the metaphysical problem of his essence, the epistemological problem of his definition, and the cosmo-ethical problem of his place in the universe.

27

Different philosophical traditions have approached the question of man in keeping with their understanding of the context within which it is formulated. Scholasticism, whether colonial or contemporary, Latin American positivism—a mixture of naturalism, Comtism, and scientism—as well as most other traditional perspectives have insisted, although for different reasons, that the discussion of the ontological status of man remain at the center of the anthropological problem. The Marxist and existentialist currents, however, are engaged in a well-defined attempt, although with negative intent, to clarify the metaphysical problem of the essence of man, whereas the vitalism of French origin and the German philosophy of the spirit, so popular in Latin America, have directed their principal efforts to the reinterpretation of the specific dimension that separates man from the rest of the universe. All of them, moreover, have given special attention to the cosmo-ethical consequences of their respective solutions, announcing a new era of genuine humanism.

It must be pointed out, however, that in spite of the preference to approach the anthropological question with a given emphasis, most of these philosophical perspectives have also developed views about the remaining dimensions of the problem of man. Each concentrates on a specific dimension of the problem, and the implications with respect to the other dimensions are often less fruitful and profound. That is to say, all of these positions, explicitly or implicitly, contain ontological, metaphysical, epistemological, and cosmo-ethical dimensions, although usually one of them dominates as a thematic center of gravity.

The ability of a philosopher or of a philosophical view to recognize the implications and interrelationships of each of these aspects of the human problem with respect to the others provides the criterion for determining the degree of originality and value of its contributions to the anthropological issue. The more restricted the orientation, the more restricted is the contribution and the less valuable becomes the solution offered. And, by the same token, the more each of these aspects is emphasized and proper attention given to its interrelationships, the more profound and lasting is the theory.

DIMENSIONS OF THE PROBLEM

The indispensable prerequisite for any philosophical anthropology, as has been pointed out by Frondizi in the preface to *El yo como estructura dinámica*,[1] is a theory of the self or, in keeping with the terminology used here, a solution to the problem of the nature and the ontological status of the conscious center of the human being. All major philosophers (Aristotle, Descartes, Hume, and others) have recognized the importance of the ontology of the self and thus have begun their anthropological discussion at this point. When we ask 'what is man?' our answer must begin with an examination of the kind of being man is and especially of the reality, i.e., the self, that constitutes the basis for distinguishing him from the rest of nature. Such a concern does not seek to set man apart from the rest of the universe, since it is not looking for the specific difference that would distinguish him within a broader genus. The latter type of emphasis focuses on what we have here referred to as "the epistemological aspect" of the problem, to which we shall turn shortly. What is sought at this point is to classify man and particularly the self within the ontological categories of reality. The question is *whether the self exists* and, if so, *how* it exists, not primarily *what* it is.

In Latin America the question concerning man is first approached in the light of this problem and its positivist solution, which in its most direct expression considers the self to be an epiphenomenon of matter. With the dismantling of positivism and the vital-spiritualist reaction to it that emerged during the second decade of this century, diverse theories concerning man emerged with some frequency. For the most part these theories reflected a partial return to an ontologically autonomous concept of the self in which the self regains some of the attributes lost in late nineteenth-century scientism. With the exception of the neo-scholastic developments, however, this tendency stopped short of substantialism. The new theories use the dynamic terminology of function, activity, and structure.

The problem of man's essence is the second most important problem. This issue has two clearly distinguishable aspects with important implications for the answers given to the anthropological question. Although the 'what is' of man is no longer interpreted as a 'whether it is' or 'how it is', but rather in the sense that is appropriate to the question to be answered by the definition of the essence, this 'what is' opens up into an initial introductory moment in which one investigates *if* man *has* an essence in order then to define and interpret *what* the essence *is*. The first corresponds to what we have called the metaphysical aspect of the issue and the second to its epistemological aspect. The metaphysical problem is similar to that of the ontological status of man already considered, but in this case it refers to an abstract rather than a concrete reality. For this reason we refer to it as metaphysical rather than ontological.

As is to be expected, this issue follows a development parallel to that of the ontological question in the history of Western philosophy. It begins with the essentialist perspective of the Greeks in which the particular and mutable man is subordinated to his universal and immutable essence. This extreme position, taken by Western philosophy in its initial stages, begins to weaken with the growing awareness of the reality of concrete existence. The doctrine that gives it the final blow is the Hegelian identification of the essence of man with his activity. Thanks to this development, it is possible to conclude that the essence of man is not some immutable universal but rather that it depends upon what man does. What man is depends on his activity. In short, man creates himself. Nevertheless, in the nineteenth century the identification of man with his activity is not complete and therefore his essence is not totally indeterminate. The *homo faber* of the 1880s still has an essence, incomplete and dependent though it be on a particular type of activity—work in Marx and the libido in Freud—but nevertheless an essence. Only in the existentialism of the twentieth century does the eroding effect of a radical nonessentialism that denies every essence to man come full cycle and identify him completely with his existence.

As these intellectual developments reach Latin America, they are incorporated into its thought and guide it toward an understanding of man's essence that is active and dynamic. Concrete man takes the place of abstract man and his essence is conceived as oriented toward the future. Nevertheless, there have been very few thinkers, even among those influenced by existentialism—perhaps Astrada is the only exception—who have gone so far as to deny completely that man has an essence. The tendency is to conceive the essence as dynamic, rather than to eliminate it altogether.

In examining the issue of *whether* man *has* an essence, we come to the third of the aspects that constitute the nucleus of the anthropological problem. In it the question *what is* becomes *which is,* with the change pointing to the search for content in the definition of man. This aspect has been referred to as the epistemological question because it includes two correlative aspects: the logical problem of stating a definition of man in terms of genus and specific difference, thereby distinguishing him from other beings, and the epistemic problem of the understanding of the definition. For example, should one accept the Aristotelian definition that man is a rational animal, the first aspect consists in formulating the definition, whereas the second consists in understanding what is meant by the rationality that distinguishes man from other animals. The answer to this twofold question properly resolves the problem of man, although this is achieved only if the two preceding introductory questions have been answered previously. For this reason, the third aspect of the question has taken on special importance in contemporary philosophy, at times at the expense of the others. The search for the specific human difference was used, especially in Latin America, to combat the scientistic position of positivism current during the last century and the beginnings of the present, in which man was reduced to something purely physiological, destroying all qualitative distinctions between man and nature.

Most Latin American philosophers have concentrated their anthropological efforts on this problem, following the example of many Europeans, such as Scheler in *Man's Place in Nature* (1928) and Cassirer in his *Essay on Man* (1944). Due to this emphasis they have neglected the ontological and metaphysical dimensions of the human problem with serious consequences for the clarity and value of some of the anthropological theories they proposed.

Neglect, however, has not characterized the interest shown in Latin America in the fourth aspect of the problem of man, namely, his cosmo-ethical status. With rare exceptions, all the Latin American thinkers who have given serious attention to the anthropological question have also examined the place that man occupies in the universe and the consequences for his moral, social, and political life. This concern is especially evident among those committed to a practical ideology, such as the Marxists, and is, perhaps, a direct result of the critical situation confronting Latin America in the present century.

Simply put, this aspect of the question is the central problem for humanism, namely, what interpretation is given to man in light of his relationship to the other dimensions of nature? The question 'What is man?' becomes in this perspective 'What place?' and 'What relationship?' The inclusion of cosmic and teleological elements makes this problem secondary to the issue of man's essence, which ultimately determines the nature of the response to the cosmo-ethical question. If the ontological and the metaphysical questions are to be resolved prior to the epistemological question and thus maintain their formal priority, the cosmo-ethical question becomes consequent to them. In short, the scope of the cosmo-ethical question is not the ontometaphysical delimitation of man or his definitive interpretation, but the problem of the cosmological and ethical consequences of the solution given to the onto-metaphysical question.

In this development, Latin Americans have followed a tendency amply illustrated in the history of Western philosophy. Due to its immediate relevance, the Western thinker has always given great importance to this problem. The Greeks began to treat this problem effectively when they placed man at the cosmological and ethical center of the universe. But classical humanism does not recur in its fullness at any time in the history of Western thought, not even in the Renaissance. With the death of Greek culture, man ceased to be the absolute center of the universe and became subordinate to a greater or lesser degree to other realities. Parallel to the development that gradually deprived man of his traditional attributes such as substantiality, essence, and reason, he was being deprived of his cosmological and ethical preeminence to such a degree that in the nineteenth century he was even denied a moral conscience. Positivism's crude scientism converted moral conscience into a mere illusion reducible to instincts that functioned mechanically. The inadequacy of such a view engendered an adverse reaction in European thought, although not a return to classical humanism. This was the moment of crisis and antiscientistic reaction with which the twentieth century opened in Latin America. Inspired particularly by the perspectivism of Ortega y Gasset and later by existentialism, Latin American philosophers, as had been the case with their European counterparts, turned again to man and restored him as the measure, indeed the center, of the universe, though no longer in the absolute sense of the ancients. A return to the Greek cosmogony and its essentialist ethic was impossible. Scientific and philosophical discoveries of the past century and the first half of the present century prevented it. Man became, then, only the relative center of the universe. He was no longer the universal man who judged the cosmos, but the concrete and historical man who constructed his world. Rather than an essential center, in this more radical contemporary humanism he becomes the transcendental condition of all things. His centrality, therefore, is relative to the individual and eminently subjective.

POSITIVISTIC ANTHROPOLOGY

Latin American anthropological thought in the twentieth century takes root in a scientistic ground, a ground often referred to as positivism. This positivism was nurtured on such heterogeneous elements as the evolutionistic naturalism of Spencer, the positivism of Comte, and the utilitarianism of John Stuart Mill. The unity of Latin American positivism, therefore, is more a matter of perspective than of content, since it reduces ultimately to an attitude that exalts the explanatory value of science to the detriment of metaphysics and other theoretical disciplines. All genuine knowledge must be based on empirical experience and not on speculation. As a result, the problem of man within this perspective is reduced to the study of psychic phenomena and philosophical anthropology becomes empirical associationist psychology or biology.

However, one must take note of positivism's philosophical wisdom in recognizing the fundamental importance of the ontological problem of man. Every positivist begins by stating the problem of the existence of the self, even though this problem is resolved negatively, in phenomenal terms. In positivism, the self ceases to be an existing and substantial entity and is conceived as a group of phenomena that, because of their interrelationship, coordination, and succession, give the impression of belonging to something that sustains them. This empirical phenomenalism is used to explain the subject-object, mind-body dualism of human experience, a dualism resolved by maintaining a parallelism between these phenomena considered as correlative but irreducible as Enrique José Varona (1849-1933) did, or by accepting a biomechanistic monism in which the phenomenal duality is reduced to the real unity of a common, energized substratum as was proposed by José Ingenieros (1877-1925).

As already stated, most positivists begin their investigation of man by focusing on his ontological status, but they preclude the possibility of continuing the investigation along metaphysical and epistemological lines. If man as an individual self is reduced to a bundle of phenomena, it is superfluous to speak of his essence or of the definition and interpretation of this essence. Some positivists, like Varona and Ingenieros, however, do attempt to offer a solution to the cosmo-ethical problem, although their attempt is a lamentable failure. The presuppositions of positivistic anthropology do not permit the construction of a normative ethic. If man is no more than a collection of phenomena that are strictly ordered according to absolute laws, his freedom is an illusion and ethics becomes a purely descriptive science. Ingenieros understands and explicitly accepts the consequences of his psychological position: "The term *to choose* is badly used and has the false connotation of an entity that chooses: the supposed choosing is simply *a natural selection* among different possibilities, in the sense most appropriate to the conservation of life and the least expenditure of energy."[2]

VITALISTIC ANTHROPOLOGY

These implications, devastating for ethics, engendered the antipositivistic reaction in Latin America. A group of thinkers influenced principally by Bergson began to attack those presuppositions of positivism that destroy human freedom. The concern with the problem of freedom emerged early in the twentieth century. In 1903 Vaz Ferreira started work on his book *Los problemas de la libertad,* and published it in unfinished form in 1907. The first serious criticisms, however, were made by Alejandro O. Deústua in Peru and Antonio Caso in Mexico. These were followed by Enrique Molina, Alejandro Korn, and others.

Deústua argues persuasively in his treatise *Las ideas de orden y libertad en la historia del pensamiento humano* (1917-22) that the idea of order, which is the basis of positivistic determinism, is logically posterior to the idea of freedom and that both are necessary to explain the intellectual history of man. Freedom is necessary for any change in order and, therefore, order is subordinate to freedom.

With the ethical limitations of positivism made explicit, Latin American thought was free to explore new philosophical horizons. Anthropology abandoned its interest in the ontological status of mind, which had been the foundation of positivistic psychology, and turned toward the epistemological problem of man—his definition and understanding. The philosophers who established the foundations for this new anthropology are, principally, Caso and Vasconcelos in Mexico.

Antonio Caso (1883-1946)

Caso's philosophy of man, as developed in *La existencia como economía, como desinterés y como caridad* (1919), can be characterized as a personalism. Man is differentiated from the rest of the universe because he is a person. The physical realm is constituted of things, beings without unity that are highly divisible. The organic realm consists of individuals, who constitute a level of being superior to the divisible thing although still inferior to man. It is only in the latter that the highest level of the spirit—or the person— appears in nature. When the individual becomes a person, he acquires unity, identity, and substantial continuity and becomes fully man. The person is the complete fulfillment of human essence because it is a creator of values. "It is proper to man to fulfill his essence continually and the essence is the person creating values."[3]

Man, however, is also an individual, and the tension between individual and person creates moral conflict. The individual is egotistical and interested only in his own biological survival and welfare. The law that governs his existence is essentially economic: "life = maximum gain with minimum effort."[4] The person, on the other hand, exists towards others, and tends to unbind his biological interests, choosing freely the ethics of disinterest and love. The person confronts the law of life with that of "sacrifice = maximum effort and minimum gain."[5] The highest expression of this free and disinterested activity is art.

José Vasconcelos (1882-1959)

Caso's trilogy "thing-individual-person" is reformulated in the *Todología* (1952) of Vasconcelos as "quantic wave-molecule-cell-person." However, the significance of the elements is completely different. In Vasconcelos's aesthetic monism each of the elements represents a different stage in the constant struggle of the cosmos to maintain its existence and to contain the tendency toward dissolution and dispersion present in every being. The quantic wave is the first elemental structure to restrain the entropological process of universal dissolution. The molecule is the second cosmic effort to restrain the disintegration; the third and fourth cosmic efforts constitute, successively, the cell and the human person. In the fourth one finds the maximum degree of coordination of the heterogeneous, namely, consciousness. By means of consciousness, man reflects and unifies within himself the heterogeneous multiplicity of the universe, becoming a true microcosm.

The "self," "consciousness," and "soul" are equivalent terms for Vasconcelos. The nature of the reality that they represent is known to us through their coordinating activity, but their being "is an unfathomable abyss."[6] The self always escapes any analytical scrutiny. We know it only through its effects.

For Caso as well as Vasconcelos, the primary concern is to characterize man's place in the universe. They both point to personality as the essential, constitutive element of man's humanity. For Caso the person is a center of free, disinterested activity. Vasconcelos identifies the person with conscious-ness and characterizes it as a coordinating element of the cosmos. Both thinkers, therefore, tend to neglect the ontological and metaphysical prob-lems of man.

ANTHROPOLOGY OF THE SPIRIT

When the philosophical domination of positivism was broken through the work of Deústua, Korn, Caso, Vasconcelos, and Farias Brito, among others, the study and acceptance of new European philosophical tendencies became more widespread. In 1916, Ortega y Gasset came to Latin America for the first time and introduced contemporary German thought. The generation of thinkers that followed the "founders" were inspired by him and his mentors, Husserl, Dilthey, Scheler, and Hartmann in the main.

Philosophical renovation took root with such men as Samuel Ramos in Mexico and Francisco Romero in Argentina, followed by Risieri Frondizi, Francisco Miró Quesada, and Leopoldo Zea, among others. Ramos and Romero focus attention on the characterization of man and his relationship to the universe although they also develop the ontological implications of their views. Frondizi and Miró Quesada develop along different lines, while Zea is concerned with another problem, as we shall see later. Frondizi is the only thinker of this generation who works extensively with the ontological question and Miró Quesada investigates the metaphysical problem from an epistemic perspective.

Samuel Ramos (1897-1959)

Ramos develops his philosophical anthropology in a work published in 1940 entitled *Hacia un nuevo humanismo.* His "purpose is to obtain an idea of man as a whole."[7] Influenced by Scheler, he rejected philosophical perspec-tives that down through the history of philosophy had conceived of man as primarily reason or will or feeling or instinct. Ramos claimed that to under-stand man, one must study him in his complex totality.

Borrowing Ortega y Gasset's division of man into life, soul, and spirit, Ramos thinks of man as an integral whole composed of a series of hier-archically ordered ontological levels. At the lowest level, life consists of all internal sensations. Proceeding inwardly, one comes to the realm of feeling or soul. Then, in the very center of the human being is spirit, composed of will and thought. The soul constitutes the subject and the private world of man's individuality. The spirit, on the other hand, is objective and manifests itself as person when one acts, thinks, or feels with complete freedom. In this personal dimension, man becomes aware of value and constitutes himself into a value that confirms his teleological nature: "Man is a being who pursues valuable ends."[8]

Ramos inherits from Caso the notion that the human is essentially related to the axiological, but he differs from his former teacher in that he does not identify the person with man. In Ramos's judgment, the individual self is also essentially human, although man does not develop completely until he becomes a person. In this sense, his view is similar to that later formulated by Romero in *Teoría del hombre* (1952).

Francisco Romero (1891-1962)

According to Romero, "duality is the constituting fact of the full man."[9] The elements of this duality are intentionality and spirit. The first in itself is a human element, although animals possess a rudiment of intentionality. Man, however, possesses intentionality in a full and essential sense. His "consciousness is organized as a differentiated structure in which there exists a subjective pole which grasps objects and projects itself actively toward them."[10] This subjective pole is the individual self that, in Romero's view, distinguishes man from the pre-intentional psychism characteristic of animals.

The intentional man or self, however, is not the full man. He is "a mere man." His humanity is completed with a second element: spirit. Structurally, there is no difference between intentional man and spiritual man. Both are men and both are structured as a self-world pair. The difference is in their direction. In the first, the direction is subjective, toward the self. In the second it is objective. The purely intentional act always returns to the subject, whereas a spiritual act comes to rest on the object.

Intentional man is part of nature and acts in accord with its laws. Spiritual man, on the other hand, is not a natural entity. The direction toward the other indicates that he has broken with nature, giving him the freedom of action that constitutes man as an axiological being.

Transcendence is the metaphysical basis of man as well as of all reality. For Romero reality consists of four orders: the inorganic, the organic, intentionality, and spirit. Each of these is structured on the level that precedes it, which in turn serves as a foundation to the level above it. Each level transcends its preceding level and is transcended by the level that follows it. Man, therefore, consists in a dual transcendence: as intentional self, he transcends toward the object taking it to himself, and as spirit he transcends toward the object and rests in it. The highest level of transcendence is spirit.

Romero's theory of man is profound and fruitful. However, it tends to ignore a fundamental problem in the human question, namely, man's ontological status. In the same year in which Romero published his major work, Frondizi published his *Substancia y función en el problema del yo,* a work that gives special attention to the ontological status of man.

Risieri Frondizi (1910-1983)

Frondizi rejects the two traditional solutions to the problem of the existence and nature of the self: the substantialist position that conceives of the self as a transempirical entity and the atomist position that dissolves it into a collection of lived experiences.

The basic error of the traditional substantialism originating with Descartes is to suppose that all activity requires a subject. This is why it went on to conclude that thinking presupposes something that thinks. Empirical atomism, finding its origin in Hume, erred according to Frondizi through "the sophism of reduction," i.e., the metaphysical postulate that seeks to reduce wholes to their component elements. The outcome of both perspectives is disastrous; the substantialist creates an artificial entity whereas the atomist destroys the self.

Frondizi finds the solution in the concept of structure *(Gestalt)*. The self is a quality that lived-experiences possess when they are taken as wholes. Immutability, simplicity, and independence, characteristics that substantialism sustained in a transempirical entity, are changed to mutability, complexity, and dependence. At the same time, however, Frondizi avoids the atomist reduction of the self to its component parts. As a structural quality, the self depends upon the members of its structure, the lived-experiences, but it cannot be reduced to them. In virtue of this condition, the self is one and permanent in spite of being mutable and complex.

Francisco Miró Quesada (b. 1918)

For Miró Quesada the basic problem in philosophical anthropology is the metaphysical question, which he approaches from an epistemological perspective in *El hombre sin teoría* (1959). The problem is not the status of human essence but the possibility of formulating an adequate theory of man.

On the one hand, it is a fact of man's experience that he cannot live without theory and that all theory concerning the world that surrounds him implies a theory concerning man himself. On the other hand, man is a reality so complex that every theory concerning him is destined to inevitable failure. What, then, must one do? One solution is to cast aside or modify unacceptable theories in favor of more truthful theories. But this procedure is unsatisfactory, since "whatever we do, our theory concerning ourselves will have the same outcome as the others."[11] The only way, therefore, is to desist from theorizing about man. But is this not impossible? Is theory not necessary for our practical life and even implicit in our language?

Miró Quesada claims this is not necessarily the case. To be sure, man cannot dispense with the theory implicit in his language, but this theory is different from scientific-philosophical theories about the world, about life, and about human destiny. The first is primitive, spontaneous, collective, and practically unconscious. The second, however, is created for the specific purposes of knowledge. It is this latter that we must abandon in order to give attention to the facts, since scientific and philosophical theories about man are artificial dividers among men. True humanism must be founded on fact and not on theory.

EXISTENTIALIST AND MARXIST ANTHROPOLOGIES

Existentialism began to influence Latin America in the 1930s. This influence was extensive, but few Latin Americans accepted existentialism uncritically. Among those most influenced by it, the more distinguished are Carlos Astrada of Argentina and Vicente Ferreira da Silva of Brazil. The work of the former reflects the impact of *Being and Time,* although about 1950 he abandoned the Heideggerian perspective and adopted a Marxist outlook. Ferreira da Silva (1916-1963), not included here, was inspired principally by the works of Heidegger's later period. Both of these men were concerned in particular with the metaphysical problem of the essence of man.

Carlos Astrada (1894-1970)

In *La revolución existencialista* (1952), Astrada identified the essence of man with its historic humanity. Heidegger's error, according to Astrada, consisted in the ambiguity latent in his thought, an ambiguity couched in the debate between the old ontological objectivity and existential-historical transcendence.

Properly speaking, man is not a determinate thing. His essence is his temporal existence and, therefore, it is more a possibility than a given reality. "Man never *is,* in the sense of something conclusive and formed in the ideal mold of a goal that was to be achieved, rather he is an eternal *coming to be* suspended in the effort in which he is projected toward historical concretions."[12] Man's mission and nature is dramatic, says Astrada in terminology reminiscent of Ortega. He can be remolded and changed because he is nothing definite. Man does not depend on the idea of man; rather the idea depends on man.

Once humanity is accepted as a mere possibility, man is able to develop free of the limitations imposed by eternal truths and essences. This is the basis of true humanism centered upon the identity of the existing man. As for Marx, Astrada maintains that the only limitation imposed upon man is his concrete existence. This does not condemn him to subjectivism, however, because the objectivity of man is given in his history.

J. G.

NOTES

1. R. Frondizi, *El yo como estructura dinámica* (Buenos Aires: Paidós, 1970), 11.

2. J. Ingenieros, *Principios de psicología,* in *Obras completas,* vol. 3 (Buenos Aires: Mar Océano, 1962), 148.

3. A. Caso, *La existencia como economía, como desinterés y como caridad,* in *Antología filosófica* (Mexico: Ediciones de la Secretaría de Educación Pública, 1943), 190.

4. Ibid., 51.

5. Ibid., 61.

6. J. Vasconcelos, *Todología,* in *Obras completas,* vol. 4 (Mexico: Libreros Mexicanos Unidos, 1961), 905.

7. S. Ramos, *Hacia un nuevo humanismo,* 2d ed. (Mexico: Fondo de Cultura Económica, 1962), 49.

8. Ibid., 44.

9. F. Romero, *Teoría del hombre,* 3d ed. (Buenos Aires: Losada, 1965), 193.

10. Ibid., 127.

11. F. Miró Quesada, *El hombre sin teoría* (Lima: Universidad Mayor de San Marcos, 1959), 24.

12. C. Astrada, *Existencialismo y crisis de la filosofía* (Buenos Aires: Devenir, 1963), 190. This text is an enlarged reedition with substantial changes of *La revolución existencialista.*

Antonio Caso
(1883-1946)

Caso and Vasconcelos are the two major figures in contemporary Mexican philosophy. Born only a year apart, they were charter members of the "Ateneo de la Juventud," which was the point of departure for new philosophical thinking in Mexico. In both there prevailed a metaphysical concern for a solution with a Christian foundation; both were presidents of the National University of Mexico and both were intensely concerned with the destiny of their country, an issue about which they wrote at length. The similarities are numerous, but differences are also significant for we are confronted with two distinct types of personality.

Caso's life had a unifying direction and hence he was admired by his supporters as well as his adversaries. Vasconcelos changed directions and his early admirers became his vociferous critics in his later years. Caso always maintained his faith in man, whereas with Vasconcelos that faith shifted with his personal fortune. Caso was a modest person whereas Vasconcelos, as reflected in his autobiography, was somewhat vain. Caso's prose is clear whereas that of Vasconcelos is elaborate and often difficult.

Caso was born in Mexico, Distrito Federal, in 1883 and he died there in 1946. He studied in the National Preparatory School and graduated as an attorney from the School of Jurisprudence. From 1907 on he was devoted to teaching and at thirty years of age he was made director of the School of Advanced Studies of the National University. In the early years when he studied philosophy, an authentic dedication and commitment as well as a spirit of sacrifice were necessary, because the preoccupation within the country was channeled in other directions.

His philosophical production is extensive and diverse with respect both to its themes and quality. There are fifteen books in addition to many articles. Some of his books incorporate university courses, lectures, and articles. In 1915 he published *Filósofos y doctrinas morales,* a work that was followed by other commentaries on contemporary thinkers.

His intense concern for his country led him to write several books: *Discursos a la nación mexicana* (1922): *México y la ideología nacional* (1924); *Nuevos discursos a la nación mexicana* (1934); and *México, apuntamientos de cultura patria* (1943). He explores the problems of history and culture in two works: *El concepto de la historia universal* (1923), and *El concepto de la historia y la filosofía de los valores* (1933) wherein he develops his social interpretation of value. *Los principios de estética* (1925) is also a solid work.

It is difficult to synthesize Caso's rich and varied thought, which developed over a long period of time. His thought begins with a positivist orientation that he overcomes through the influence of Boutroux and Bergson. Kant, Plato, Schopenhauer, and William James also influenced his work. Later he studied contemporary German philosophers such as Husserl, Scheler, Hartmann, and Heidegger, but this did not sway him from his earlier position.

The bedrock of his thought is a metaphysical spiritualism with a Christian outlook that finds its most important expression in *La existencia como economía, como desinterés y como caridad*, first published in 1916, but amplified and revised in 1919 and again in 1943. Here he conceives of man as a spiritual reality that surpasses nature. His philosophical anthropology is united with an ethical conception of life. A variety of activities makes its demands upon man. The lowest level of activity is the *economic*, which is instrumental and utilitarian, governed by the principle of efficiency: "A maximum of gain with a minimum of effort." *Disinterest*, an activity of the aesthetic sort, represents the second stage and in the last place we find *charity* that represents "the fundamental religious and moral experience" supported by sacrifice and love. This level of activity is summarized in the norm "Do for others more than what you would like others to do for you."

Although he dedicated his life to philosophy, he maintained through his teaching and his conduct that the most important knowledge is the knowledge for living.

Caso's personality transcends the realm of philosophy. Throughout his native land, he is respected and admired. As an expression of this esteem, one of the principal streets in Mexico City bears the name "Maestro Antonio Caso."

R. F.

The Human Person
and the Totalitarian State*

PERSON, INDIVIDUAL, THING

There are three levels of being: thing, individual, and person. What are the differentiating attributes of each level of being? . . . Thing is being without unity. If a thing is broken, nothing in it has died. Things are inevitably associated with this divisibility.

This is the region, the realm of the physical, where life does not exist. Things do not have life, therefore they can be divided without changing their intrinsic nature. They continue to be things. Dividing them does not modify their nature.

If one moves from this lower level of being to that immediately above it, a fundamental difference appears that mediates between the physical world and the realm of organic nature. When things are divided, we still have things, but when we come into contact with life, existence is endowed with profoundly different properties.

The being gifted with life is called an "individual." By its structure, the individual embodies something essentially different from the nature of things. Individual means what cannot be divided. The idea of indivisibility lies in the very name of an organic being. Individuality can be more or less energetic, but the living being is always indivisible, always individual, always assuming in its own substance a level of being superior to the thing. This superiority is indivisibility.

Among the individuals endowed with life, there are also hierarchical differences, differences in the intonation of the vital potential. Within the bound of both natural realms, plant and animal, individuality does not reflect the lively differentiation that it takes on in the forms that are superior to those of plants and animals.

---

*From Antonio Caso, *La persona humana y el Estado totalitario* (Mexico: UNAM, 1941), 187-90, 198ff.

The most perfect form of individuality is the animal organism. Man is an animal organism, the most perfected of all organisms. However, his obvious superiority does not stem from his biological nature, but from his intellectual and moral superiority. Man is a microcosm; in him individuality surpasses physical nature, but an additional nature is also present that cannot be reduced to pure individuality. Man is individual, an admirable biological individual, but he is more than that, he is a person.

The biological individual takes on the characteristics of substantial unity, identity, and continuity. Only man, however, plays the role of a social being, therefore he is referred to as a person, which means specifically to play a role, as it is played by actors in the theater. In this same way, man, as a social unit, inevitably plays a role in history.

What other being in the world is capable, as is the human being, of exercising and fulfilling a social function? Only man conceives the ideal, he alone is capable of making his spiritual faculties, such as reason, science, and feeling, work in support of those ideas that the will affirms. And what is an ideal but a firmly cherished idea?

The purely psychical nature of man is not sufficient for defining the concept of the person. Over and above the psychical is the spiritual. Man is not only a psychical being, he is also a spiritual being. He is a "creator of values," as Nietzsche expressed it so magnificently.

Human spirituality cannot be achieved in the isolation of the psyche. That is why Aristotle defined man as "the political animal." So-called animal societies are similar to an individual, not to a person. In them, each of the component beings performs a constant function, an activity repeated tenaciously. There is a stereotyped, organic division of labor. A beehive is an individual that reduces each of the individuals within it to the law of the hive.

The error of individualism and the error of socialism are very much alike because in their extreme forms both the social theories and the philosophical creeds ignore the superior nature of the human being, they ignore the quality of his spiritual reality.

Individualism and communism lower the dignity of the person. Person and culture, however, are concomitant, for the person requires a society for his development. Society, in turn, needs the person for its very being. The spirit flourishes above life, in the same way that life flourishes above physical nature.

At issue are the various levels of existence. The highest level is personality. In scholasticism every substance complete in itself but lacking reason is called a supposit. The etymology of the word refers to "what is underneath." The person is not what is underneath, but what is above all. Human personality, in Dante, Newton, and Plato, is the highest level of being. The greatest powers in history, the most famous nations, as well as the cities of the most refined culture, such as Athens, Florence, or Paris, have personality. However, great as they may be, their spirituality cannot be compared with that found in the work of such geniuses as Plato, Dante, or Newton. The human person is the highest level of being. . . .

PERSON AND CULTURE

1

Person is a *sui generis* essence that rests on the mode of being characteristic of each subject and is also unique in its being. Personality then is the world of irreducible spiritual being. The universal in personality is its unsubstitutability, the uniqueness of its existence. Each actualization of personhood is singularly unique. . . .

2

The greatest error of contemporary civilization is the lack of respect for the human person, its preeminent attention to groups, to sums, to the anonymous, the collective, and the common. . . . If man sacrifices himself to the standards of contemporary civilization, his destiny, his sense of humanity shall have been lost forever. Humanity and personality are the proper and genuine dimensions of the species in its historical development. The recognition of the personality of human beings obliges society to accept their real inequality rather than an impossible uniformity. . . .

3

We are engaged in a new enterprise: personalism. We would like that each one be recognized for what he is: a human person. The idea of person requires respect because it implies respect. Respect must be the first virtue to emerge from the accumulation of evils characteristic of contemporary war. In this day we are referred to as human beings, as biological unities. One hears talk of the "masses"; everything is anonymous, collective, gregarious, unreal. The human person, the exquisite work of individual and social culture, cannot interact with the disregard for the unconquerable spiritual reality of its own nature. . . .

4

Every person is such to the degree that it is itself and not another, for personality is a *sui generis* essence that rests on the mode of being characteristic of each individual, that is unique in its being. . . . What is characteristic and unique cannot be replaced, for this would imply a contradiction. Things are exchanged, individuals are substituted, but persons cannot be replaced. . . . Contemporary civilization works against human essence, against personality. This civilization thinks in terms of groups or sums rather than in terms of real, personal subjects who cannot be equated with each other. . . .

5

It is proper for man to achieve his essence gradually and the essence proper to us is the personality that creates values. Being is not moral or juridical reason. To exist is to be contingent and perishable. Individuals and communities are contingent and perishable! To be valuable, however, is what must be stressed. For which is of more value, the individual or the community? Neither the individual nor the community, but the society based on justice, that is, the moral union of men who respect values. The community that tyrannizes man forgets that we men are persons and not "biological units," we are "spiritual centers of cultured action." The individual who opposes the community, conceiving himself as absolute reality, forgets that above the individuality nurtured on egoism is human culture that is always a synthesis of values. Values were not elaborated by the individual or the community, rather they were reflected by the historical continuity of generations and the moral solidarity of peoples. Inevitably, culture is tradition and solidarity. Solidarity is impossible without tradition and tradition is impossible without solidarity. . . .

6

Culture is the continuing work of human societies. Culture, however, implies a synthesis of values, and values are constant relationships reflected in thought and action. Further, value or religious experience can never be postponed. In order for man's social life to take on full meaning, value must be the predominating influence in human consciousness. The evil of this century is to postpone the holy because of the profane, believing that man can save himself and does save himself. This is the error and the hidden sophistry of contemporary social and political movements. Humanity has forgotten love. It no longer thinks of works of charity, but of works of egoism. Social distribution is the universal preoccupation, because love, which would give all if it were asked, is confused in the consciousness of our contemporaries. Spengler says "Since contemporary man does not know how to renounce, he aspires to distribute." . . .

7

If personality is not integrated by means of a cultured knowledge that recovers humanism, social endeavor remains incomplete. Only persons deserve to be saved. Things are not saved. Thus, in order to recover the knowledge of salvation, it must be grounded in the cultural integration of personality. Without salvation as its purpose, without God, culture cannot be organized with reference to its essential harmony. God is the kingdom of ends and the center of values. . . .

8

Man is not a *factum,* rather he is the possible direction of a process, and at the same time a task, an eternally luminous goal that hovers above natural man. Man is rebirth. Humanism is more true than man, because man exists only as a process, as humanization. Man is reborn and then gives birth to himself, but he is not merely repetition for he humanizes himself and becomes more of a man. The rebirth of man constitutes his essence. We are not a *factum* but a development, a coming to be, a perennial process; we die and are reborn in the episodes of history.

9

We long to return to the true self, metaphysically as well as morally. The values of being have been obscured. Man lives leaning toward the outside, away from himself, tending toward the external. This is evil, therefore good should result from an inverse action, with people turning toward themselves. They must be taught to examine the awareness they have forgotten. The public plaza cannot be one's inner dwelling. To return to the inner dwellings, to rejoice in the pleasure of one's own self, to feel one is the work and agent of one's own will, capable of one's own substantivity. . . .

10

The possibility of being, of developing as a man, of putting essence in harmony with existence can be destroyed by a corrupt, unjust, useless social environment. One must recover the being of the human person in the face of the conditions of contemporary life. Our concern is for being, which we explore along the pathways of contemporary philosophy, because the human person finds a model only in joint action with others.

Existence as Economy, Disinterest, and Charity*

LIFE AS ECONOMY

Life cannot be perceived without the recurring idea of purpose. An organism always implies the subordination of a whole to its purpose, but it is not only the organism as a whole that presupposes the subordination in question. Each organ, each apparatus of the organism, expresses this intrinsic purpose. The eye has a purpose: to see; the ear also has its own purpose: to hear; and so with each organ. If one makes an abstraction of purpose, the organism cannot be explained, since it can be explained only by referring to cause; the cause of the several organs and functions that are interconnected and which constitute organized beings is a final cause. We are not referring to a transcendent principle. We are not thinking of the universal purpose of every living thing. At this point, we are not inquiring nor do we wish to inquire why life exists. We are referring to life itself in its ordinary integration and action and we affirm that life cannot be understood without the idea of an inherent purposiveness, whether conscious or unconscious. . . .

The economy of existence rules with absolute dominion over life and its manifestations: to nourish, to grow, to reproduce, to struggle, to play, and to die are all a complex yet diverse expression of the fundamental equation of the universe as economy: life = the maximum gain with the minimum effort.

Nevertheless, in this interplay an important fact intervenes. Superior animals have an excess of energy, energy that the life of each individual being does not require. We have seen how, in spite of this vital excess, and because of the absence of even a suggestion of a disinterested act in the animal, the excess is used in imitation of the struggle that strengthens and develops the athlete.

---

*From Antonio Caso, *La existencia como economía, como desinterés, y como caridad,* in *Obras completas* (Mexico: UNAM, 1972), 3:25, 43-44, 70-72, 95-97, 100, 102, 106.

Life is the energy of egoism and egoistic sexual appetite that continually attempts to resolve the complex problem of hunger. As such, if it does not find a different thrust, a principle of a different order, life is always consumed within itself, much as it may accumulate and capitalize what is acquired.

The excess energy displayed in games can be an indispensable vital condition for purposes other than those of a purely biological life. If man does not possess this vital excess, if he did not produce energy beyond that needed to achieve his end as a mammal *sui generis,* he would lack the organic foundation for the intellectual, aesthetic, and moral orders. This does not mean that science, morality, and art are mere copies or even the equivalent of a purely vital force, as will be fully established later. The superior animals are expended in being animals, but the surplus in man makes of him the possible instrument of culture, heroism, and sainthood.

ART AS DISINTEREST

He who is aware that human consciousness is not so bound and constrained by biological action that it does not have its metaphysical moment for accepting the world as an object of contemplation, is well on the way to understanding artistic activity. Life is always bound to interest. It is an economic, egoistic, assimilative, and dissimilative activity. To nourish, to grow, to reproduce, to play, to make tools, to die, all of this is pure economy, the pure effect of egoism, the formless imperialistic thrust.

It is wonderful, therefore, and according to biology simply inexplicable, that a being such as man, that is, a superior animal, one more avid than any other, who is aware that he is so and could be so increasingly, would proceed, without denying the biological interest, to dedicate himself to contemplating what would have served to nourish and develop him had he decided to take advantage of it. Economy of effort cannot explain this innate disinterest, as Bergson calls it, disinterest or artistic individuality whether very ordinary or that of a genius. Art, when compared with even the least biological imperative, appears as a shocking waste, as a violent and arcane antithesis. . . .

Inheritance and struggle, the laws of adaptation that together produce natural selection, serve to explain many aspects of existence but they do not explain them all. Nevertheless, intelligence pursues the line of least resistance and far from confessing the impossibility of explaining disinterested activity in terms of economic principles, it tends to refer all experience to only one of its forms, to refer all being to one aspect of being. In so doing, it is forgotten that the reality to be explained by intelligence does not exist, rather science exists to interpret, as least imperfectly as possible, a multiform and diverse reality.

Art is not an economic activity. The more one gives oneself to contemplation, the better is the artistic spirit that is acquired, so that if one exercised all one's senses disinterestedly, one would become the supreme artist.

In art, one breaks the circle of vital interest and as an immediate consequence the soul is loosed from its biological bonds and reflects the world hidden from its egoism. Because the soul was egoistic, it did not know, it thought of itself; because it wanted whatever existed for its own designs, all else was ignored. Now the soul has ceased to want, therefore it begins to know what surrounds it and becomes aware of other goods. Before, the soul was an enemy of the world, it wanted to dominate it and therefore the world was not given for its contemplation. . . .

EXISTENCE AS CHARITY

The artist sacrifices the economy of life to the objectivity of intuition, which is innate; and the good man sacrifices egoism to help his neighbor, although such sacrifice is free. That is why Pascal said, "All bodies taken together, the firmament, the stars, the earth and its kingdoms, are not worth the love of the spirits and all their fruit is not worth the least act of charity."

By way of summary, humanity's scale of values is this: one becomes more noble the more one sacrifices, the more one overcomes the difficulties of sacrificing the merely animal life to disinterested ends, until, through aesthetic contemplation and simple acts of goodness, one reaches heroic action.

Disinterest, love, and sacrifice cannot be reduced to the economy of nature. If the world were only will, as Schopenhauer claimed, it would be impossible to explain how the will would deny itself through sacrifice. The world is the will of egoism but the good will is a contradiction to the former and cannot be reduced to it. Thus experience itself established that there is order and life other than, but given with, the order and life that so rigidly govern Darwin's barbarous imperative, the struggle for life. A concise formulation of the good would be: sacrifice = maximum effort with a minimum gain.

The good is not a categorical imperative, a law of reason, as Kant thought, but rather an enthusiasm. It does not impose, it does not come from the outside, but emerges from inner consciousness, from the feeling whose roots take hold of the depths of spiritual existence. It is like music, which subdues and charms; it is easy, spontaneous, intimate, the most intimate part of the soul. It is neither compulsion of pure reason nor of external life. It cannot be induced nor subdued. It is created. It is liberty, personality, divinity. In a word, to use the expression of an illustrious Mexican thinker, it is "the supernatural that is experienced as the most natural thing in the world."

Herein is the ground for rejecting every idea of compulsion, of conditional or categorical imperative. The essence of every commandment pre-supposes two acts of will, one that orders and another that obeys, one stating the command and another executing it. However, the experience of the good is that such development does not exist except as a representative fiction, as an *a posteriori* rationalization of a unique and indissoluble spiri-tual process. One is not good because someone else wants it, rather one is good because one wants it oneself, because one is free to be good, because one is good; in other words because one is creator of goodness, law, and action.

The three classical Christian virtues are widely known. Love is not demonstrated or inferred. It is the fundamental religious and moral experi-ence. It consists in going out of oneself, in giving oneself to others, in yielding oneself, lavishly, without fear of exhausting oneself. This is the essence of what is Christian. . . .

Love is an act, in the sense that a struggle is an act. Love is not demonstrated, it is practiced; like life, it is doing. Yet, it is a different life. You will never intuit the order that stands opposed to biological life. You will not understand existence in its profound richness; you will inevitably mutilate it if you are not loving. You must live the fundamental intuitions. He who does not sacrifice himself does not understand the world as a whole nor is it possible to explain it to him, just as it is not possible to explain sound to the deaf or light to one born blind. There is no optics for the blind nor acoustics for the deaf nor morality or religion for egoists. This is why they deny there is such. But just as the deaf do not argue against music and the blind do not argue against painting, so the evil do not argue against love, for love is an incomparable work of art. One must have all the facts, be human in an integral sense and not an angel or a beast, in order to encom-pass existence as economy and love, as interest and sacrifice. . . .

He alone is good who does the good. He alone is free who attains the incoercible personality of giving; of giving because he has strength above and beyond the negative causes, laws, and conditions of his action. Life says: Do not give what is your own. Reason says: To give is foolish. The good says: Give what your egoism asks you to hold on to because reason does not discover your true, deep self, your real, autonomous personality, emanci-pated from biological life. If you deny your extrinsic self, you will find your transcendental self. Sacrifice yourself, for thus will you abide eternally. Only in this way will there be nothing above you. Your egoism is a whole. If you give it all, you will have it all. If you retain a portion, you will be enslaved to another law. Only he who has no property possesses himself. Existence of love is the fullness of existence. No law governs self-denial. Sacrifice is victory.

And, as the culmination of virtue we have hope, the *sagesse* of the Christian, the most philosophical and lovable of all the virtues, greater even than Socratic wisdom. . . .

Reader: What is said here is only philosophy, and philosophy is an interest of knowledge. Love is action. Go and act in love. Then, in addition to being wise, you will be holy. Philosophy is impossible without love, but love is perfectly possible without philosophy because the first is an idea, a thought, but the second is an experience, an act. Your century is egoistic and perverse. Nevertheless, love the men of your century that appear not to know how to love, who act only out of hunger and covetousness. He who does not love in this way will never know love. All of the philosophies of the men of science are worth nothing in the face of the disinterested action of one good man.

José Vasconcelos
(1882-1959)

Vasconcelos must undoubtedly be considered one of the most interesting and controversial figures in the history of Latin American philosophy. A profound philosopher, an excellent writer, a dedicated educator and political activist, he represents in his life and in his work a profound sense of Mexican destiny and of Latin American culture in general. In a series of works that attained great popularity (*Estudios indostánicos*, 1920; *La raza cósmica*, 1925; *Indología*, 1926; and others), he optimistically prophesies concerning the future of Latin America. The foundation of this future is constituted by the cosmic race, a synthesis of the four basic races of the present world that will emerge in the region of the Amazon and fulfill "the divine mission of America." In contrast with the ethnic egoism and nationalism incarnate in the Anglo-Saxon people of Europe and North America, the new race will be characterized by a universalist spirit based on love.

Vasconcelos was born in Oaxaca, Mexico, in 1882. From 1897 on he lived in the capital of his country, where he studied in the National College of Jurisprudence, graduating in 1905. His thesis, "La teoría dinámica del derecho," published later in *Revista positiva* (1907), reflects the positivist perspective that dominated his thought at the time. His sympathy for positivism, however, was transitory. A year later, 1908, along with a group of young men of like mind, he founded the Ateneo de la Juventud, which became a center of artistic and philosophical ferment from which the Mexican national intellectual movement emerged. From that time on he was no longer identified with the ideological positivism that had dominated the Mexican intellectual environment throughout the dictatorship of Porfirio Díaz. During the revolutionary commotion of 1910 and the years of political chaos that followed, Vasconcelos actively participated in the national struggle. He was exiled on two occasions, 1910 and 1913, and was obliged to remain in the United States for some time, but he returned to Mexico in 1914 to assume the position of minister of public education. Some time later, during the government of Venustiano Carranza, he left the country again. In 1919 he was appointed president of the National University and later minister of education for a second time. During this period he began the intensive activity that provided the foundation for the Mexican educational system. His unsuccessful candidacy for the national presidency in the elections of 1929 brought an end to his political ambitions. From 1939 on, his public activity was limited in great part to serving as director of the National Library. He died in Mexico on June 30, 1959.

Parallel with his intense political activity and his teaching responsibilities, although the latter were not major, Vasconcelos developed a philosophic system inspired by Bergson, Schopenhauer, Plotinus, and Pythagoras—a system he characterized as "aesthetic monism." Its development begins with *Pitágoras, una teoría del ritmo* (1916) and continues through many books and essays, among which the most important are *El monisimo estético* (1918) and *Tratado de metafísca* (1929). *Todología* (1952) concludes the development of Vasconcelos's system and constitutes the most important synthesis of his thought. In it he provides the final statement of his philosophical system and attempts to integrate it with the principles of Christianity to which he had been converted shortly before. Within this system man is the highest expression of the principle that makes reality intelligible. The highest degree of coordination of the heterogeneous flux is carried out by man's consciousness through the synthesis of knowledge. Thus Vasconcelos can go on to say that man is a genuine although small reflection of the universe and that therefore he constitutes a true microcosm.

J. G.

Todología*

[MAN IN THE COSMOS]

Our system begins with the atom, or going back still further, with the quantic wave length that is sometimes expressed as light and at others as one of the eighty or so forms of the electromagnetic variations. These variations are the foundation of all that occurs in the physical world. The wave and the atom are the first constructive efforts of the Cosmos, the elemental structures that oppose the second law of thermodynamics, that of entropy, and thus restrain the process of dissolution from which the Universe has suffered since its creation.

The second stage of this process toward construction and architecture, toward coordinated heterogeneity rather than disintegration, destruction, and homogeneity, is found in the molecule that joins two or more heterogeneous atoms to form elements, of which at present, chemists have identified approximately ninety-eight. Through compounds of these elements, which are always heterogeneous and asymmetrical, the molecular world leads the architecture of the Universe one step beyond the wave and the atom in its task of opposing entropy, that is, in the struggle against dispersion into homogeneity.

In the third place we have that unique activity found in the living cell. Through combinations that are also asymmetrical (male, female; heat, cold; assimilation and disassimilation of elements), the cell gives rise to animal species and at the end of these, the human person appears as a conclusion and yet also as a transition toward another stage. With or without evolution, man represents a break in the Cosmos, a break similar to that of light quanta that create waves, or to that of the molecule or of the cell, although it is much more profound because with man a new element appears: consciousness. We say consciousness because it is dangerous, after all, to speak of intelligence if by intelligence we mean intuition of essences or forms. Rather

*From José Vasconcelos, *Filosofía estética. Todología,* in *Obras completas* (Mexico: Libreros Mexicanos Unidos, 1961), 4:836-43, 900-905.

than formal intuition or even ontological intuition, consciousness is characterized by the living act that permits it to *coordinate the different elements of knowledge* that come to one through the various instruments of knowledge. These elements are the senses, intelligence, will, and feeling. Their number may increase as investigation probes deeper into the psyche and into psychology, but what constitutes the center and the specific character of consciousness is the *act coordinating the heterogeneous acts* that form knowledge. This coordinating act gives rise to a special type of unification, the unification for action, that differs from the unity derived from intelligence, which is the product of purely conventional abstractions and common denominators. The coordinating action integrates perceptions of the external world into a form of behavior. When this behavior inquires where it is going, it engenders an activity of a transcendent nature, a metaphysical activity. This metaphysics, as over against the ancient metaphysics, does not consist in intuiting abstract, logically related essences set over against a changing reality; nor does it consist of an ontology that is supposed to be most real because it is unchanging and which for that very reason seems to us to be dead and completely alien to the real nature of creation. On the contrary, by metaphysics I understand a system of knowledge of the parts or of the beings that make up a realm of existence of the relationships that bind the parts together, the particular purpose of each part and the common goal of the distinct groups, all intended to achieve a comprehension of the whole. This is a living whole, however, within which the parts are not elements that can be summed up as in the case of arithmetic or geometry, rather they are functions, properties and factors that, although remaining heterogeneous nevertheless give rise to a whole that is always something more than the sum of the parts. It is more than a formal whole because it constitutes a hierarchy and a hierarchy is a more accurate image of the Universe than any purely quantitative image.

In any case, let it be clear that we are attempting to identify the person with the psyche of the Greeks and more specifically with the soul of the Christians. However, we reject at the outset the pretension of reducing the soul to pure intellect, because the soul is a portion of life itself that is brought to perfection as a miniature of the Universe. We do not find possible nor desirable the hypothesis of a pure intellect. We also reject the old Aristotelian concept of the pure act because, in its excess of abstraction through paring away, instead of God one is left with nothing. There are no abstractions in nature. Verbs exist only as conditions for nouns, but only nouns possess being.

In any case, the soul is the supreme achievement of action that, through structures and a variety of architectures, initiates the action of beings in order to combat the entropy of the Universe. The best instrument that creation had to begin the struggle that enlivens the spirit was man, but for some mysterious reason, akin to original sin, he was filled with pride, became blind and therefore useless. Since then, nature and souls themselves have been in need of redemption. Redemption is a cosmic process that works against entropy through the redeemed man who returns to himself upon uniting his will with the one who said, "I am the way and the life; he who follows me will achieve immortality."

From this perspective, man represents a fourth stage, which is that of the soul. Differentiated from the rest of the Cosmos and alien to entropy as long as his soul is active, it is through man that the brilliance of the spirit bursts over creation. The quanta produce light; the atom engenders movable structures; the cell is the beginning of life that contradicts entropy; the soul is the beginning of the spirit; and by means of souls the Holy Spirit renews the Universe. At the same time, with the soul there appears for the first time a certain affinity that enables us to be aware of the presence of the matters of the spirit with something like instinct—the precursor of intelligence in the species—and in much the same way the soul anticipates the ways of the other world and attempts to relate to the beings that possibly inhabit it, such as angels and archangels.

We have said "beings of the other world" and not "essences of the other world," as the usual Platonist or idealist would have expressed it, because we have repudiated the thesis of two worlds: the world of essences and the world of concrete life. We do not accept nor do we conceive anything other than one world made of structures, organisms, and souls, that is, of fully integrated beings and beyond which are even more perfect beings. Thus we avoid the pseudo-Platonic operation that first abstracts so it can postulate essences and then, to cope with these ghostlike essences, clothes them with fleshly attributes and in art resorts to humanized forms of angels, virtues, potentialities, and so on. We find this mental game neither necessary nor useful. . . .

Having traced the panorama of existence, from the magnetic wave to God, what yet remains as a major task is to establish the relationships of these parts to each other, which is the responsibility of science, and the relationships of the parts with the Supreme Person, which is the purpose of Theology.

THE ONE AND THE MANY

The human person represents the first act of knowledge in the Cosmos, if by knowledge we understand not only adapting the thing to an idea, and the image to the material object, but also the act of *cognoscere* itself that is the coordination of heterogeneous factors in a common, possibly concurrent purpose. In the highest spheres of existence, the human person, in coordinating various dimensions, carries out a function similar to that of the amoeba as it captures and apprehends the nutritive corpuscle necessary for maintaining the construction that is life. Lower in the scale, the wave and the atom are the first acts of the elaboration of necessary structures for the architectonic foundation of the Cosmos. . . .

Each of the ways of our psyche or personality is a system of order that gives rise to a method of investigation and action. And corresponding to each of these systems is a partial vision of the nature of the psyche. If we give preference to intelligence, we will have rationalism; if we make feeling predominate, we are converted into materialists; if we balance our vital functions, our systems of investigation, we will attain a harmony that is more than the reason of the idealists and more than sensualism. We will achieve an awareness of totality in which each of the particles of the Cosmos will find its place according to the proportions and hierarchies of the Universe.

An equilibrium of this sort is not given in its entirety by reason, sensation, or art; nevertheless, it is achieved within us when we live in keeping with the fullness of our consciousness. In an effortless way, consciousness carries out its unifying function at each moment and thus reveals a power that is both above reason and the senses. It is a power of adjusting and harmonizing what is below with what is above, what is far with what is near, but it is no longer natural since it is above nature, as if it belonged in fact to the realm of the spirit. It presupposes an immaterial consciousness that transcends corporeal consciousness. Without separating one realm from another, because it is useless and because every dispensable hypothesis borders on confusion, let us say that it is proper to man's consciousness to understand what is below him while receiving its requests and yet give what is below him an orientation that leads to superior ends while at the same time anticipating and divining the directions and goals of existence from above, like an immaterial amphibian that participates in two natures, the sensible and the invisible.

However, what does the head of this amphibian perceive as it looks into incorporeal regions? To be sure, it discovers a world in which notions concerning matter are no longer applicable, whereas ideas and feelings satisfying eternal demands are applicable. In the new world of the invisible, physics and chemistry are no longer valid, neither are mathematics and logic but only the highest visions of poetry, philosophy, and religion. And it is the last that in the end is the indispensable interpreter, the only idiom enabling the soul to communicate with the invisible. For religion, after all, is nothing other than revelation, the contemplation of the whole in all its infinitude though no longer according to what is above or below, but according to mental operations of proportion, harmony, and love. God is in the center and the creatures are in their respective places within a world that is a perennial dynamism, while still a rich and complete concert of disparities and asymmetries.

Revelation is thus the ultimate philosophy and even as Christ is the highest, most authoritative religious seer in all History, the only one in whom, as Saint John saw, the Word itself is incarnate, we must conclude that in the Gospel we find the principles and the ends, the columns and the archways of the true and total philosophy. This permits us to explain and connect what has occurred, occurs, and is to occur in the Universe, between the creatures and their Creator.

[BEING AND SELF]

The notion of beings belongs to the experiential order. It is not an idea, rather all ideas proceed from it. It is not a vision because all visions proceed from being, nor is being a rumor since all sounds find their source in being. The notion of being is not negative but the most positive that exists. The I Am Who I Am is the foundation of the world. When we attempt to come to being through analysis, through subtractions and abstractions, this foundation escapes us. Being is a synthesis from which all flows. Ideas, memories, premonitions, feelings, sensations, all stem from the complex singularity of Absolute Being and from our consciousness, which is its image. We are therefore a microcosm, an abbreviation of the Universe, unique, extraneous to the generic, yet made to understand all genders. The notion of being possesses density, like a weight that holds itself up in a vacuum; it supports existence itself. It conquers gravity, even as spirit transcends the body. Firmer than steel because it is unbreakable; heavier than weight and faster than the wing, Being is reality itself and the source of the confidence in which the Universe rests. . . .

We participate in Absolute Being and therefore we feel like small kings of the Universe. Experience informs us of our fragility so we seek the center of power: the Absolute from which the particle that we are proceeds. To find this Absolute in any of its manifestations gives rise to confidence and rejoicing. When we lose contact, our being bursts like a soap bubble that has reflected the Universe, but does not incarnate it; it has not been part of life. The soul survives if it is inserted into the processes of the Universe and carries out a function in them, but that function is so limited compared with the vastness and complexity of the Universe, that our being recoils and is alarmed, it is overwhelmed and disturbed and feels it lacks support. It therefore needs an infusion of substance, a new generation, a rebirth, and this is the grace of faith. Our fragility converts us into eternity because the promise of life eternal and resurrection is fulfilled. . . .

Being in itself is the soul and the soul is an organized portion of what is. We understand the Divine Person to be what is, for he defined himself as He who is. The soul is a creature, made in the image and likeness of its

Creator and thus in its constitution there is a coherence that is an imitation of the divine coherence. In their special nature, all microcosms are varieties of the original being; each being is a part of the whole of creation, but not like a part of an abstract whole that when added to other parts yields a quantitative whole. The parts of a being cannot be added because they are heterogeneous; they coordinate their particularity to engender wholes with new qualities. The parts enrich, concur, and harmonize, they are linked through harmony not geometry and thus engender partial wholes that possess life. . . .

It is the essential for the soul to coordinate the internal elements with the external in order to affirm within the Universe the presence of an autonomous quantum of energy, a living factor, a unity that operates within the physical but belongs to the spirit.

The individual soul makes use of different instruments and means for knowing: the sensitive, the intellectual, the ethical, the aesthetic, each of which operates by means of specific *a prioris,* as we have insisted in various parts of this work.

BEING IN OTHERS

Much depends on first impressions. He who knew the caress of a mother, the adoring eyes of a father, or the attention of a relative or friend, some loving person, has an impression that others are a blessing. The other is our guardian and support, there within reach. A gesture or a call and he will come, seeking to help us in our need. Even before we know our own self, we contemplate, recognize, and give structure to the other, be it father, brother, or neighbor. Our being is complemented by, rests in, and trusts him. Only later, much, much later, do we recognize that, for all the help, consolation, and comfort, all of which are good, the other is also suspended in the same emptiness in which we find ourselves. Both of us lack a foundation, a support, some branch to hold on to and prevent us from sliding into the abyss. Where shall we find the support, the base, the branch that will prevent us from falling without end? The little corner of the world that is our planet provides gravity, a pitiful support, but thanks to it we do not fall endlessly and hopelessly through space. Where does one find gravity for the soul, the equilibrium of a living eternity?

The other is a body. All at once in a sudden involuntary reflection, we discover that the other, even the highest of the others, a mother, is also a body. Each of its shaping lines responds to a disagreeable secretion. In vain does it lift its shoulders because it cannot fly and its condition is such anguish that no one, unless he is beside himself, disrobes willingly before a multitude. . . .

The being like myself is the only one it would be natural for us to know. Yet when I turn toward being, it escapes and leaves me, and I am like an insane man who turns quickly so as to catch a glimpse of his back. It is useless, I will never be able to see my being, perhaps because I am within it, for it is not at my back but in the unexplored dimension of depth. Furthermore, it is not a substance to be seen since it is that with which I see. What is my being? The pivot of the machinery, the pilot of my directions that gathers whatever I look at and feel, whatever I hear and think and love. To picture it to myself I turn to the nature of God as seen in the mystery of the Trinity. God is the Unity of the Trinity. My being, a spark of his, is the invisible unifying power of everything that enters into the realm of its own operation. We speak of the metrical field in electricity. The Universe is the metrical field of the unique monad that each being is. But the mention of the Universe takes us away from being as self. So let us return.

What is to be found in the depths of my living, acting monad? Nothing, if I proceed by analysis, because I am neither sensation nor color, sound nor vibration, thought nor feeling, but all taken together. This is to say that at each moment, unlike the atom, I need polarity in order to subsist: electron-neutron, my consciousness is always invaded by the thousand demands of the external world, and in order to subsist it needs to classify and then coordinate sensations, ideas, images. But what is coordination? An irregular, periodic act at times tenuous and at times resplendent, produced in my consciousness, which is itself the coordinator.

Consciousness, the invisible factor of coordination, is not an entity in the body, just as God is not the soul of the Universe. The soul possesses a destiny that is other than being consciousness. God is the Creator of the creation, but he is not immersed in it. He does not depend upon it. He could destroy his work, and perhaps may destroy it several times, as the Hindu Kalpas claim or he may simply let it die, as in entropy. For the soul, however, God has different norms from those that govern the Universe. Between the soul and God there is the terrible covenant of the free will and if I had the opportunity to choose, I would reject it. The responsibility of the free will was inserted into our nature, but the consequences of its abuse are so cruel that I feel the need for help. I draw near to divine mercy, without whose grace the poor worm that I am would never develop into a chrysalis.

The being of the self is an unfathomable abyss. We extract from it something new each time that we go down into its infinity. A chasm of desires without potential, there is yet one sense that draws us to its obscure reality, the sense of touch, since the being as myself is felt through kinesthesia. Internal sensibility is a tension. The electron is also a tension capable of explosion when its counterwave, its polarity, appears. Being as myself experiences this same necessity for emerging, for manifestation, when it encounters another being like itself. The order of being is thus divided into three great realms: Being as myself in the world that surrounds me, the being of others, and the being of God. . . .

Philosophy Manual*

[SOUL, VALUE, AND CONDUCT]

Just as the cell develops ways of conduct that break the harmony of its environment in order to create a harmony of its own in keeping with the needs of its development, so the soul appears as an organism that from the invisible dimension of its environment takes elements to structure its development and conduct. These elements are ethical and aesthetic values. They are values, modes of conduct that have nothing to do with nutrition. The soul makes its energy demands upon the body that is made of cells and functions like an organism composed of cells, but the higher aspect of conduct does not stem from the cellular system, because it is a process. To use a word that a contemporary school has put in vogue, we will say that it is intentioned conduct. The soul moves by intentions. The study of these intentions would lead us to discover, by means of generalized induction, certain laws of conduct that, according to the materialists, are founded in habit. We believe, however, that their origin is to be found in the delightful discovery by the initiators and creators of ethico-religious values. These creators proceed by revelation that operates in consciousness and submits us to a will that rules and surpasses our own. . . .

Consciousness lives expressing itself in three spheres that are often decentralized and may rotate in a discordant manner. However, it is possible to imagine a moment of perfection in which they would coincide to produce a singular impression, like a light of several colors, in which the colors remain individual and separated by a prism or by the vapor in the rainbow. For the soul the forms of unity are intelligence, will, and beauty. Depending on which form predominates, we have the wise man, the saint, or the artist, although it should be understood that in the case of the saint, the will finds its fulfillment in the beauty of love, which is superior to the purely formal

*From José Vasconcelos, *Manual de Filosofía,* in *Obras completas* (Mexico: Libreros Mexicanos Unidos, 1961), 4:1271-78.

beauty of the artist. It is also certain that as on inferior levels and in the biological world so in the human world, triumph belongs to the more intelligent and daring and by virtue of that triumph we have the creation of the norm of virtue or the norm of the good for politics and history, as in the case of the patriotic or social hero. Thus, we should not expect the masses to abide by superior rules of conduct nor should we expect to find these rules as habits in those who are inferior. In thinking about human conduct, we must adhere to what the great personalities of the species have thought and to what its heroes and saints have done. Within the human species, individualization is more sharply defined than in the inferior species. Among fish, for example, there is no individual distinction, whereas our species is characterized by the infinite differentiation between individuals, and among them the example is set by those who are superior. The ethical norm is what they have seen, what they have commanded, and it is valid to the degree to which they capture the revelation of something that, in order to remain within the realm of biologico-philosophical terminology, we call the consciousness that surpasses us. If psychology believes in the subconscious, religion and art believe, with sublime faith, in the much more positive reality of the superconscious, which for the creators of ethics is the supernatural will that sustains the worlds. In effect, each time the creators of morality formulated a rule of conduct, they have had the impression of being transmitters of a supreme thought, that is, they seem to confirm through their experience precisely that theory referred to earlier, namely, the theory of the Word. It is as if in the environment, in that plasma of consciousness that the spirit is, there should already be formulated norms, not in the air, but abiding in the consciousness of the archangel or of other mysterious persons that ritual calls Virtues, Thrones, Powers, Dominions. Suddenly a superior individual in the species achieves communication with the Fullness, that is to say, with the persons of wisdom or with God himself. Such is the phenomenon of revelation. . . .

Values, for us, are the boundaries within which the soul moves. Just as the naturalist studies that group of processes in the animal's mode of behavior, which is often admirable and permits the animal to live and develop within its environment, so it is natural to conceive that this new being of the spirit, this cell of the spirit that is the soul, should have its group of reflexes and operations so that, let it be said clearly, it can attain its own salvation, as various religions have seen so profoundly. These are the values, this group of operations and reflexes that the soul needs for its moral life and ultimately for its salvation. In animals, the reflex is a nerve process that can be measured because the animal is something concrete and palpable, but in the soul we can only conceive of these values as *a priori* or as structures that govern conduct and are inseparable from it. The invisible self is inaccessible to our senses, but to the mind it is reality itself. Thus it should not be strange that we should not be able to locate where values operate within the nervous system. The soul does not have nerves, but it does have modes of operating that if violated lead to disaster but if fully actualized lead to salvation. In like fashion, when we turn to aesthetic values, we see that they govern the production of beauty in the sensible world, that they make things according to the spirit and not as is done in the physical world, where things are made after the pattern found in lower material dynamics.

We have been studying ideas and values in keeping with the method of contemporary science that begins from below in order to build upward. Science begins with the primordial cell and later leaps up toward the spirit. This method is the inverse of that followed in ancient philosophy, which began by postulating the absolute in order to descend then to the study of the particular. Both ways lead to identical results.

It is a more viable hypothesis to suppose that things proceed from above and degenerate toward what is below than it is to begin, as is done today, with what is inferior in order to reach what is above. Nevertheless, it is a comfort to establish that these two ways converge toward the same absolute truth. At present we are led to imagine human personality, human consciousness, as a—I was going to say mechanism but we must avoid the word—as a system of operations that can be separated precisely into three great branches: the system of sensibility justified by intelligence; the Kantian forms of the spirit can be applied to sensibility that is measured and defined by the norms of time and space. Whether we conceive these norms in keeping with the ancients or according to the modern concept of relativity, we are speaking of norms adapted to the object, as Bergson has made us see with such clarity. It is our good fortune that in the last analysis, physics is an effort to adapt matter to intelligence, but not in the rigorous fashion proposed in Aristotelianism and scholasticism, which both failed. Today, intelligence recognizes events that are not an intelligent consequence, yet neither are they absurd; they are events in experience, contingent events, that can occur or not without reason being trampled in the process. So, in order to give meaning to some events, intelligence must turn to other elements of awareness, for example, the will. Now the will brings with it intention, and transforms the entire mechanism of the Universe so as to adapt it to the world and purposes of the will. The whole operation of the will, beginning with its appearance in the cells that lengthen the cilia in order to acquire nourishment, is a process and an effort to subdue the environment to the purposes of an obscure or clear intention that operates in organisms, from the cell to the soul. In order to explain this intention, reason is not sufficient; one must also observe the operation of the will in order to determine its common tendency. The superior impulses of consciousness are the creators of the norm; they define values. By the same token, in the third operation that is the operation of joy, the operation that complements the others and is being's prize for its achievements, we also have to suppose a system. In joy we discover a system that is not rational but has its own ways of operating. These ways are rhythm, melody, harmony, and counterpoint. Each of these three systems of living, the intellectual, the moral, and the aesthetic, have in the human person, in consciousness, their proper place and means of action. . . .

Samuel Ramos
(1897-1959)

Ramos is the most outstanding Mexican philosopher in the generation that followed the "founders," i.e., Caso and Vasconcelos.

He was born in Zitácuaro in 1897. He studied in the National High School at San Nicolás de Hildalgo and later in Mexico City under Antonio Caso. In 1920 he collaborated with Vasconcelos in the ministry of public education. He lived for a time in France and Italy and later became part of a group of professors of philosophy at the National University in Mexico City. There, he held the chairs of aesthetics and history of philosophy and letters and became a member of the Colegio Nacional, an institution that brought together the intellectuals of major importance in the country.

In his first work, *Hypothesis* (1928), he tells of the vicissitudes of his spiritual pilgrimage and of his debt to and his break with Caso. Ortega y Gasset, Scheler, Hartmann, and Adler and the historicists were also important influences.

The perspectivism of Ortega helped to provide a foundation for his preoccupation with a national philosophy and to clarify the "Mexican nature." Ramos was attracted to two apparently contradictory impulses that he attempted to reconcile. He sought to remain true to the particularity of Mexican reality and yet he aspired to knowledge and values that were universal. He succeeded in avoiding both an abstract universalism and a false folkloric nationalism, maintaining that "the norm of 'nationalism' must be to purify our own life without impairing it as it approaches the level of universal forms."

He analyzes these problems in his work *Perfil del hombre y la cultura en México*, published in 1934 (*Profile of Man and Culture in Mexico* [University of Texas Press, 1962]). In applying the psychoanalytic theory of Adler, he believed to have discovered that the fundamental characteristic of the Mexican, taken individually as well as collectively, is an inferiority complex. This interpretation is continued later by Octavio Paz in his well-known book *El laberinto de la soledad* (1947).

Ramos maintains that the spiritual renewal of his country would be achieved by a profound educational reform based on a new theory of man. He states the fundamental ideas of the reform in various articles that later were published in a volume entitled *Veinte años de educación en México* (1941). His philosophical anthropology is found in his principal work, *Hacia un nuevo humanismo. Programa de una antropología filosófica* (1940), from which the selections that follow have been taken.

In this work Ramos seeks to surpass the dualism between materialism and spiritualism, conceiving of the whole man as constituted by body and soul or, in the language of Ortega, by vitality, soul, and spirit. With spirit as the highest level of reality, he places the foundation of the spirituality of the person in the objectivity of values, understood in Max Scheler's sense.

Ramos was also interested in the philosophical past in his country and he wrote the first *Historia de la filosofía en México* (1943). This book inspired the research on thought in his country later carried out by Leopoldo Zea and other scholars under the direction of José Gaos.

R. F.

Toward a New Humanism*

AXIOMS OF HUMAN ONTOLOGY

Human life is not a mere existing as is the case with things that surround it, for it is, and this must be stressed, a knowing that it exists. Human existence is distinguished from all other existence in that it is conscious of its existing. A stone, an insect, or a tree exists but without knowing so. Consciousness, one might say, is a revelation of being. However, consciousness is not an "epiphenomenon," a mere addition that accompanies existence in order to acknowledge it; it is not a reflecting surface destined for contemplation. Consciousness gives to human existence its characteristic mode of being, and is an inseparable dimension of man's ontological structure. When I become aware of my existence, I am not aware of it alone, as if surrounded by a vacuum; quite to the contrary, my existence is given to me in the midst of a host of realities that act upon me and at the same time are the focus of my action. Consciousness makes me feel, therefore, like one existence in the midst of others, occupying a specific place among them. The basic trait of human existence in Heidegger's words is "being in the world." Further, I do not feel that I am a fixed, immovable existence, but something that is constantly flowing. My consciousness is not only of my actual state, of the "here" and the "now," I also have memories and expectations. I remember my previous states, what has been, but through representation I also anticipate what is not as yet. In a word, I have intentions, projects, hopes. Consciousness is precisely the capacity to retain images of the past and to project the imagination toward the future. However, the acts separated in this analysis—because one cannot speak of everything at once—are actually interwoven in the living present, enriching its content and forming the uninterrupted continuum that constitutes time. Consciousness, then, gives temporal dimension to human existence. The things outside ourselves that constitute our world also appear to us in time although for them time does not

*From Samuel Ramos, *Hacia un nuevo humanismo* (Mexico: Fondo de Cultura Económica, 1962), 40-43, 46-47, 49, 56-58, 78-79, 84-88, 89-90.

exist. However, time is with us, our existence *is* time. The notion of time, then, has a twofold significance, depending on whether we apply it to the external world or to our own life. In the first case time, properly speaking, is not a reality but a mere relationship characteristic of entities as they flow through the channel of our sensibilities. For us, however, time is not the channel but the river itself that runs through the channel. Time has in this last sense an ontic reality as an integral part of human existence.

Like other living beings, man is a continuously developing process. In the plant and animal worlds, however, this process invariably follows the same curve, with each species adhering to a mold that each individual faithfully reproduces, since these beings have a prefixed destiny governed in all details by an unavoidable law. In human existence there is also an element of inevitability. Basically, human existence appears as a task directed toward its own survival, since every man concerns himself first with structuring his own life and in so doing he must think of the future, for through anticipation he perceives what may happen. For this reason, Ortega says, man is an essentially "pre-occupied" being. First, man must do something in order to live, for life is given as a majestic problem that must be resolved, and the demand to guarantee existence is pressed upon him as an inevitable necessity since life is given as a continuous risk, the risk of being lost. The possibility of death emerges and leads to the feeling of anguish present to a greater or lesser degree in all human existence.

The uncertainty of human life indicates that it is not completely predetermined. Within a great measure of determinism, life contains a margin of liberty for man is a being of multiple possibilities with varying degrees of breadth in his choices; he can voluntarily propose some specific goal and accomplish it. The basic principle of human life is not reduced to mere conservation and assurance of existence. If animal life is a vicious circle, appearing as a tendency that starts with life only to return to it, human life searches for a meaning that transcends mere living and represents enrichment in addition to the conservation of life. We shall return to this point later, however. For the present we only conclude that in the realm of being man appears as a teleological entity, for he can consciously propose goals for himself and attempt to achieve them. This characteristic can exist only in man because of his knowledge and foresight. Whereas animal existence is shaped like a series of points, a discontinuous succession of present moments, human existence is amplified into a continuous becoming that goes from the past to the future through the present. Memory is the instrument of his past, whereas that of his future is foresight.

THE THEORIES OF MAN AND
THE CURVE OF HUMANISM

Greek metaphysics exhibits a marked anthropomorphic propensity to conceive the universe in the human mode, as is seen in the great teleological and soul-filled system of Aristotle. Modern philosophy, however, influenced by natural science, tends to conceive man in the mode of nature. From a theoretical perspective, the Greeks elevated nature to the level of man whereas the moderns have lowered man to the level of nature; only Christian philosophy has placed man above nature, attributing to him a religious, supernatural meaning. These errors in perspective have been denounced by contemporary philosophy, for it has discovered that reality is divided into ontological realms that are diverse in structure. Philosophy will not fall into the error of explaining nature from the anthropological point of view or vice versa. Its aspiration is to explain each realm not from outside but from within itself in terms of its own categories. The problem in philosophical anthropology stems from the fact that man is an archway in which several categories of being are joined. But in which is his essence found? There seem to be almost as many conceptions of man as there are elements that constitute his existence. Each conception takes a single dimension and would make of it the whole of human existence, with the result that man's existence is mutilated by the one-sidedness of the vision. Man is conceived as reason, as will, as feeling, as instinct, etc. These ideas stem from three main sources: religion, philosophy, and natural science. . . .

In no way do we belittle the value of scientific studies concerning man. Undoubtedly, thanks to science we possess a knowledge of human life that is more complex and profound than any there has ever been. We also possess some measure of understanding concerning man's relationship to nature. Science, however, proceeds by abstraction, dissecting human life into parts; life as physical, psychical, social, juridical, and so on. The aspiration of philosophical anthropology differs, for it seeks to obtain an idea of man as an integrated whole. The range of the diverse historical conceptions of man corresponds to a limited series of empirical types, no one of which represents the whole of human kind. So it is justifiable that anthropology should attempt to formulate a suprahistorical and supraempirical idea that will contain only those elements that can be ascribed to any man regardless of his temporal coordinates and empirical particulars. If man is a composite of diverse elements, anthropology is not going to concede special privilege to one of them, thereby downgrading the others. She accepts all of these elements with the privileges that belong to each, since the purpose and the problem of anthropology is to determine how these particular elements are integrated into a unity, what relationship they bear to one another, and what their essential structure is. She inquires whether it is possible to order these elements into a hierarchy according to an objective scale of values. . . .

LAYERS OF THE HUMAN BEING

Some human beings live primarily on their vital energy or are pure vital energy, as is the case with children and some primitive peoples. When vital energy is pervasive we place ourselves outside the center of our personhood. At times of play, in games, in living that is bound by the senses, the individual forgets the self and finds he is as molded with the rest of nature. From this treasure of vital energy, man's personality is nourished. However, if from this peripheral corporeal zone we turn inward, two separate territories appear: the soul and the spirit. The reason for distinguishing the soul from the spirit is the following: we perceive within ourselves movements that do not stem from our own inner will, movements of which we do not feel we are the authors. Emotions, feelings, passions, sympathies, and dislikes are awakened in us without our assent, produced in spite of ourselves but nevertheless they are in us. We would prefer not to have them, but we do. They are *my* sentiments but they are not *me*, because I do not identify with them. Here we find the passions of love and, generally, the life of feeling— the private world of the individual life. The movements of the soul, however, can be suppressed or set free by other forces over which our person has control. The spirit is made up of will and thought. It constitutes in the strict sense what is called the *self*. The self is the central focus of our person that resolves and decides, it is that in the actions of understanding and knowing that is placed in direct contact with the known. Another difference between soul and spirit is that spiritual phenomena do not last, whereas those of the soul occur in time. We may take a long time to understand something, but the understanding itself is the work of an instant, just as preparation for action may take time, but the decision to act is made in a moment. Everything, however, that belongs to the soul is carried out in time. "To be sad, to be happy for a while, a day, or for all one's life."

The spirit is the center of the person and yet it is governed by impersonal norms. In order to think the truth one must abide by logical norms and adapt one's intelligence to the being of things. That is why pure thought is the same in all individuals and, in thinking formally, all think the same. The will also acts in accord with objective norms, with what ought to be, with value. The soul, then, is the realm of subjectivity and the spirit of objectivity.

It should be clear that this notion of spirit does not correspond to the traditional concept of a metaphysical entity hidden behind phenomena. What we affirm concerning the spirit is fully justified by experience, for it is from experience that these statements have been drawn. Even when we no longer accept the old metaphysical doctrines concerning spirit, the direct observation of phenomena places us in the presence of a series of activities that is peculiarly human, that cannot be reduced to others, and thus deserves to retain that name. Evidently intelligence, will, and intuition of values are functions not governed by psychophysical laws. Scheler defined spirit as "objectivity" or "the possibility of being determined by objects themselves." Spirit, then, is the life of a subject that transcends his individuality in order to seek its law in the objective world, whether real or ideal. The spirit is a direction of human life that is personal at its point of departure but whose goal is supraindividual. This should not be interpreted to mean that spirit exists as a universal something outside the individual. Spirit exists only in that singular concentration that we call person. We live with the Spirit in those moments in which we do not live for ourselves as individuals. There are two possible forms of life, in one we live as isolated beings, in the other we live with the world. The latter represents spiritual life. . . .

MAN AS FREEDOM

Freedom should not be sought in what transcends the individual but in what lies within; strictly speaking, his will is free, in the proper sense. However one should not identify this view with "indeterminism," even if that freedom is seen as the capacity at the beginning of a reflection to disobey a command from one's values or to elude one's natural impulses. To do so would be to conceive the essence of freedom as something negative as in the scholastic notion of *liberum arbitrarium indifferentiae*. Freedom is either a positive force, a decision of the will that results in self-determination, or it is an empty concept deprived of all content, making freedom incomprehensible. Freedom does not constitute a violation of the principle of causality. What is needed to explain it as Hartmann says is an added determination that introduces will into causal complexes. Such liberty "in a positive sense" would then be possible if in the world the causal nexus is constituted by different types of determination, each of which has a certain autonomy.

In this sense, freedom is not an exceptional phenomenon to be found only in man; it is common to all beings insofar as they find themselves hierarchically arranged on different levels of existence. An animal, as compared to inanimate nature, is free as can be seen in its movement and sensibility; consciousness is free compared to the organic life to which it is bound, and so on successively. By placing the problem of moral liberty within a broad perspective, the dualism of determination is resolved into a pluralism. Every level of being appears endowed with a characteristic type of structure. In the ideal sphere of being we find logical necessity, which might be described in Leibniz's words as "the principle of sufficient reason." Following this would come mathematical necessity that governs all calculation according to specific deductive laws. In the realm of physical reality we find a stratified series of independent structures: mechanical, biological, and psychological structures. And finally, spirit emerges as the highest level whose processes are interwoven also in accord with its own laws. The freedom that corresponds to each level is not absolute, for each is conditioned by the previous level. Thus, there is no personality without consciousness, no consciousness without organic life, no organic life without natural mechanical structure, and no mechanism without mathematical order. In each level, however, an element appears that cannot be reduced to the preceding level and this element constitutes precisely what is new in each level. If the organism lives as a corporeal being, bound to the physico-chemical order, the life in it, manifested as nutrition, development, or reproduction, is a phenomenon that can only be explained by specifically biological principles. The biological structure is relatively free with respect to mechanical structure. Hartmann does not consider that a "contingency of natural laws" is acceptable, although Boutroux had maintained that it was, explaining that liberty can only be understood in this fashion. Here one may fall into the error of identifying liberty with indeterminacy, giving to liberty a negative meaning. Within each level the specific law is necessarily fulfilled in all cases. Liberty is understood as the new structure that each being introduces into the inferior structure that supports it. This is liberty in a positive sense.

PERSON AND PERSONALITY

The person is a general phenomenon through which human spirituality is expressed whereas personality is the highest degree that spirit achieves in some individuals. The value of personality was discovered during the Renaissance and since then the idea, representing the highest goal of humanization, has been incorporated into our culture. Apparently, there is nothing more obvious than personality, since with no previous impression of it we are able to discern its existence in those who possess it. When we try to isolate it conceptually, however, the clarity of its profile vanishes and its essential traits escape formulation in precise statements. Related to this issue, a series of problems emerges that philosophical anthropology must work with, because they concern a condition that belongs exclusively to the human being. The category of person is applicable only to human beings to the exclusion of all other living things.

Linguistic usage seems to establish a difference between person and personality. In principle it is accepted that all men are persons, but only to a select few is personality granted, for 'person' is a qualifier that can be applied to the whole human species, whereas the term personality has a more limited range of application.

We call a man 'person', not because he is a physical or psychical entity but because he is a moral entity. Person is a characteristic manner that the subject gives to himself by the spontaneous exercise of his inner will, as when he acts, thinks, or feels with full freedom. This characteristic manner can be distinguished from another that stems from the individual character of each man. Character is given to the individual by birth, whereas he gives himself a personality by superimposing it like an ideal mask upon his psychophysical character. . . .

Personality undoubtedly has its root and foundation in the psychophysical character of the individual, but it is something different from mere individuality. Personality settles over individuality like a necessary complement giving it order and direction, like a governing force. Individuality and personality are two distinct levels of the human being arranged in a hierarchical manner with the superiority given to the latter. Personality is not, therefore, a phenomenon determined by laws immanent within the individual nor is it a biological or psychological fact, but it is a phenomenon of the spiritual order.

Personality awakens the desire of the individual for dominion and control over the acts of his life; it belongs to the man who is not a servant to his inclinations or the circumstances that surround him; it rather superimposes itself on everything and gives its own direction and individual seal to his activity. Personality is the man who over and above his subjective motives always obeys the norms of truth, morality, and aesthetics and in this way reveals the dominion of a superior will. Through personality man's most intimate voice is heard and it is the revelation of his highest values. The true self is found in the center of the personality. Only the decisions made here have a spontaneous and active nature in contrast to all passive movement. That center is the high court that approves or disapproves of motivations of every kind, apparently in every dimension of the human being.

If personality emerges within the individual self, its bearing nevertheless is essentially centrifugal. Some impulses in man are centripetal, directed exclusively to the affirmation of individuality. For the personality, however, what is individual is only a means for affirming supraindividual values. To be sure, personality belongs only to an individual and it cannot be transmitted nor reproduced, for each has to create his own. However, personality can be achieved without awareness of individuality, as in the case of the Greeks. The awareness of individuality is a discovery of the modern era that, at times, attempts to make use of personality to affirm individuality. Personality is one of the many resources that so-called individualism makes use of to impose itself, but in the end it is quite different from aspiration to personality, whose roots are not found in the *being for itself* of the subject, but in its being *for the other*. A condition for acquiring personality is to be unmindful of it and not to make it a deliberate purpose for one's life. When it is postulated as a consciously pursued end, this attitude almost certainly hides an inclination toward individualism. Such an internal contradiction will bring about the failure of achieving the desired personality. With frequency this false attitude is turned toward the vain imitation of some other personality that is taken as a model.

Personality is experienced as a coherence or unity throughout the conduct of the individual. It appears as a steady bearing that directs the most heterogeneous activities of existence. I do not mean to say that in order to appreciate a concrete personality it is necessary to take into consideration the whole history of the development of the individual. The subject does not reveal his personality in all the acts of his life, but given a few of his acts, his personality as a whole can be seen. Acts of the personality are those that the individual performs with the intervention of his whole being. In them personality is seen as a unique standard impressed upon completed work like an identifying seal. Essential to the life of the person is the quality of singular unity that appears as distinctive in isolated psychological phenomena (Dilthey, Stern). In addition, among various parts of the psychological life a functional connection exists, which according to given proportions, causes psychical structures to be configured into "psychological types" (intellectual, intuitive, sensitive, and so on). On this structural base a modification determined by the *ethos* can be built. Now the *ethos* consists in the value relationships formed by each individual, for it is a system of evaluative election, a persistent manner of preferring or rejecting that acts in a consistent mode in the tastes, sympathies, and dislikes of each individual. Such tendencies in evaluation have a bearing on psychical composition for they provide a specific structure determined by the class of preferred values. The hues of personality are seen above all in the things that the individual selects and draws to himself to form his own world.

Interaction undoubtedly occurs between psychical character and personality. Character is the prime matter of the personality as well as the boundary limiting its possibilities. Within a psychophysical type only a specified form of personality is possible, although the latter is a potentiality that governs the forces of character and channels them toward given objective values. . . .

METAPHYSICS OF PERSONALITY

Personality is an ontological category of human existence, even if it is difficult to grasp within the accustomed forms of thought. It must not be thought of as a substance located in the obscure inner recesses of man, nor as a pure abstract essence that hovers in view of an individual's thought to serve as a model for his conduct. The entity of the person manifests its real existence in action and not only in a special mode of action, such as practical conduct, whether moral, political, or economic. Intellectual, artistic, and religious life is also action. In all of these vocations man can reveal a personality, for there are personal ways of thinking, feeling, imagining, believing, and loving. Spranger attempts to classify and define the different types of personality since for him personality is a "structure of meaning" originating in the intuition of a value.

Personality is not, as could be supposed, a fixed spiritual structure, representing an *a priori* form of action. Rather it is the meaning of an infinite process that moves toward a goal that is almost achieved. One might say that in this sense it shares the pragmatic character with human life in general.

Max Scheler, to whom we owe the most complete study of this topic—a topic that he includes in his analysis of ethics—identifies the concept of spirit with that of person. This is the necessary form of the existence of the spirit. The idea of an impersonal spirit seems contradictory to him. The spirit is by its very essence a pure actuality that exists only in action; it is a complex of acts ordered within a unity. The person is, one might say, the center of the acts of the spirit or the unified flow of these acts, but not their point of departure, for the person is something that is born and lives in the midst of these acts. Every concrete and real act, for example, of thinking or loving, carries within it the *totum* and the particular essence of the personality from which it proceeds.

Francisco Romero
(1891-1962)

Romero and Korn are the two major philosophers in Argentina and they are among the most important in Latin America.

Romero was born in Seville in 1891 and as a child came to Argentina, where he remained the rest of his life. He was educated as a military engineer and attained the rank of major in the army. During his youth he began to explore the bounds of his professional training, tending first toward literature and then toward philosophy. In these areas he was his own teacher. His philosophical interests and self-discipline led him to study philosophy on his own during long nights in the barracks after he had completed his professional duties, although the barracks were not the most propitious place to study philosophy. He began by reading Spencer and later turned to the study of German philosophy. Husserl, but principally Scheler and Nicolai Hartmann, were major influences in the formation of his philosophical perspective. His close friendship with Alejandro Korn was also a guiding factor in his life.

In 1939 he resigned his commission in order to work full time in philosophy. He was promoted from assistant professor to full professor of epistemology and metaphysics at the University of Buenos Aires, replacing his friend Korn who had retired the previous year. He was also professor at the University of La Plata. He resigned from all his positions in 1946 and returned to them in 1955. In 1962 he was appointed professor emeritus and traveled to Europe. Upon returning, he suffered a cerebral hemorrhage and died on the seventh of October that same year.

His creative work ran concurrently with the teaching he carried on both in and out of the university. From 1937 until his death he was director of the philosophical library of the Losada Publishing House. He was the organizer of the chair of philosophy in the Colegio Libre de Estudios Superiores, and he published numerous popular essays that came to create an environment propitious to the development of philosophy as a "normal task." Romero was the last of the philosophers to live in a heroic age, when philosophical activity was carried on in the face of public indifference or official opposition.

Until 1952 he had not published a systematic work, although for more than twenty years he had developed his philosophical ideas and published articles sketching his later thought. His most important essays were "Vieja y nueva concepción de la realidad" (1932); "Filosofía de la persona" (1935); "Programa de una filosofía" (1940); and "Trascendencia y valor" (1942). The last two were published in *Sur,* numbers 73 and 92, and were incorporated in *Papeles para una filosofía* (1945). The majority of his important essays were also incorporated into books.

If we leave aside his *Historia de la filosofía moderna* (1959), his only systematic work is *Teoría del hombre* (1952), in which he develops a philosophical anthropology "within the context of a metaphysics of transcendence."

The concept of "transcendence" is fundamental for his thought. Hierarchical levels depend on the degree of transcendence, with the least to be found in the physical and the most to be found in the spiritual level. The intermediate levels are those of life and intentional psychism. What is human is found on the third level, that of intentional psychism, and this is perfected in the spirit, which is "absolute transcendence." The most important characteristic of the spirit is "absolute objectivity" and the second is "universality." To these must be added freedom and historicity.

If indeed the numerous works published throughout a period of twenty years had not been enough to insure that Romero would be an outstanding philosopher, his *Teoría del hombre,* considered by many to be one of the most solid works in Latin American philosophy, insured his position as an original thinker.

R. F.

Theory of Man*

INTENTIONAL CONSCIOUSNESS

Preintentional Psychism and Intentional Consciousness

It is best to conceive of psychism[1] in its earliest stages as an undivided succession of states, a kind of psychical repercussion of life. No distinction between subject and object exists in such psychism, nor can one properly speak of it as consciousness. Life is recorded psychically; it resounds and multiplies in a clouded psyche. This psychism is, so to speak, inherent in life from its beginning, being a direct echo of life and the instrument of the living entity to be used for its internal coordination and external conduct. The superior or intentional psyche is based on this foundation, and its distinguishing characteristic consists in the objective direction of its acts. Also resting on this foundation, though in less direct fashion, is the spirit, the principle whereby man passes beyond the natural realm.

Our sole concern at this point is to make clear the nonintentional character of animal psychism, yet at the same time, conceding to some species of animals a vague rudiment of intentionality that is limited and detained in its first stages. As a normal function, true and complete intentionality carries with it, of necessity, both nomination and objective communication, in preparation, as we shall see, for that inversion of interest of which the spirit consists. If intentional consciousness actually operated in animals, it would manifest itself in a language of objective content; it would give rise to the beginning of self-consciousness, and that being would not then be an animal, but the sketch of a man. Provisionally, we accept Max Scheler's conclusions concerning the psychism of animals as it pertains to affective impulses (which would seem to be apparent in plants), instinct, and associative memory. We do not share his opinion concerning what he calls practical intelligence. We disagree with his supposition that practical intel-

*From Francisco Romero, *Theory of Man* (Berkeley: University of California Press, 1964), 3-4, 6-7, 33-35, 83, 96-97, 122-23, 133-37, 139-42, 162-65, 167-74, 177-78, 180-81, 207-209.

ligence is similar in animals and in man—that there is only a difference of degree between a chimpanzee and an Edison (as inventors of technical artifacts). We believe that the difference—or the primary difference—between man and the animals must be sought in this aspect, yet without denying the statement that it is the spirit that completes and perfects human nature. . . .

It is proper for man to perceive objects, to recognize reality as a conglomeration of separate entities endowed with existence and consistency. Man is, in the first place, an intentional consciousness—without it he is not man. What is characteristic of intentional consciousness consists in a cluster of intentions or acts projected toward objects in the function of cognitive, emotional, or volitional apprehension. "States" or psychical acts without intentional character, that is without objective direction, occur in man as in animals, but it is man's prerogative that many of his states lose their condition as such by becoming the content of intentional acts. Of these, the cognitive acts enjoy an undoubted priority and preeminence in the shaping of human nature, for they are what establishes intentional consciousness. Simultaneously these acts create or distinguish the object and present it to us as perceivable, for they have the concealed ability to give objective form to sensible material and the evident capacity to present this outcome to us as objects existent in themselves. The common observations concerning the priority or superior strength of the emotions or the will with respect to the intellect do not succeed in invalidating the former assertion, as will be seen later.

Intentional activity transforms the states into objects. The exploration and description of the mechanism and function that produce that transmutation are the concern of the theory of knowledge. We use the word "object" in its most inclusive sense—it takes in everything that comes into the cognitive glance, everything that is apprehended by the subject. . . .

We are able to conceive the attribution of objectivity only as an act similar to judgment. The state is merely lived, endured. It is neither accepted nor rejected; it is not apprehended and, properly speaking, there is no consciousness of it. When one turns toward a state, it automatically becomes an object, and the 'turning onward' is a becoming aware that the state is there, that it is, and subsequently that it is of this or that form. To perceive, to apprehend something, is to attribute being and consistency to what is apprehended. The subject, therefore, is born as the ability to assign presence to states, to judge that they are. This objectifying judgment, however, is not conscious, formulated, and explicit, since we are not conscious of it. Yet this judgment provides us with the consciousness of objects. Further, the lack of consciousness of this act of judgment does not argue against it, because, even in the ordinary activity of the intelligence, we are not conscious of the major part of our judgments.

The objectifying judgment is similar to the existential judgment dealt with in logic, and though this similarity has been noted more than once before, there is considerable difference between the two. One must keep in mind that for both the characteristic of judgment is assertion and not the attribution of predicates. Yet we do not become trapped in insurmountable difficulties if we insist—contrary to the opinion of Meinong and others—in maintaining predication as a *sine qua non* of judgment, since what constitutes the object may be thought of as the predication of existence, or, as we prefer to state it, of presence. The objectifying act may be conceived according to the formula "that is an existent" or "that is present," whereby one expresses that "that" (which was a state until the intentional glance fell on it) is an existent or something of the class of that which is placed before a subject. . . . As has been previously stated, man is the being for whom there are (or who perceives) objects, and he is the being who is a subject. Let us now add with equally strong emphasis that man is the being who judges. For, as we have seen, the subject unfolds as the being capable of judging, of attributing objectivity to states. In fact, we might say that this capacity to judge becomes substance or is structured into an entity. The subject is the judging entity, but he himself seems to appear in order to embody the judging attitude, as though awakened or called up by an obscure power in the preintentional psyche which would assert itself and thereby rise to the level of consciousness—the level it achieves as soon as it forges an adequate instrument.

To dwell on problems limited to the sphere of knowledge would lead us astray from our primary aim—the elucidation of the idea of man—so we will add only those comments that seem indispensable to our purpose. For us, as has been firmly asserted, the essential activity of the subject is judgment. This is not the only function in which the subject is engaged, yet it is the function which, so far as he is a subject, bestows being on him, and which through reiteration confirms him as a subjective entity and increases his stature as such. . . .

The subject-object structure is not only essential and determinative in man—in what might be called his individual constitution; it is also essential in the community or collection of men and in man's objective product, that is, his culture. The capacity of this basic structure to provide a satisfactory explanation of everything human is precisely what assures us of its truth.

What is proper to the human community derives, without exception, from the fact that man is a subject and that he perceives or conceives a world of objectivities. Social life, as such, is not exclusively human. Not only do many species of animals live in societies of diverse kinds, they also reveal some of the conditions investigated in human society by sociologists—positive and negative tensions, leadership, stratification, division of labor, and so forth. The parallel can be drawn with particular reference to family complexes. No animal grouping, however, regardless of the aspects which it may have in common with human society, can reasonably be equated with it; only human society is a grouping of subjects, each with its own world of objects, and each one, therefore, capable of objectifying the group and of objectively conceiving each of his companions. . . .

CULTURE

Our primary intention is to show how culture stems—one might say by necessity—from the objectifying capacity and, therefore, is a part of the fact that man is a subject who grasps and conceives an objective world. The unity of man and culture is manifest in many ways, and we are especially interested in pointing out, in the correlation between them, culture's influence on man.

Let us first define the distinction between objective culture and cultural life. Objective culture includes all of man's creations that achieve substantiality and autonomy with reference to their creator and thus have a relatively separate existence, such as institutions, works of art, theories, and customs. By cultural life is understood the life that man lives in the midst of the objects he has created. If the merely organic—in which man coincides with other living beings—is left aside, then the whole of man's life is cultural life. What continues to be purely organic in man is not clear, for, since man is immersed in culture, much in him that originally was organic has taken on cultural implications. For example, the digestive functions are modified by diet and regularity, which are the products of culture; sexual activity stems in part from peculiarly human motives occurring within a framework in which the agents are subjects, and their activity takes place in specifically defined situations usually under strict social regulation.

The reference to culture at this point provisionally sets aside its spiritual aspect. From our point of view, culture is not necessarily spiritual, even though throughout it seems to be dominated from above by spiritual motives, and even if in effect it is spiritual in many of its expressions. The spiritual implications in culture will be discussed later.

All specifically human activity is cultural. It presupposes cultural objectifications and it manipulates them in the processes of creation, modification, comprehension, and development. Human life is inconceivable apart from culture. The notion of culture includes, then, every human product and all human conduct. The strictly organic is not human, just as the physical is not organic. Yet weight, a physical trait, is something no living body can escape. . . .

THE SELF AND THE WORLD: THE NATURAL MAN

In the previous chapters we have tried to describe the fundamental structure of man. We have shown that this structure presupposes a judging attitude, that it introduces into the most profound levels of man what later becomes the explicit judgment. We have attempted to show that intelligence and significative language, just as much as the human community and culture, are based on that fundamental structure; and we have referred to the role of intentionality in the acceleration of activity and in the process of individualization which seem to provide the essential directions to the cosmic process. The problem of the spirit has remained a separate one thus far, since it is to be the theme of Part Two. But it has been indicated that intentionality leads to the spirit and is perfected in it, and that intelligence, society, and culture, if indeed they can be maintained on the level of pure intentionality, take on the forms in which they are familiar to us as well as their characteristic human dimension when they are integrated with the spiritual dimension.

To be constructed on the intentional structure yet to be deprived of the spirit, is neither to be an animal nor, strictly speaking, to be a man in the full sense of the word. It is not legitimate, on the other hand, to deny absolutely a human condition to such a being. Perhaps we might say that we should attribute that condition to him in the light of the promise of the spirit which is latent in his intentionality. Such a being has undoubtedly existed in the inferior stages of humanity, perhaps existing normally in minimal cultures and, perchance, in isolated instances, enduring in the superior cultures. We refer to it as *natural man* and, as we have stated, characterize it by the total lack of the spiritual factor. We do not preclude that the spiritual attitude may arise suddenly and unexpectedly in intentionality, influenced by inner motives, by an example, or by some external appeal. The natural attitude is maintained only until the first spark of spirit appears. Habitual persistence in overtly natural attitudes, if in some way one has assented or assents to the spiritual attitude, does not constitute a true natural attitude, but rather a special situation related to the duality peculiar to man. This duality is discussed in Part Three.

Let us consider the principal traits of the natural man—that is, man so far as he is deprived of spirit.

This man, built on the subject-object structure, is a self surrounded by a world of objectivities. The self-world pair represents a step up from the subject-object pair. The subject is converted into a self through the reiteration of intentional acts which organize the subjectivity, granting it consistency, continuity, and identity with itself. The world is the result of habitual objective experience.

The self can be dissolved into the 'we' or affirmed individually. The consciousness of the self is just as natural when the individual incorporates himself into a natural complex with which he identifies himself as when he sharply distinguishes his own natural individuality from that of his fellows. The universal projection, the turn toward the "other," exclusively constitutes the nonnatural or the spiritual attitude. . . .

THE SPIRIT IN GENERAL

Intentionality and Spirit

In preintentional psychism, the individual lives his states obscurely, without referring them to a subjective center. In intentional psychism, consciousness is organized as a differentiated structure in which a subjective pole exists that grasps objects and projects itself actively toward them. The subjective pole, in keeping with its normal function, is constituted as a self surrounded by a world, that is, an environment of objectifications linked together objectively. The acts of the self—cognitive, emotional, volitional—flow into this world, which determines them in part, both by the situations that it presents to the self and by what the latter owes to the accumulated experiences of that world with respect to its own constitution. In merely intentional psychism, the world is only the objective field in which the self affirms and develops its existence, governed entirely by practical interests, by incentives of an individual sort which are referred to the concrete and unique being of the self. The situation does not change fundamentally, as has been said, when these interests are referred to complexes or groups with which the individual is concretely identified rather than directly to a single individual. This is true only to the extent to which the identification with the group stems from concrete and practical motives and not from ideal intentions, for in the latter case one crosses over from the natural to the spiritual attitude.

Merely intentional activity creates objectivities for the subject but subordinates them at once to the immediate goals of the percipient, who catalogues them under the earmark of interesting or indifferent, useful or useless, agreeable or disagreeable, attractive or repugnant, and so on. The emphasis on some of these objectivities and the blurring of others, the direction and energy of the objectifying glance, depend on practical factors. These concrete incentives are at work, primarily, in subsequent cognitive activity, in intellectual elaborations. The emotional and volitional acts are oriented in the same manner, depending on and yet to the advantage of the psychophysical reality of the agent. Thus, intentional acts are launched toward given objectivities, but a return to the subject is within them.

The principal characteristic of the spiritual act is the lack of this return.

The spiritual act is projected toward the object, and it remains there. In cognitive, emotional, and volitional activity, the self is concerned with the objectivities for what they are in themselves. In merely intentional activity the subject places the objects and then takes them to himself, whereas in the spiritual act he places the objects and then yields himself to them. In order to give profile to the spiritual act at this point, let this provisional and incomplete definition be offered: the spiritual act is that intentional act in which the subject yields himself to the object. A more precise specification of this kind of act requires that one determine its what, why, and how—that is, its internal nature, the presumed motive of its appearance, and its manner of functioning.

Because the spiritual act is an act of a special nature, of a superior kind, hereafter, when we refer to nonspiritual intentionality, we will say "mere intentionality" or "pure intentionality," or we will use some other expression distinguishing it from intentionality made spiritual.

At first glance, according to the preceding summary description, the spiritual act seems more simple, more direct, and less complex than the act of mere intentionality. Actually, one element in the nonspiritual intentional act is lacking in the spiritual act—the subjective return, the practical reference of what is objectified to the individuality of the agent. When the naked acts are taken in themselves, they undoubtedly present this difference. But this is not so if, as is only just, attention is focused on the self and its corresponding behavior in mere intentionality and in intentionality made spiritual. In the first, the self lives its natural state spontaneously, leaning over the object and bringing to bear its own reality as a concrete individual who takes himself as the universal and ultimate point of reference. As can now be well seen, what we have referred to as subjective return is not something that can be superimposed on its act by the self; rather, it is an intention operative within the act itself—it is the final polarization of the act toward the agent which is inherent in the "natural" attitude of the agent. In the spiritual act, on the one hand, this intention is suppressed, but what occurs is not, properly speaking, a simplification, but a purification of the act. On the other hand, the spiritual act enlarges its radius with respect to the nonspiritual act, because, in freely turning to its object, it finds a more extended area than that circumscribed by the relatively limited register of the practical interests of the agent. Mere intentionality redirects reality to the midst of man's natural state, whereas, in the spiritual attitude, man turns to whatever is and participates abundantly in totality. The self, particularistic in the first attitude, rises above itself and is universalized in the second.

The difference between the psychism of states and intentional psychism is self-evident if one accepts the proofs or assumptions we have previously set forth. The first is a flux of psychic matter with no clear distinction between cognition, emotion, and the will, and without a subject before whom objectified instances might appear. Intentional psychism is an intimate aspect of the activity of a subject to whom objectivities are presented, who recognizes them intellectually and projects on them, as objectivities, his acts of emotion and will. The difference between these two psychical realities is enormous in itself, even if one considers only their internal structures. Such a difference is increased when one considers its mode of functioning. Preintentional psychism finds itself inevitably at the command of organic life. It is an instrument of regulation and adaptation for the individual, in that it adapts the individual to the surroundings and also in that it partly adapts the surroundings to the individual—so far as it limits the environment and makes it functional in view of the implicit demands in the constitution of each species. High as one may ascend the scale of this psychism, though occasionally and exceptionally the rudiments of intentionality may be found in the individual, such an individual never passes beyond the level of the purely vital, it does not come to be a self surrounded by a world that it can recognize and within which it conducts itself with a free choice, taking into consideration the wide perspective of objects extended in space and time. Intentional psychism, however, draws the individual out of the strictly organic level, converting the individual into a self gifted with a world in which he develops an action overcoming the biological levels to the extent that the incentives of this order are partly transformed into motives of another kind. It is essential not to ignore that intentionality entails cultural objectification whereby a realm of a new kind is constituted around the individual, the realm of culture, thus creating a complex, untested situation; for the subject lives simultaneously in the world of the spontaneous natural state and in that of culture, and he works in virtue of them both. Even in the lowest levels of civilization, however, a notable preeminence of the cultural influx exists, an influx that defines his evaluation of basic, natural reality and his behavior in its presence. The distance between the nonintentional and the intentional entity, from the point of view of structure and activity, is sufficiently large to justify a strict ontological separation.

The preintentional psychic field and the intentional psychic field differ profoundly. No structural difference between the merely intentional and the spiritual exists, however, because the foundation, the self-world pair is the same in the second as in the first. Intentional consciousness is the common field of the purely intentional and the spiritual acts, so that one cannot speak accurately of a spiritual consciousness that could be opposed to the other. The spiritual act is an intentional act of a special kind, an act that not only turns toward objects but is governed by them and is exhausted in them, though this should be said with the reservations that will emerge later. What is essential in it is the full objective direction. In functioning as the agent of such an act, the subject does not change in what we might call his subjective makeup but rather in his implantation within reality, in his meaning, in his posture or attitude. One cannot say, however, that for the subject the spiritual state is only a mode of working and not a mode of being, because the subject is constituted by his acts, and what he is depends on the character of his acts, with reference both to actuality and to acquired habit. The differences to which we have been referring find support in the awareness that nonintentional acts are easily distinguished from intentional acts on the basis of external factors, whereas an intentional act may appear spiritual without being so and vice versa. At times one may be in error about the nature of one's own act.

From one point of view, then, the difference is minimal, from another, and undoubtedly more justified standpoint, however, it is immense. The difference between the merely intentional act and the spiritual act seems minimal because many times the two are confused, and the only difference between them may rest in the final subjectivist intention of the former and the objectivist intention of the latter—nothing more. But with the step toward radical objectivism which defines the purely spiritual act, the natural level is abandoned, and even a particle of the divine—nothing less—is restored in humanity.

It follows that between the purely intentional and the spiritual there is an identity of real contexture, but a difference of intention or purpose. In other words, we might say that there is an identity of matter or content, but a difference of relation or form. The same occurs in the two previous strata of reality—the inorganic or physical and the organic or living. The constitutive matter of the inorganic and the organic is the same. Not one single component can be discovered in the organic level that cannot be reduced to elements existing in the physical order. But the relation or form differs, and, with its functional consequences, it serves in each case to define the entity, to locate it in the level of organic reality or that of life. . . .

Passing from pure intentionality to spirituality not only carries with it a distinction capable of giving shape to a new ontological species, but it produces one of the greatest separations imaginable. This separation is between the two great orders into which reality is divided, that of nature and spirit, concerning whose heterogeneity something has already been said and which will be treated extensively in the following pages.

The great distance—a truly unbridgeable abyss—open between nature and spirit, however, does not hinder our attempt to understand the motive for the appearance of the latter, with the former serving as a foundation. The meaning of that appearance will be discussed when we attempt to establish the relation between spirit and transcendence.

Removed as spirituality may be from natural intentionality, basic though the novelty be that it introduces into the picture of totality, one must recognize that it was already present as a possibility, even as a seed, in the first intentional attitude. What we have referred to as mere intentionality is an imperfect intentionality. In the light of spiritual demands it even appears as frustrated because the subjective return does not emerge as a *plus,* but rather as a decrease in the objectifying intention. In general, intentionality characteristically constructs objectivities, perceives them, thinks them, and directs itself toward them in emotional and volitional movements. The objective direction is thus inherent in intentionality. What happens before the appearance of the spirit is that the objective direction, not entirely fulfilled, is delayed by a ballast that hinders its free advance. That ballast is the structure of the self as a sheaf of individual interests. Mere intentionality, therefore, is revealed to us as something incomplete and mutilated, as an impetus of the subject toward what he is not—an impetus that later weakens and returns to the subject, bringing to it, one might say, the usable spoils of the object. Basically, the intention of the subjective return, the "vested or interested interest," constitutes the purely intentional act and defines it from the beginning, although this return may indicate an obstruction of the objectifying impulse. The naturalness of the nonspiritualized intentionality is rooted specifically in the final reference or the redirecting of the acts toward the self as a particular center, whereby it shares the particularism that, as we shall soon see, characterizes everything natural in contradistinction to the radical universalism of the spirit. With its vested interests in the world, the nonspiritualized subject shares in its own way the condition of the organic entity, which is only interested organically in its surroundings, for its own specific and individual goals. The attitude is the same, although the actors and the stage may change. One must admit, however, that although particularism is the general law of nature, its forms allow for degrees of extension and dignity, and that intentional particularism at times approaches spiritual universalism, as when the objectified world is enlarged and the self broadens into a 'we' which may come to include all humanity and even elements in addition to man which are accepted for purposes of an interpenetrating sympathy. Many times, no doubt, the self is enlarged and ennobled when it is broadened into a 'we,' but any act ultimately referred to that 'we' is purely intentional—though of a superior intentionality—because the open and cleanly objective direction is basic to the spiritual act, a projection toward something as "other."

Thus mere intentionality, which in itself is on a high level in the scale of reality, on occasions comes to border on the spirit through the broadening of the subject into a 'we'—to which, for all practical purposes, the subject's acts are referred. The 'we' of which we speak here is not the social complex to which the primitive refers his behavior before he has lived as a true and individualized subject. Rather, it is the 'we' that is constituted after there has been an actual subject; it is the 'we' that presupposes the self. Yet this bordering with the spirit does not suppress the enormous difference in level between the two. One need only keep in mind that with the self broadened into a 'we' the subjective return is the same as it was before, except that the center to which the action is directed has changed. The particularism acquires a much broader base, but it does not cease to be particularism.

What defines the spiritual act is not that the subject swells and is enlarged, but that it gives up the subjective return of the act. The notion of the 'we' is always relative: we, the living human beings, Americans, those of our class, our family, the doctors, the athletes, the contributors, the pipe smokers—we, who now agree in something and feel bound by that tie, which can be fundamental or accidental, permanent or temporary. The notion of pure objectivism, however, which is the mark of the spiritual state, is absolute. It is the absolute projection toward the other, conditioned only by the mode of being and of the other (and of the objectified subject itself as an other). In the spiritual state, as well, the subject has become larger, but in a special sense that is not akin to the broadening of the circle of concrete interests of the 'we.' The subject has become larger because he has turned loose of his battery of individual interests and has converted otherness as such into his own interests. He has not evaporated as a subject, as one might imagine; he has only annulled himself as a subject who functions as a single unit, which, for all practical purposes, redirects every existing thing toward himself. The purely intentional subject works naturally. Nothing is more *natural* than this: that each one work according to, and as a function of, what he is with intentions that terminate in himself because he is a self. The spiritual subject is no longer a natural entity. It is not *natural* that a self yield itself definitely to the other. The spiritual state is freedom, it is evasion. This freedom, this evasion, is above all the destruction of the walls of particularism that enclose each self in a private enclosure and, generally speaking, enclose every natural instance in the special regulation that pertains to it. . . .

THE UNIQUENESS AND SIGNIFICANCE OF THE SPIRIT

Traits of the Spirit

The central, founding event of the spiritual act—the projection in this act of the subject toward the object—has certain consequences and is manifest in certain modes that can be considered as the principal traits of the spirit. These traits, however, are not to be considered as independent properties that meet in the spiritual act, as something added to it, forming part of it, or making it complex; rather they are to be considered as different expressions of its most genuine and profound character, as diverse aspects of a single reality.

The first of these traits is *absolute objectivity,* which is the fundamental condition of this kind of act. The merely intentional act is also of objective scope because it gives form to objectivities and manipulates them in various ways; all intentionality is a working with objectivities. But this objectivity is not absolute. In it the subject functions with the particularism of a living, intentional being, keeping continuously in mind his particular concrete being; and this gives a highly subjective quality to his act. The subjective interest imposes its direction on the intentional glance: heightening some aspects of the object and darkening others, it circumscribes the realm of objectivities according to its own standard. In addition, the object is given in a modified form because the practical intention of the subject is included in it. It is understood as "something for the subject," and to the extent that this occurs, it diminishes or annuls the autonomous condition of the object, which is an undeniable part of it and on occasion the fundamental aspect, since the object can signify its own unchangeable meaning, its very heart. In spiritual or absolute objectivity, the *whole* object is objectified, without its being altered with subjective innovations, and without neglecting the ultimate and independent significance of anything that is not the object itself. Knowledge of a spiritual kind is concerned with what is only because it is; the interest thus projected toward the object deserves the characterization "disinterested," because it is not governed by any interest peculiar to the agent, but rather by an interest engendered in the agent by the mere fact of the object's existing or by its being given. In ethical behavior, a given objective situation may be disvalued in a moral judgment, or the attempt may be made to correct it through actual intervention. But this is not equivalent to an interference of subjective particularism in the objective situation; rather the subject, facing a complex situation characterized by a conflict or an encounter with something given as real and something considered as an objective value or duty, decides for the latter—that is, for an order he recognizes as justified and valuable above the given reality.

Absolute spiritual objectivity does not permit the elimination of the subject as the terminal for its acts, but it does permit the elimination of the subject as a complex of subjective interests. The spiritual subject does not deny itself; rather it recognizes in itself an objectivity parallel to others. It is doubtlessly concerned with itself, but only as its being and meaning are conceived objectively.

Universality is another trait of the spirit; it has already served to distinguish the spirit from nature because of the particularism that is akin to everything natural. The spirit is universal in various ways, and all these stem from total objective projection. The subject, deprived of actual reference to itself, of the intention of redirecting everything to its own concrete being, feels universalized, cleansed from any existential particularism. This universality does not mean self-denial, as was indicated previously; on the contrary, the subject lives with a new intensity in this new situation, which, at the same time that it opens him to reality, in a sense brings the whole of reality to him. . . .

The *freedom* characteristic of the spirit, which Max Scheler considers to be one of the three traits that define it, is only the evasion of natural particularism; it is autonomy with regard to the interests and incentives of the living human being as a single concrete entity. Freedom, therefore, is absolute objectivism and universalism as viewed from the relation of the spiritual subject to the nonspiritual subject that sustains it and with which it lives. One should keep in mind that, properly speaking, it is not a matter of the spirit's independence from "life" in the biological sense—from the strictly organic and animal complex—because the section of nature most closely related to the spirit is not organic nature, but intentional nature. The freedom of the spirit is affirmed against the propensities and attitudes of what we have called the natural man—the man subject to intentional, nonspiritualized acts. It is not opposed to some animal-man who does not exist in the human race. The essential duality of man is rooted precisely in the difference and the frequent conflict between the natural conditioning of what is merely intentional and the freedom of the spirit or, what amounts to the same thing, between full subjectivism and full objectivism, between particularism and universalism. . . .

From this radical objectivism also stems a *unity* of the spirit, which is primarily perceivable in the most general and consolidated spiritual attitudes, such as the cognitive and the ethical attitudes. . . .

The *historicity* of the spirit has been previously discussed. The spirit has a historical source; it emerges in a determined season, probably when the merely intentional function has been consolidated. Spiritual acts are absolute—that is, they either have the distinctive features or they are not spiritual acts. But their "habitualness," their frequency, is undoubtedly a historical conquest. . . .

Respect and interest (the "disinterested interest") are the secondary traits of the spirit. The spirit respects everything and is interested in everything, and obvious signs of the absence of spirit are lack of respect and indifference with regard to beings and things. The pragmatic stamp that mere intentional consciousness imposes on its objectifications is a lack of respect for what they are in themselves and a lack of interest in their own, nontransferable character. From a certain point of view, to behave spiritually is to be aware that everything is worthy of respect and everything is interesting. Philosophy, pure science, and art are born of a disinterested interest in things, of a respect for what is and for what is imagined. It is not difficult to discover in the moral attitude the confluence of the high potential of interest and respect. For common eyes the only hierarchy of beings and things is that given by reasons which pertain to the practical order. . . .

Responsibility is a trait of the spirit that has received little attention. There is a feeling of responsibility that tends to reach very elevated forms and, though not belonging to the sphere of the spirit, almost borders on it. We do not refer to the responsibility that primitive man experiences toward his group, for he is hardly individualized; rather it is that felt by the subject when he lives as an identical and continuous self. This responsibility to one's own individuality, to one's own life as reality, whether as fictionally imagined or as projected, at times reaches the heroic and the sacrificial. The same is true of responsibility with respect to others when a solid nexus of interests and affection exists. Spiritual responsibility has special characteristics. The responsibility of the subject to himself as a spiritual subject, as a person, presupposes responsibility to other persons conceived as entities of equal worth. The spirit, as we have repeatedly stated, is an absolutely objective projection, and it feels, as an intimate obligation, that it must act as such. . . .

Self-consciousness has been considered by Max Scheler as one of the three principal traits of the spirit. But self-consciousness is not an exclusive attribute of the spirit. In nonspiritualized intentionality, self-consciousness is to be found as soon as the subject is firmly constituted as a self. An unprecedented intensification of subjective interests tends to reenforce self-consciousness without taking into account that there are more or less morbid psychic dispositions that turn the subject toward himself and stir up a watchful and even exasperated self-consciousness. In general, the adolescent, the timid person, and the introvert turn toward their own inner reality. There is also a frankly pathological complacency in self-contemplation in some psychic types (the one who analyzes himself, the one who feels sorry for himself, the one who suffers from an excess of intense scruples, the one who feels inferior) that leads to a constant probing and, as a result, an exaggerated self-consciousness which abounds in erroneous interpretations and a defective appreciation of the context in reality in which the self is found. . . .

Finally, we hold *absolute transcendence* to be the essential trait of the spirit.

Spirit as Absolute Transcending

As we have repeatedly asserted, the fundamental difference between the spiritual act and the merely intentional act consists in the fact that the former is directed toward its object without a subjective return, whereas the latter has a subjective intent, a subordination of the object to the particular goals of the subject. Such a difference may also be expressed by saying that the nonspiritual act is transcendent to the extent that it has an undeniable, objective direction inseparable from its intentional character. Yet it partly denies or shifts its transcendence by referring the object, in one way or another, to the interests of the subject. The spiritual act, however, is absolutely transcendent because it goes out to the object and remains with it, in no way actually referring the object to the existential uniqueness of the subject.

The spiritual act thus achieves pure transcendence. Its reference to the subject is only the inevitable connection between the subject and his act. . . .

The absolute transcendence and the full objectivism of the spiritual act come to be the same thing. But the introduction of the notions of transcendence and immanence makes possible the sounding of the spiritual act to its very depths, the placing of it in relation to metaphysical hypotheses that help in understanding its place and meaning in totality. It also offers a new interpretation of values that recognizes their objectivity without falling into the error of disconnecting the realm of values from that of being, an error incurred by most axiological systems of an objectivist bent.

Although, as we have indicated, absolute transcendence and complete objectivism come to be the same thing, strictly speaking they are not identical. In our opinion, absolute transcendence is primary, basic, and original in the spiritual act. Thus, one should not say that an act is fully transcendent and objective, rather that it is completely transcendent; and, as a consequence, it is completely objective, because absolute transcendence is what provides the foundation for complete objectivity. In the merely intentional act the transcending toward the object is accompanied by the domination of the subject as a cluster of interests which leads to the modification of the object, its practical subordination to the subject. The transcendence is, therefore, weak and incomplete, and it is ultimately defeated by the subjective demands. In the spiritual act, transcendence works without obstacles or limitations; its strength yields to no opposition. The spiritual subject is the one who is identified and the one who coincides with the transcending impulse of the act. The objectivity is a direct expression of that transcendence, of the lack of subjective return; and all other qualities of the spiritual act, as they have been previously set forth, can be equally understood as manifestations or consequences of absolute transcendence.

Something will be said later concerning transcendence in general and freedom. Transcendence is always a setting free and, in its turn, freedom is a mode or an aspect of transcendence. The constitution of the intentional order undoubtedly points to the appearance of a regime that is much freer than the organic order. The intentional individual enjoys an autonomy superior to that of the animal. . . .

As for self-consciousness, lived though its content may be, it is only conceivable through "reflection," by the return of the subject to itself. The subject goes out of itself in order to fall back on itself; it is the point of departure and the destination of the act. Self-possession confers on the self a dual role, as possessor and as possession. However it occurs, it presupposes that the subject steps out of himself in order to return again to himself. This going out of oneself is a transcending of oneself. And in the same manner as we have already done for freedom, we must distinguish here between restricted and total transcendence, between a transcendence that later becomes immanent and a pure or spiritual transcendence. There is a transcendence accompanied by a tendency to immanence when the reflection which grants the self-consciousness does not take the subject out of the natural level; when in it and through it the subject continues to live, in an absolute sense, as the supreme reality to which everything else, for all practical purposes, must be subjected. There is spiritual self-consciousness when the subject, as he transcends in his reflection of himself, perceives himself in full objectivity—which is close yet at the same time distant—and therefore can possibly refer to himself with that "disinterested interest" of which full objectivity consists. The reflective transcendence that this self-consciousness affords is obviously absolute.

Spirit in the Context of a Metaphysics of Transcendence

Reality is arranged on four different levels or orders: the physical or inorganic level; the level of life; the level of intentional psychism; and the level of the spirit. Each is the foundation of the level that follows it, emerges from it, feeds on it, and surpasses it. A notable increase in transcendence is evident in this succession of levels. One can best imagine a pure immanence on the physical level here, transcendence is least visible. It is at this point that the attempts at a strict rationalist interpretation have felt the preference for "downward explanations," that is, for the idea that the physical order is the only one with substantial or metaphysical worth and that all the rest is a manifestation of the physical, a mere accidental result of the interplay of matter. Transcendence is quite evident in life. Living beings are active centers of transcendence, not only as individuals and species but, above all, as they make up the whole current of life, multiplying on the inorganic level as they colonize it. Living beings succeed and reproduce through the series of generations in which the progenitors transcend themselves and seem to continue to transcend themselves, even after they have disappeared, through the continuity of a vital message entrusted to the farthest reaches of time. In intentional psychism transcendence is even more evident: intentionality consists precisely in the transcendence toward the object. The subject is the point of departure of innumerable, continuous transcending acts, and the horizon for such acts is practically unlimited because everything is objectifiable—everything is or may be the target of intentions. The whole of reality with all its elements, real and nonreal, has been converted into a stage where the intentional individual acts out his role, which consists of nothing other than acts of intentionality, of transcendence. This transcendence, however, is not complete. The intentional individual refers his acts to himself; as an existing individual, he holds himself to be the ultimate concern to whom all his acts are tied by the bonds of his own interest. Such a limitation or relativization of transcendence disappears in the spiritual attitude, so that all actual reference of the act to the subject is severed—except that the act still remains that of the subject. The subject, we might say, is the point of departure of the act but not its goal; this is true, however, of the purely intentional act, because of the concrete and individual interest in the purpose of the act. The spiritual subject, therefore, is a focus of pure transcendences; in him transcendence reaches its highest possible attainment. The animating thrust of the whole of reality thereby achieves its triumph and functions with total autonomy, free from any remainder of immanence. This functioning consists in reaching out to the whole of reality, unhindered by bonds or compulsions; it consists in turning in a special way toward oneself as the informing principle of reality, in cognitively apprehending oneself and in achieving an ethical wholeness with oneself. . . .

The three orders of reality that form an echelon above the physical level reveal a gradual increase in transcendence. There is more transcending on the organic than on the physical level, on the intentional than the organic level, and on the spiritual than the merely intentional level. Spiritual transcendence indicates the apex and does not allow for a higher level; it is absolute and total transcendence. Spiritual acts are defined by their completely objective direction, and the spiritual focus—the subject—is immediately identified with his acts. As self-consciousness, the subject is constituted through acts of pure, reflected transcendence, which do not form kernels of immanence. Spiritual self-consciousness is fully objective, and the only 'lived' factor found in it is the direct impression of transcendence, which is the specific feeling that accompanies every spiritual act. One might conclude from this that when the concretely immanent disappears from the subject, all effective individuation also disappears. But we have already made clear that transcendence is not the annulling of the center that transcends, rather it is action that stems from that center, a going beyond oneself without ceasing to be that self. Spiritual individuality is assured by the unity and continuity of the subject, by its reflexive reference to itself, and by the distinctness of the spiritual processes, so far as they form an organic complex that constitutes the activity and experience appropriate to each self. . . .

DUALITY

Duality is the constitutive event of the complete man. The being we properly refer to as man, who has a destiny, who develops historically and is determined by individual and group motivations—yet he also obeys certain demands that are foreign to these motivations which shape an ideal order— this being, we say, is fundamentally a dual entity. In principle we have maintained that man is created when the intentional function is normally organized, bringing with it the appearance of the subject, the constitution of an objective world for him, and the elaboration of culture with the in- dispensable, objectified creations. All this carries with it something new with respect to the animal kingdom, and it is sufficient to provide for man's separation from the zoological scale, justifying that a new section within the bounds of reality be marked out for him. If what is human rested solely on intentionality,[2] as defined in Part One of this book, that special section kept apart for man would be within the natural sphere. When intentionality is dispossessed of spiritual demands, it is no more than the highest expression of natural activity. From his beginning, however, man is capable of spirit, and he seems to be gifted with spirituality from the first stages of history. Perhaps what we currently call history is the human process beginning with the emergence of the spirit. The man we know, and the one to whom we attribute the characteristics which define the species, is man with the spirit, though we do not absolutely exclude the existence of men lacking in spiritual- ity. The complete, finished man, not some fiction or idealized image, but a historical reality, is he who comes to us as a complex in which mere inten- tionality and spirit alternate and are joined together. Man permanently deprived of the spirit may subsist in the lowest levels of the species, in the midst of embryonic cultures or even sporadically located in middle and high cultures. In any case, at least in some degreee, the spirit is indispensable if we are to recognize what it is in man that we call human in the full sense.

Without spirit, man is already something more—rather, much more than an animal. He is a subject who through his continued, subjective activity is converted into a self; he contemplates and conceives a world of objectivities which is extended in space and time and which leads him to live, taking into consideration what is present, what has happened, and what is foreseen, and is thus in keeping with the past and the future. He makes use of the rich accumulation of objectifications of the community, which he receives through significant language, and he creates and uses culture, which in its elemental forms does not necessarily presuppose the spirit. There is nothing similar to this in the animal kingdom. Natural man, or man without spirit, is, then, a being different from any organic entity, because he encloses his organic life in, and makes it conform to, intentional lines, in keeping with the general situation traced by the enumerated elements whose extra- organic character seems quite evident. Demanding as the biological require- ments may be for natural man, they echo throughout a structure which imposes its own special mode of being upon them. Preintentional psychism comes to be an echo or a psychical modulation of the organic realm.

Intentional psychism responds to its own laws and is governed by them, strong as the organic ingredients may be that are introduced in it.

As was stated, spiritual projection is latent in intentionality. Intentionality perceives objectively, it recognizes what is perceived as subsisting. The spirit radically strengthens the objectification, showing that what is objectified enjoys a fullness of being and autonomy when confronting the objectifying subject, making it possible for the latter to act without the subjective return. In order to understand the significance and scope of spirituality in man, one must keep in mind that it does not consist of a principle completely alien to his primitive nature. It does not consist of an element which comes to primitive human reality from the outside and is inserted into it in some mysterious manner. We might say that it is the fulfillment of the promises contained in the most unpretentious intentional attitudes; it is the completion of what was already present as a seed in the first objectifying acts.

However, this does not set aside the radical difference between mere intentionality and spirituality, for this difference points to a profound break between the spirit and all natural reality. With the spirit, a new order in reality is established; the enclosure of each part of reality within itself, which is characteristic of nature, is broken, and centers heedful of totality are organized, centers which lean toward totality, receiving it in keeping with their universality. Stated in another way, they are centers which transcend themselves and radiate to every horizon, giving whole-hearted attention to whatever is, through different spiritual attitudes yet without being dissolved or even weakened thereby, but rather purifying and strengthening their condition as personal centers. Spirituality, as we have already seen, imposes a complete inversion in the direction of the interest of the subject, whose behavior changes, through the work of the spirit, from subjectivism to full objectivism, from particularism to universalism, from partial to absolute transcendence.

The duality of man is a fact widely recognized in religious and philosophical concepts. . . .

NOTES

1. [Romero uses the word "psychism" and its adjectival form "psychical" with a meaning similar to that developed by Brentano. Husserl's discussion on pp. 249-50 of his *Ideas* (New York: Macmillan, 1931), clarifies the use of this terminology.—Trans.]

2. Personal spirituality is always intentionality. For the sake of convenience, when we use the word intentionality by itself, we are referring to what at other times we have called mere intentionality—that is, an intentionality not spiritualized.

Risieri Frondizi

(1910-1983)

Frondizi belonged to that generation of Latin American philosophers born around 1910 whose contributions to philosophy began in the 1940s. His writings are not extensive, but his work was sound, original, and stated in a meticulously clear style. This last characteristic was the result, at least in part, of the contact he maintained with Anglo-Saxon philosophy.

Frondizi was born in Posadas, Argentina, in 1910. His education, however, took place in Buenos Aires, where he received the degree of professor of philosophy in 1935. He also received a master of arts from the University of Michigan in 1943 and the doctorate in philosophy from the National Autonomous University of Mexico in 1950. Some of his graduate work was done at Harvard, where he studied under A. N. Whitehead, C. I. Lewis, and R. B. Perry, among others. In 1933, he studied in Buenos Aires with Romero, with whom he maintained a close relationship until Romero's death.

His teaching career began at the University of Tucumán in 1938, where he also served as chairnman of the department of philosophy and letters for two years (1938-40). In 1946 he was forced to abandon the country for political reasons. During this period he was visiting professor of philosophy at the Central University of Venezuela (1947-48) and the Universities of Pennsylvania (1948-49), Yale (1949-50), Puerto Rico (1951-54), and Columbia (1955). He returned to Argentina in 1955 and resumed his teaching responsibilites as professor at the Universities of La Plata (1955-56) and Buenos Aires (1956-66). In the latter university he was elected dean of the faculty of philosophy and letters (1957) and president of the university for two terms (1957-62). His heavy involvement in university reform forced him to relinquish his philosophical work for a time. When the military government of Onganía put an end to the autonomy of the university, he resigned from his positions in protest, and accepted positions at the University of California in Los Angeles (1956-68), at the University of Texas (1968-69), and at the University of Southern Illinois at Carbondale. He retired in 1979, but subsequently was appointed distinguished visiting professor at Baylor University, a post he held until his death.

The importance of Frondizi's work both within Latin America and internationally was recognized on various occasions. He was elected president of the Inter-American Society of Philosophy and of the Argentine Philosophical Society as well as a member of the executive council of the International Federation of

Societies of Philosophy and of the International Institute of Philosophy in Paris. In addition he was a member of the Institute of Advanced Studies at Princeton and lectured at several of the most important universities in both Americas and at leading European universities. In 1980, twenty philosophers from around the world presented him with a volume in his honor entitled *Man and His Conduct* and published by the University of Puerto Rico Press.

His main works were published in several editions: *El punto de partida del filosofar* (1945-57); *Substancia y función en el problema del yo* (1952-70, under the title *El yo como estructura dinámica*); and *¿Qué son los valores?* (1958: 5th ed., 1972). The last two works also appeared in English as *The Nature of the Self* (1953, 1971), and *What is Value?* (1963, 1971). In addition, he published approximately fifty articles on various philosophical topics and several books on the mission of the university in Latin America (1971).

In Frondizi's first work we are able to find a general sketch of his thought. He maintains that philosophy is the theory of human experience constituted by the self, its activity, and objects. In the book devoted to the problem of the self, he is opposed to Descartes's substantialism as well as Hume's atomism, and develops a concept of the self as a dynamic structure. Later he applied this approach to the study of values, taking a position opposed to both axiological subjectivism and objectivism. For Frondizi, value is a structural quality that emerges in the relationship between the subject and its objects and is present in every situation. His axiology leads to a situational ethics, although in his judgment this does not imply an ethical relativism. On the contrary, the existence of an axiological hierarchy for every situation strengthens ethical feeling as well as man's creative activity.

J. G.

The Nature of the Self*

THE BEING AND THE DOING OF THE SELF

Experience shows us that the self does not depend upon any obscure or hidden substantial core but depends upon what it does, has done, proposes to do, or is able to do. The self is revealed in its action; it reveals itself and constitutes itself by acting. It is nothing before acting, and nothing remains of it if experiences cease completely. Its *esse* is equivalent to its *facere*. We are not given a ready-made self; we create our own self daily by what we do, what we experience. Our behavior—in which both our actual doing and our intentions should properly be included—is not an expression of our self but the very stuff which constitutes it.

What holds experiences together, what gives us personality, is not, therefore, a substantial bond but a functional one, a coordinated structure of activities. The self is not something already made but something that is always in the making. It is formed throughout the course of its life, just as any institution is formed—a family, a university, a nation. There is no aboriginal nucleus of the self that exists prior to its actions; the self arises and takes on existence as it acts, as it undergoes experiences. The category of substance must be supplanted by that of function if we wish to interpret adequately the nature of the self. The concept of function connotes, in this case, the concepts of activity, process, and relation.

The functional link by no means includes only our past experiences. The self is memory, but it is not memory alone. Our personality depends upon what has happened to us, but it cannot be reduced to our personal history; the self is not the blind aggregate of our experiences. We get the push of the past, but we also get the pull of the future. There is, in the self, a note of novelty and creativity, a free will, an ability to control the eventual course of our experiences. Activity, therefore, contains an element of novelty; it cannot be grasped or comprehended by referring exclusively to its past.

*From Risieri Frondizi, *The Nature of the Self* (Carbondale, Ill.: Southern Illinois University Press, 1971), 145-147, 158-63, 170-77, 181-84, 188-93, 197-200.

The self is not inert matter, deposited on the shore by the tide of experience, but creative will, plotting its own course for itself. It depends upon its past history but is able to mold its own history-to-be, to orient its life according to new courses. It is memory but memory projected toward the future, memory hurled ahead. The future conditions the nature of our self not only as it merges with the present but also while it is still more distantly future. What we plan to do, even if we never get to do it, gives sense to our activities. The future, however, is not a part of our self merely as a system of ideas and intentions; it also enters into the formation of the self through our emotions. In times of confusion and disaster the thought of the future of our country, our child, our own lives grieves us. Though it is true that this suffering is a present and not a future experience, its object is the future. It is like the pain caused by a splinter; the pain is not the splinter, but it could not exist without the presence of the splinter. Hope, despair, and many other experiences would be impossible if the future were not an element in our lives.

The self is a function already performed but also a function to be fulfilled, a capacity, a potentiality. Our being consists of what we have done but also of what we intend and are able to do. The past creates ability; the ability gives a sense of direction to the past. Even the capacity that was never realized, the potentiality that never had the chance of becoming actual, forms an integral part of our self.

The past and the future of the self are not, strictly speaking, separable parts; they form an indissoluble whole. The past acquires meaning in the light of the future; the future, in turn, depends upon the past. We cannot do whatever we want; our abilities depend upon our past experiences.

Some people have denied the dynamic character of the self or have relegated it to a position of secondary importance, thinking it to be incompatible with its unity. Unable to conceive of the unity of a changing being, they have considered that the process of alteration of the self only scratches its surface and that the self keeps an immutable central core. It is true that there is only one Ego for each experiential stream, but it is also true that the self is not immutable. We have seen that the self is constantly changing, that everything that happens to us enriches and modifies our self. But change does not mean substitution; rather, it means an alteration of the inner pattern. Thus, former experiences never quite disappear completely, though they can change their nature and meaning with the development of the self.

ANALYSIS AND ANALYTICISM

As is well known, the method that is used conditions the nature of the object under observation. If, blinded by the prestige acquired by the scientific method, we commit the stupid blunder of the modern tourist who tries to examine under the microscope a city which he is visiting for the first time, we shall not succeed in seeing the houses, the people, the plants, and the flowers. It would imply an even greater blindness to maintain that in the city there are neither houses nor people nor flowers, without realizing that they have disappeared as a consequence of the instrument chosen. The naked eye, in such a case, is a better instrument than the microscope, which, though it shows us the detail, keeps us from seeing the whole.

The analytic method has often worked like a microscope. It has revealed details which no one had ever seen before, but it has impeded our view of the whole. Again, the naked eye and the free-ranging glances of the spirit are superior to the intellect provided with the perfected technique and instruments of analysis. We need only to glance within, if we hold no prejudicial theories, to see what is hidden from the philosophers using analytic methods and blinded by the postulates of their theory and by their technique of observation.

Why should we be surprised that the wholes are not perceived if it has already been accepted in advance that analysis is the only form of apprehension? That which has been previously eliminated cannot be discovered, and it is impossible to reconstruct what should never have been destroyed.

The analytic philosophy which sprang from Hume's atomism is subject to an almost demoniac desire for destruction—destruction by reductions. When confronted by a whole, these philosophers make no effort to comprehend its nature and find the sense of the whole. They proceed immediately to chop the whole into as many parts as possible and to submit each part to the thoroughgoing test of analysis. It is like the little boy who wants to find out what makes his toy work and ends up defiantly facing a heap of loose nuts and bolts.

This destructive drive is based upon a metaphysical postulate from which another postulate, an epistemological one, is derived; these two postulates support what we might call "the fallacy of reduction." The metaphysical postulate may be stated thus: elements have a more actual reality than wholes. The epistemological consequence is obvious: the goal of philosophic knowledge is to come to grips with the basic elements which constitute reality.

From these two postulates a series of principles is derived and conditions the whole attitude of the analytic philosophers. There are two principles which particularly concern us in the study which we are making: a) that the "parts" or elements can be separated from the "whole" without undergoing any change; b) that these elements can be discovered by analysis and defined in such a way that leaves no room for doubt. . . .

I am not proposing, of course, the abandonment of analysis as a philosophic method. It is not clear how analysis could be abandoned without falling into an attitude of contemplative mysticism, which would bring as its immediate consequence greater confusion and obscurity to the field of philosophy. What I am criticizing is *analyticism*, if we may so call it, which attempts to reduce to analysis every philosophic task and actually analyzes away what is really important.

Analysis involves the disarticulation of a complex reality whose unity is destroyed when its component members are separated. It can be used in the realm of psychic life with a great deal of profit and very little danger, provided that one is constantly aware of its limitations and consequences and never loses sight of the fact that the elements which have been separated by analysis are members of a totality which must, of necessity, remain united. Analysis should therefore be used—always, of course, keeping the totality in mind—only in order to make clear the meaning of the whole and to comprehend its inner mechanism, not in order to eliminate the whole or reduce it to a heap of disjointed pieces. Hence analysis should be applied to a structure only after the structure has been taken in and recognized as a whole; reality should not be sacrificed to the method used. . . .

The analytic attitude is moreover complemented by a mechanical conception of the psychic life which tries to "explain" everything by means of simple elements and the forces that move them. When the psychic life has been put together again in this way, it has lost its organic unity, its spontaneity, its very life—all that characterizes the human being. Hence the final result seems more like a robot than a man: the parts that make it up remain unalterable, and the forces that move it are completely mechanical. The process of reconstruction cannot give us what analysis has previously destroyed—the organic coherence of the inner life. Reconstruction is neither necessary nor possible, for this organic unity is a primary reality and not the conclusion of a system.

THE CONCEPT OF *GESTALT*

What is the self before its unity has been broken down by analysis? In what does its organic or structural unity consist?

Let us first make clear that this unity is not one that transcends the empirical world, the world of experiences. It is a unity derived from the very experiences themselves. There is nothing under or above the totality of experiences. If one overlooks the word "totality" or interprets it in an atomistic sense, this statement would be equivalent of subscribing to Hume's theory. But we should never interpret the totality or structure of experiences as a mere sum or aggregate of the same. The experiential totality has qualities which are not possessed by the members which constitute it. Consequently the characteristics of the total structure of the self cannot be deduced, necessarily, from the characteristics of each of the experiences taken separately. . . .

What is it that characterizes a *Gestalt?* Like any other fundamental concept, that of *Gestalt* presents a degree of complexity which does not allow one to enunciate in a few words all the richness of its content. Nevertheless, there are certain characteristics which seem to be fundamental. First, there is the one that has already been emphasized: a structural whole—a *Gestalt*—has qualities not possessed by any of the elements which form it. In this sense, a *Gestalt* or structure is set in contrast with a mere sum of elements. The physical and chemical qualities of a cubic yard of water are the same as those of each gallon that makes it up. The whole, in this case, is no more than the mere sum of its parts. In the case of a structure, on the other hand, this is not so, as we have seen in considering the character of a melody; it possesses qualities which cannot be found in any of the notes, for it can be transposed without being changed into another melody.

The above-mentioned characteristic does not mean, of course, that a *Gestalt* is completely independent of the members which constitute it. In the first place, there can be no structure without members. But the dependence of structure upon members does not stop here—the removal, addition, or fundamental alteration of a member modifies the whole structure, as can be seen in the case of an organism. Any important alteration or suppression of a member alters the totality of an organism and may even cause its disappearance. This does not happen in the case of a sum. We can remove one, two, thirty, or forty gallons of water without causing the rest to undergo any important change in quality.

But not only does the structural whole suffer alteration when one of its members is taken away, the member that is taken away is also basically altered. A hand separated from the body is unable to feel or to seize an object—it ceases to be a hand—whereas the gallon of water separated from the rest retains practically all of its properties. This characteristic, taken along with the foregoing one, will suffice for the definition of a member of a structure. A member of a structure is that which cannot be removed without affecting the whole structure and losing its own nature when separated from the "whole." Conversely, we can characterize the "mere sum" as something made up of "parts" or "elements" that undergo no change when joined to other "parts" and which can be removed without producing any change either in itself or in what remains. The relationship between the parts is that of mere juxtaposition.

The difference between structure and mere sum does not stem solely from the fact that the parts of the latter are independent of the whole and that the members of the former are conditioned by the structure. There is also the fact that the parts may be homogeneous, whereas the members must offer diversity and even opposition of characteristics. One gallon of water is just as much water as any other gallon or measure. The same is true of one brick in a pile of bricks or of each grain of sand in the desert. On the contrary, in an organism each member has its own specific nature—the heart is the heart and cannot perform the functions of the liver or kidneys. There is not only diversity among the members but also opposition; and this opposition is subsumed into the unity which organizes them. The unification and organization of the members which make up a structure do not come about at the expense of the peculiar and distinctive qualities of each member. Organization is not the equivalent of homogenization, and unity does not contradict the multiplicity and diversity of the elements. This multiplicity and diversity must always be maintained as absolutely essential. Thus we find structure to be the result of a dialectic play of opposites, of a struggle between the members; it seems to hang by the thread which establishes a dynamic balance. But this unity is not of an abstract sort. A concept which organizes different members into a unity by grouping them in agreement with a common note does not constitute a structure. One essential aspect of the structure is lacking: its unity must be concrete. For that reason I use the term "structure" rather than "form" or "configuration" to translate the German word *Gestalt*, which, besides carrying the connotation of these two latter concepts, designates a unity that is *concrete.*

THE STRUCTURAL UNITY OF THE SELF

When we considered the applicability of the category of substance to the self, we noticed that none of the three classic characteristics of this concept—immutability, simplicity, and independence—belonged to the self. We obtained a similarly negative result from the consideration of the atomistic conception. In the first place, the supposed psychic atom is a poorly defined unit which, when one attempts to fix it with any precision, vanishes into thin air, becoming a mere arbitrary instant in an uninterrupted process. In the second place, the aggregation of atoms, which can have only a relationship of juxtaposition one to another, looks like a grotesque caricature of the real organic unity of the self. Let us now see if the category which we have called *Gestalt* or structure is any more successful.

It seems unquestionable that the psychic life is not chaotic, that each state or experience is connected to all the rest. This connection, however, is not of experience to experience, like the links of a chain, for if this were so there would be a fixed order of connections and in order to get to one link we should necessarily have to go by way of the preceding ones. But in the same way that Köhler showed that there is no constant relation between stimulus and response, it would be easy to show that in like manner there is no constant relation between one experience and another. No laboratory experiment is needed to prove this, for our daily experiences supply all the material we require—the sound and sight of the sea is exhilarating one day and depressing the next; the same piece of music arouses in us different reactions according to the situation in which we hear it; our arrival at the same port and in the same ship can start altogether different trains of reflection in us, depending on whether we have arrived to stay for the rest of our life or only for a short vacation; the memory of a disagreement with a friend, which irritated us so much when it happened, may now provoke only an indifferent smile. The relations of experiences to each other resemble the relations between stimuli and responses in the fact that they arise within a given context.

These undeniable data of the psychic life are founded on the fact that the self is not a sum of experiences or an aggregate of parts in juxtaposition but a structure—in the sense defined above; whatever happens to one of its elements affects the whole, and the whole in turn exerts an influence upon each element. It is because the whole reacts as a structural unity and not as a mechanism that a stimulus can provoke consequences in an altogether different field from the one in which it has arisen. Thus, a strictly intellectual problem can give rise to emotional torment, and a fact of an emotional sort can have far-reaching volitional consequences. The self is not departmentalized—like modern bureaucracy—but constitutes an organic unity with intimate, complex, and varied interrelations.

The self presents itself, then, as an organized whole, an integrated structure, and experiences are related to one another not through but within the whole. For that reason, when the structure is modified the nature of the experiences and of the relationships between them are also modified. The interdependence of the different experiential groups shows that the self is a structure which is organized and "makes sense" and that each member occupies its proper place within the structure.

This does not mean, of course, that the structure which constitutes the self cannot be analyzed and broken down, theoretically, into less complex structures. It does mean, however, that we are in fact dealing with a unity that is formed upon substructures and the intimate and complex interrelation of these substructures.[1]

And here we notice another characteristic of the concept of structure which is directly applicable to the self: the members of a structure are heterogeneous in contrast with the homogeneity of the parts of a non-structural unity. Let us state, first of all, that the structure which constitutes the self, being a very complex structure, is made up not of "simple members" but of substructures; it is consequently to the heterogeneity of these substructures that we are referring. It must also be kept in mind that the substructures are not of an abstract nature, like concepts, and that we are not trying to reconstruct a reality by juxtaposing abstractions such as the so-called "faculties of the soul."

The complexity and heterogeneity of the structure are twofold: on the one hand there is the complexity which we may call transversal; on the other there is the horizontal or, better, the temporal complexity. In actuality the self embraces the combination of both complexes, which do not and cannot exist in separation. . . .

This diversity and opposition among the elements which constitute the self should not lead us to forget the unity which characterizes every structure. The self is no exception. Its multiplicity does not exclude its unity or vice versa. And this is not the abstract unity of a concept which points to what is common; it is a concrete unity, of "flesh and blood" as Unamuno would say, for there is nothing more real and concrete than our self. Diversity underlies the structure but is in turn lost within it, for the elements uphold each other mutually in an intimate sort of interweaving in which it is impossible to distinguish warp from woof. This is not because the three types of sub-structure have equivalent strength and no one of them dominates the other two—as in the theory of the so-called balance of power—but because they vary constantly. At a given moment one element stands forth as the figure and the others form the ground; after a while there is a change of roles. These changes are explained by the fact that the self is a dynamic structure and thus resembles a symphony rather than a painting.

We should perhaps stress the point that the changes undergone by the self are not due exclusively to a different distribution of the members, for the members themselves are of a dynamic nature. Moreover, the self is constituted not only of members but also of the *tensions* produced by the reciprocal play of influences. The breakdown of the equilibrium of tensions is what generally produces the most important changes.

It now appears obvious that the relations between the experiences are not fixed, for each experience as it is incorporated into the structure modifies its former state. This member in turn undergoes the influence of the whole, which is another characteristic of a *Gestalt* easy to find in the self. Thus, the perceptions which we have at this moment depend upon our former state. The new experience immediately acquires the coloration given it both by the basic structure of the self and by the particular situation in which it finds itself at that moment. If we are happy and in pleasant company, for example, the color of the spectacles we happen to be wearing has very little effect upon the emotive state of our spirit. This is not because visual perception ceases to have emotional tonality but because a greater affective tone—the happiness which results from a different cause—completely overshadows it. What is more, the stable nature of the self colors the transitory state. There are people who give the impression of seeing the world in the rosiest colors, whatever the tint of the spectacles they wear, and there are others who see clouds in the clearest sky.

This is the influence of the whole upon the member which is incorporated, but there is also an influence of the member upon the whole. We must not forget that a structure is not suspended in thin air but rests solely upon the members which constitute it. A symphonic orchestra is something more than the sum of the musicians that go to form it, but it cannot exist without the musicians. A self without the experiential structures that go to make it up would be the same as an orchestra without musicians, that is, a pure fantasy, the fantasy of a spiritual entity that would be unable to love, hate, decide, want, perceive, etc., and would pretend to be immutable substance. Such a concept would be immutable without doubt, but it would have the immutability of nothingness.

In the same way that the total suppression of the experiential structures would mean the suppression of the self, any change or alteration of a member has repercussions on the whole structure. By this I do not mean a man lacking in emotional life, for example, for it is obvious that he would not be a man but a mere caricature, or projection on a plane of two dimensions, of a three-dimensional reality. I am referring to the alteration of a structural subcomplex. Abulia, for example, is a disease of the will, but the changes which it provokes are not limited to the volitional—it has immediate repercussions in the emotive and intellectual spheres and consequently in the total structure. Its intellectual repercussions are easily seen, for the person suffering from abulia is unable to concentrate his attention, and thus his intellectual processes break down completely. And the emotional sphere is impaired too, for the sufferer is unable, by an act of the will, to get rid of the emotion which has taken control of him, so he lets himself be so possessed by this emotion that it changes his whole personality.

Of the characteristics of the structure that are applicable to the self we have only to consider now the first and most important, that is, the fact that the structure possesses qualities not possessed by the members that make it up. At this stage in our inquiry it seems a waste of time to insist that this is one of the characteristics of the self. Let us consider only the most obvious reasons. The self has a permanence—in the sense of constant presence—and a stability that the experiences and experiential groups do not have. Experiences are totally unstable; transiency is their characteristic. The self, on the other hand, remains stable in the face of the coming and going of experiences. If experiences do not have stability, even less can they have permanence, which is the fundamental characteristic of the self. And this is not all. The structure of the self is such that the members that make it up cannot exist in separation from it. There is no experience that does not belong to a particular self. The self depends, then, upon the experiences, but it is not equivalent to their sum. It is a structural quality. . . .

PROBLEMS SOLVED BY THE STRUCTURAL CONCEPTION

A. Permanence and Mutability of the Self

At the beginning of this chapter we saw that both substantialism and atomism were unable to give an adequate picture of the self because they could not comprehend how its permanence and continuity could be compatible with the changes that it undergoes. Substantialism emphasized the permanence and atomism the mutability.

The structural conception that we are here proposing allows us to see that the two characteristics are not only compatible but also complementary. The historical survey of past thought on the subject, which occupied the first part of this book, showed us that substantialism could not understand the changing nature of the self because it held fast to an irreducible and immutable nucleus and that Hume's atomism, in its effort to destroy the doctrine of a substantial nucleus, confused it with the very real permanence and continuity of the self.

If we free ourselves of the limitations of both historical positions and observe reality just as it presents itself, we shall see that the permanence and continuity of the self are based upon its structural character, for it is a dynamic structure made up not only of the elements which we can isolate in a cross section of our life but also of the substructures that form the complex longitudinal bundles that constitute the self. And change occurs each time a new element is taken in, which alters but does not destroy the structure.

In this way the constant alteration of the self insures its stability. It is undeniable that a new experience modifies, or can modify, the structure of the self. The loss of a child or a friend, a war, a religious experience, etc., can produce such an inner commotion that they may alter the total structure. From that time on we are not the same person as before. We act in a different way, we see life in a different perspective, and it may be that not only the future but also the past is colored by the new attitude. But it is just this experience causing us to change which gives endurance to the self. From now on we shall be the man who has lost his son or his friend or who had this or that religious experience. Other children that we may have or the new friends which we may take into our hearts may cover up but can never completely obliterate the existence of an experience that at one time shook us deeply and persists in the structure of our spirit despite all that may happen to us in the future.

What happens on a large scale in the case of experiences that are profoundly moving happens on a smaller scale in all the other experiences of our life. Each new experience alters the structure or substructure to which it is connected, and thus it is incorporated "definitively," so to speak. Whatever happens afterward may alter the meaning of the experience within the whole—increasing it or diminishing it—but it can never erase the experience completely.

An analogy of a physical sort, even though inadequate to characterize our psychic life, may perhaps make clear the meaning of what I am trying to put across. The self resembles, in this respect, a mixture of colors. If we add to the mixture a new color—for example, blue—the mixture will be altered to a degree that will depend upon the quantity and shade of blue added and upon the combination of colors that were there before. This quantity of blue which produces a change in the former mixture is incorporated definitively into the whole, and however many more colors we add we shall never be able completely to counteract its presence.

The nature of the whole and the influence of the element incorporated into it are controlled, in the case of the analogy, by certain stable physical laws in which quantity plays an important role. This is not the case with psychic structures, in which quantity gives way to equality. Psychic structures obey certain principles, carefully studied by the *Gestalt* psychologists in the case of visual perception, which also exist in all the other orders of life and in the constitution of the total structure of the self. These general principles governing the organization of our total personality are what the most psychologically acute educators use as the basis for their choice of one type of experience rather than another in their endeavor to devise a system of corrective education for an aberrant personality.

Every self has a center or axis around which its structure is organized. When the personality has already developed, this axis is what gives direction and organization to our life, not only in that new experiences do not succeed in dislodging it from its route but also in that it chooses the type of experience that it finds to be in tune with it. But it is not a nucleus immutable in itself or fixed in relation to the rest of the structure. In the first place it undergoes an evolution which we can consider normal. The axis that predominates changes at the different stages of our life. In our earliest childhood the predominant experiential substructure is that related to alimentation, later it is play, and so on through life.

What is more, the center undergoes sudden displacements caused by new experiences that shake and modify the total structure. This is the case with the soldier who, according to war records, after devoting his life to the acquisition or intensification of his capacity for destruction and after exercising this capacity for years at the cost of many lives, suddenly discovers "the truth," "finds himself," decides that "we are all brothers." The center of his personality is completely displaced. His technical capacity as a killer, in which he formerly took pride—and centered his whole personality—is now a source of humiliation and shame. His personality must retrace its steps and choose another route.

These changes are due to many varied and complex reasons. Usually they have a long period of germination, as it were, in the world of the subconscious and burst forth full blown at a propitious moment. I recall the case of an American pilot who fought for several years in the Pacific; all of a sudden "the truth was revealed to him" while he was reading, more or less by chance, certain passages in the Bible. At other times the change comes about because of the intensification of the means of destruction; the explosion of the atomic bomb produced a psychological shock in many of those who had launched 200-pound bombs under the same flag. Most commonly it comes about because of the shock of contrast; the soldier, in the midst of hatred, destruction, and death, comes across people who are devoting their lives to healing, in a spirit of disinterested love, the physical and moral wounds that other men cause. These external situations usually act as the immediate cause for the eruption of subterranean currents; at other times they stir up for the first time currents that burst forth later on, if a propitious situation presents itself.

We should not be surprised that an apparently insignificant fact may be able to change the total structure of our personality after it has been stable for many years; in the psychological realm quantities are of no great importance. The principle, *causa aequat effectum,* is not valid in the interrelations of the different elements. *Gestalt* psychology has shown us how the constitution of the structure and its alteration are governed by principles that have nothing to do with the principle of causality in its simplistic interpretation as the equal of cause and effect. . . .

B. Immanence and Transcendence of the Self

Another apparent paradox—similar to that of permanence and mutability— which is resolved by the structural conception is that of the immanence and transcendence of the self. For both atomism and substantialism, immanence and transcendence are incompatible. Either the self is equivalent to the totality of experiences—and in this sense is immanent to them—or it is something that transcends the experiences. Atomism holds the first position and substantialism the second.

According to the theory that I am proposing, the self is immanent and transcends experiences at the same time, though admittedly the terms have different meanings from those attributed to them both by atomism and by substantialism. The self is immanent because it is, indeed, equivalent to the totality of experiences; but this totality, in turn, should be interpreted not as the sum or aggregate of the experiences but as a structure that has properties that cannot be found in its parts. According to this interpretation of the concept of totality, the self transcends the experiences and becomes a structural quality, in the sense in which Ehrenfels used this expression. Nevertheless, this is not the transcendence defended by the substantialists when they affirm the existence of a being that supports states or experiences. Mine is a transcendence that not only does not exclude immanence but actually takes it for granted.

Let us look at the problem from another point of view. The relation between the self and its experiences is so intimate that every experience reveals some aspect of the self; what is more, every experience forms part of the self. In this sense, the self seems to be represented in each one of the experiences, to be nothing but them. No experience, however, is able to reveal to us the self in its entirety. Not even the sum of all the experiences can do that. The self is able to transcend its autobiography; hence the possibility of a true repentance, a conversion, a new life. In the first instance the self seems to be immanent; in the second it is seen to be something that transcends its experiences.

The problem is clarified considerably if one turns his attention to those two propositions which Hume, and many others after him, considered to be incompatible: *a*) that the self is nothing apart from its experiences; *b*) that the self cannot be reduced to its experiences. I, of course, affirm that both propositions are true. When Hume maintained that the self should be reduced to a bundle of perceptions because it could not exist without them, he let himself be misled by the substantialist prejudice in favor of the so-called independence of the self. But the self, though not independent of the perceptions, is not reducible to the mere sum of them.

The paradox of the immanence and transcendence of the self, just like the paradox which we examined before, has arisen as a consequence of the way in which substantialists stated the problem of the self, a statement that the atomists accepted without realizing its consequences. The problem, as stated, presupposes a metaphysics and a logic which our conception rejects. First, it conceives of real existence as substance, independent and immutable; and second, it interprets the principles of identity and of noncontradiction in a very rigid way. My concept, on the other hand, gives a very dynamic interpretation to both principles, to the point of seeing in contradiction much of the essence of the real. What is more, I believe that there is nothing independent and immutable. I can hardly believe, therefore, in the independence and immutability of the self, the stuff of which is relationship and the essence of which is creative process.

C. Unity and Multiplicity

A variant of the preceding paradoxes is that of unity and multiplicity. When atomism took over the analysis of the self, its unity was destroyed forever and the self was turned into a great mosaic of loose pieces. Each perception became a reality in itself, independent, separable, sharply delimited. With this conception of the elements it proved impossible to rewin the lost unity. Atomists maintained, therefore, the plurality of the self, even though they sighed from time to time for the unity that they themselves had destroyed. When atomists—and men like William James who criticized atomism without being able to free themselves from the source of its confusion—ask what unites the different parts constituting the self, one must simply answer that the self never ceased to constitute a unity. Atomism's difficulties in reaching the unity of the self are merely a consequence of the arbitrary way in which it was dismembered. First they build a wall; then they complain they cannot see beyond the wall.

Substantialism, on the other hand, takes as its point of departure the postulate of unity and relegates multiplicity to accidents. The self is only one, although many different things happen to it.

With the importance that these "happenings" have for us—the self is made up of what it does—the whole statement of the problem collapses; the self is one or multiple according to how one looks at it. It is one if one focuses on the whole; it is multiple if one focuses on the members that constitute it. The self is the unity of the multiplicity of its experiences. . . .

NOTES

1. By substructure I mean any of the structural parts that constitute the total *Gestalt* that makes up the self.

Carlos Astrada
(1894-1970)

Astrada is one of the outstanding representatives of Heideggerian existentialism in Latin America, although toward the end of his life he shifted to a Marxist orientation.

He was born in Córdoba, Argentina, February 26, 1894, and died in 1970. He completed secondary education in the Colegio Monserrat and then began the study of law in his native city. In 1926 he obtained a scholarship to study in Germany for two years, a scholarship that later was renewed for an additional two years. He studied at the University of Cologne and Freiburg with Max Scheler, Husserl, and Heidegger.

Upon returning to Argentina, Astrada was designated associate professor of the history of modern and contemporary philosophy in the University of Buenos Aires (1936-47) and professor of ethics in the University of La Plata (1937-47). He assumed Francisco Romero's position as professor of epistemology and metaphysics when the latter resigned in 1947 in protest against the Perón government. Romero then replaced Astrada in 1956 when the government of Perón fell. Astrada traveled to Moscow in 1956 where he gave lectures and in 1960 he traveled to Peking for the same purpose.

He wrote extensively and produced several perceptive works. His writing began with an article in 1931 and continued until his death. His main works are *El juego existencial* (1933); *Idealismo fenomenológico y metafísica existencial* (1936); *La ética formal y los valores* (1938), which has an incisive criticism of the axiological absolutism of Scheler; *El juego metafísico* (1942); and *Temporalidad* (1943). After this there is a tendency to abandon existentialism and turn toward Hegel and Marx as is evident in *La revolución existencialista* (1952). The second edition of this work bears the title *Existencialismo y crisis de la filosofía* (1963) and has a "Conclusion" in which there is an even sharper turn toward Marxism. He also published *Hegel y la dialéctica* (1956), *El marxismo y la escatología* (1957), *Marx y Hegel* (1958), *Humanismo y dialéctica de la libertad* (1960), *La doble faz de la dialéctica* (1962), and other books that were collections of important essays. Unfortunately, in his later publications there is a decrease in the intellectual rigor that characterized his early work and he often falls into political rhetoric of a noble inspiration but lacking in theoretical foundation and significance. He proclaims that "Western culture" is crumbling inevitably and religious fervor, so modestly and ingeniously praised, can do nothing to counter this phenomenon. The downfall is due to the demise of capitalism.

An able and passionate man, Astrada placed his thought at the service of his convictions. His philosophical formation was wholly German. He relied primarily on Hegel, Nietzsche, Marx, phenomenology, Heidegger, and to a lesser degree on Scheler and Hartmann.

Astrada's conception of man is primarily Heideggerian, and takes on a strong social concern when his thought is reoriented under Marxist influence, as can be seen in the selections included in this anthology and in the passage quoted below, which is taken from the "Conclusion" of the 1963 edition of *Existencialismo y crisis de la filosofía*.

We have therefore, on the one hand, an existential ontology (Heidegger) that is anchored in an irrationalist solipsism and, on the other hand, an existentialism (Sartre) that can be reduced to an ontological phenomenonalism without any foundation. . . . Within western, class-oriented philosophy, although they did not intend to do so, these two positions . . . have actualized the vigorous, radical problematic of dialectical materialism, giving emphasis by contrast to the perceptive insight of the philosophy of Marx.

This turn toward Marxism is reminiscent of Sartre, whose existentialism Astrada criticized on numerous opportunities.

R. F.

Existentialism and the Crisis of Philosophy*

[THE PROBLEMATIC OF MAN]

Within the diversity of positions included in the common meaning of "existentialism," within its points of contact and divergency, one should take note of a perspective of great philosophical breadth and rigor represented primarily by the thought of Heidegger, in which the rhythm and direction of the new problematic is to be found.

One of the most significant dimensions of the phenomenological analysis of human existence *(Dasein)* focuses on that existence as it is present in this world in its naked facticity, as a temporal process that in itself is conclusive. Thus, *Dasein* is no longer conceived as mere transition, as a function of some other world of blessedness to which it might be destined. Within this focus emerges the affirmation of concrete existence with its socio-historical environment and of man's destiny as ground of being, making clear for man the way that leads to full humanity without transcendentalist interference or calls from the beyond.

Since man comes to existence in virtue of the ability to accede to the truth of being, what is at stake is nothing less than the actualization of the human essence of man as a being in this world, consigned to the world's finite dimensions. Man can be conceived only in his *humanitas* and is able to tend toward it because he thinks the truth about being and becomes the ek-sistent through accession to his own being.

Man's essence is in what he actually is, and not something beyond that, therefore he only wants to be what he can be, but this essence of man—his *humanitas*—is historical and not an ontological structure or nucleus of a supratemporal character. This is to say that the being of man must be

*From Carlos Astrada, *Existencialismo y crisis de la filosofía* (Buenos Aires: Edit. Devenir, 1963), 42-43, 65-69, 110-12, 128-30, 189-203.

accomplished in history through all its contingencies, necessities, and changes. In the midst of these, immersed in historical time, man will always be bound to his unpredictable earthly adventure: becoming human. To become human he directs himself toward the fullness of his own being in virtue of the relationship that in the midst of his own selfhood, that is, the temporal environment of his ek-sistence, he establishes with *being,* as the permanent dimension in the process of his historic humanity.

Being and Transcendence

Dasein possesses a structure that is both open to other things yet also endowed with a comprehension of them. The comprehension characteristic of *Dasein* draws a sketch in which things (the entity) are discovered in their possibility. To the things thus discovered, it attributes a *meaning.* "When the intra-mundane entity is discovered with the being of *Dasein,* when it is comprehended, we say it has meaning."[1] Therefore, what is articulated in a reference filled with comprehension we call meaning; meaning is that in which full comprehension of something is maintained. However, what is comprehended in the ultimate instance is not meaning but the entity itself, the thing to which we grant meaning and, correlatively, *being.* On this basis Heidegger says "meaning is an existential dimension of *Dasein,* not a property which, adhering to the entity, resides behind it or floats in an intermediate domain somewhere."[2] *Dasein* thus has meaning. This indicates that to ask for the meaning of being is to ask for being itself, since being can be understood by *Dasein.*

In following the two roads headed in opposite directions, which is a quest that Heidegger pursues, a difficulty or one might even say an ambiguity emerges that affects the direction and the ultimate consequences of the investigation. The outcome of this situation brings us to deciding on the possibility of a fundamental ontology in one of two directions: either in the direction of a transcendence that ends up in the objectivity of the old ontology (with the danger of falling back into the naturalist idea of being or into a theologically personalist idea of the same, with the added alternative of a mythical conception of being); or in the direction of an existential-historic transcendence, beyond the subject-object relation and the idea of being as the predicate of a suprasensible object. Such an ambiguity in Heidegger's thought, with its oscillation between two directions, gives rise to an ambivalent idea of being as well as of the historical essence of man.

The thread of all questioning, including questioning about being, begins with *Dasein* and returns to it.[3] When the problem of being is focused on its ontological root, that is, on the temporal structures of *Dasein,* it can only be stated on the basis of the ontic as well as ontological preeminence of *Dasein,* of all the possibilities embedded within it. The problem of being is the philosophical radicalization of the understanding of being appropriate to *Dasein*. The problem is that philosophical thinking, ontological thematization, in straying from this root tends to hypostasize in a naturalistic direction or in that of a personal entity, the latter being the *summum esse* of religions, the understanding of being that is articulated in the unified concept of *being* as the unity of all existential things. All predication of being, all truth is relative to the being of *Dasein,* to its existence. In saying that it is relative, however, we are far from affirming that it is subjective, since its relativity is not bound to subjective will or discretion.

Dasein, as discoverer of things, is not placed in an empty happening without a world, like a "subject" facing a correlative "object," rather because it is in the world it places itself through understanding itself in its own existence, in the presence of its own factual objectivity. The interrogation concerning being will be formulated beginning with the concrete situation of the entity that interrogates. That is to say, that "we interrogate here and now for ourselves."

Transcending in the comprehension of being, *Dasein* sketches its own being and the being of things through the articulation of the concept implied in an existential unity that permits it to predicate *being.* Such a concept is implied in the comprehension of being. This particular transcendence in which the comprehension of being moves is not a flight into the "objective," rather it is the way that conduces to an ontologico-existential interpretation of the objectivity of the *Dasein,* which is located *objectively* because of its de facto placement in the world, this side of "objectivism" and "subjectivism." That is to say, that the effective transcendence of *Dasein* is transcendence in existential immanence. The direction toward which this transcendence points is not the ontic polarity that stems from the subject-object relationship, but being as a relation installed through existence. Its horizon is temporality.

Transcendence is thus interwoven with the elemental temporality of *Dasein* within which all being is constituted. However, it is not appropriate to affirm of *Dasein,* as classical ontology did, that it is a *constancy* in the *present* or permanent presence indicative of an extratemporal "now," conceived as *eternity.* As the horizon of the comprehension of being, time can no longer be considered the "moving image of eternity" as is said in Plato's *Timaeus.* On the contrary, "eternity" is the *crystallization* or stagnation of a now that is absolutized in an artificial manner, segregated from finite temporality, that is, from originating time.

Being as Finite Temporal Progression

If a fundamental ontology, one with foundations in ek-sistence, were limited solely to explaining what has been stated above without exploring its ultimate consequences, it would be an ontology in every way inoffensive, stationary. However, the step forward is the incisive possibility of thinking of *being* in the sense of a temporal-finite progression, centered in the ek-sistent man, in virtue of which it is given to him to actualize himself in his own being, that is, in his historical essence. For man to be able to maintain himself in ek-sistence, he must accede to his being, that is to say to *being*, through remembering and through a prospective thinking that is inserted into the future as a mode of primary temporality. In these two temporal dimensions ek-sistence moves in its own realm—*being*—because if the present procures for *Dasein*, through its being-in-the-world, openness toward being and thereby its accession to ek-sistence also to forget *being*, since, through the primacy that the perceptive and representative contents in this mode of temporality have, the present is scattered in the entity. The temporalization of being occurs, thus, primarily in the past and the future, and it is thus that the "instant" can be actualized as present or as a mode of primary temporality, which permits us to recover the "instant" (maintaining the unity of the three modes of temporality) and to distinguish it from the "now," which is absorbed and scattered in the entity. In its historicity such an event is remembering what abides, which has neither passed by nor been completed but is at the same time an exploration, that is, an inserting into the future, wherein the existential decision is anticipated, attentive to *being* and to the plenitude of ek-sistence. This decision is not the anticipated decisiveness of which Heidegger speaks and through which *Dasein* reaches its limit in order to take hold of itself as a whole, rather it is a decision that is more elementary, in which that decisiveness finds its foundation, a decision that governs man (and here the *ethos* is revealed, the root of all ethic), as ek-sistent, to be and to maintain himself in ek-sistence, in the home of *being*. It governs him in the degree that his remembering and his thinking are primary acts, laden with his historical essence, with his human destiny.

The Rescue of Man from Alienation

The humanism of freedom is defined above all as the affirmation and rescue of the being of man. Therefore, it is founded on an existential ontology, directed toward a conception of human life as ek-sistence, and concerned with all of life's essential aspects, ethical, political, and economic, as well as others.

   Such a rescue of man can be effected only by the forces residing within the human being himself. If this recuperation of his being implies that man has the nontransferable task of saving himself, then the humanism that leads him to salvation is opposed to Christianity that, in defining man in relationship to the *Deitas*, conceives salvation only as a work of God. The humanism of liberty begins with what man effectively is, excluding as spurious and contrary to its basic presuppositions everything from which man has alienated himself through the influence of the dominating powers in historical evolution. These powers also determine the type of man developed historically in the different ages, as well as the particular anthropological views of each age.

The objection made against so-called "pure humanism," i.e., that it falls into naturalism, cannot be made against the humanism of liberty, except in error, because the latter neither recognizes nor accepts the artificial and unfounded separation of man from nature. Centered as it is in existence, which is the essence of man, humanism of freedom thinks of him as leaning toward *humanitas* without abandoning the entitative or psychophysical support of his *Dasein*. Only in the latter does one find through its accession to existence, i.e., the opening toward being, the opening that presupposes man's coming to his being. There is a traditional type of humanism that only accentuates a "properly human" nature derived from the separation in man of the body from the soul, of a will and a self that are superior from a will and a self that are inferior, that is to say, on the supposition of the separation between human nature and animal nature. This humanism rests on presuppositions of Christian dogma and therefore derives inspiration from the duality of body and soul, of terrestrial life and celestial life. Herein man is conceived in relationship with the *Deitas*.

The humanism of liberty, however, affirms the being of man over against what alienates him from himself, whether this be subjection of his spirit to supposed truths, essences, eternal values, or superhuman powers, all of which reduce him to an infrahuman level by seeing him primarily as a means for the production of goods and riches, as is the case in capitalist economies.

For Christianity, therefore, man is at the same time nature, since his body is a natural entity, and supernature, since his soul has been infused by divine creation, granting him a free immortality. For existential humanism or humanism of freedom on the other hand there is no split in man's being in the fashion described above, rather man is a natural entity, an individual in a biological species with the functional ontological possibility of raising himself, an entity that has already yielded to its being, selfhood, and freedom, even to its *humanitas*. However, he raises himself to *humanitas* without annulling his nature or pretending to escape it, because to exist and to exist as a person impelled in that direction by the spirit implicit and generated in *humanitas*, presupposes the ontic conditionality of *Dasein* (of the human entity).

We must concede to Heidegger that the humanism or humanisms referred to as such thus far, because they are under the dominance of metaphysics, focusing only on the entity, on defining man as a rational animal, and not on the being, think about man beginning with *animalitas* and not in the direction of *humanitas*. They claim that existence can never be thought of as a specific mode among other modes, and that the body of man is something different (but not "essentially different," as Heidegger affirms) from an animal organism. This distinction does not prevent existence from conditionally supposing and requiring the ontic of the "being there" *(Dasein)*. Man, to the degree to which he is humanized, makes of his body an instrument for his humanity. His humanity is pre-formed, as Herder maintains, in the biological organization of man. Therefore, this humanity does not make its appearance in man as if it were blown in from the essential truth of an extraexistential being, for in that case existence would emerge ecstatic in man.

Man in the Crisis of Philosophy

Man has changed the direction in which he searched for himself; his demands have become radical and the process of becoming human has become more profound in all aspects. This being the case, the philosophy of existence, now in the process not only of giving complete expression to this change but also of opening the way and making its acceptance genuine, proclaims and embodies a *crisis of philosophy*. It is now clear that man's fundamental struggle can be understood in terms of rescuing his being from its alienation in the Platonistic categories and products of every kind; in recuperating his being from its alienation in "eternal" essences, values, and "absolute" truths and to rescue him also from the alienation he suffers from infrahuman conditions that reduce him to a mere means for the production of material goods and wealth. With due attention to affirming his selfhood and the fullness of his *humanitas,* he leaves behind as a *caput mortuum* the philosophy of the past and the image it forged of him, which he no longer recognizes. Thus, turning his back on conceptual transcriptions of his being and his potentialities and possibilities offered in that philosophy, he pursues the path indicated by his most intimate human needs and desires.

   If man finds himself in crisis and in the midst of it asserts himself in his own being and freedom, of necessity he must nourish the new life germinating within him from the substance, resistance, weakness, and even the vital forces remaining in these last stages of the past. Therefore, in its determination to recover, and even though it is pulled along in the flow of contemporary events, his thought must frequently revert in its polemic, denial, and criticism to the philosophical jargon of the conceptions from which he seeks to be separate and free. To give human shape to this image in gestation, the image of a man with viscera, blood, and historic and earthly substance, he must still refer to the philosophy of the past, to its conceptual instruments. That is to say, he must engage philosophically and therefore debate combatively with the ideals concerning himself that were left to him by the world views of the great systems, in which he was included as just one more element.

Philosophy of existence has brought to the forefront the crisis in which contemporary man is debated. While struggling and divided, contemporary man tries to free himself from the ontologically hypostasized structures of the "objective spirit" (the technical term coined by Hegel), within which he has been transcribed, schematized, and pressured to conform to a rigid system of values, to a cultural ideal, and to a specific cosmic image. In this struggle to return to himself, man discovers, through the progression of his being as he seeks to direct himself toward the fullness of his *humanitas,* the possibility of giving a new turn to historical becoming.

THE HUMANISM OF LIBERTY AND ITS IMAGE OF MAN

Man in the Unexpectedness of His Becoming

The age in which we live, with its thrust toward the mutation of economic and social structures and of the qualitative content of life, gives an accelerated tempo to human becoming in the individual as well as the collective dimensions.

Before our very eyes, with the pressure of an intense desire and of a need for change, a transformation, revolutionary because of its extensiveness, is at work in the whole political order. Activating this process and at the same time impelled and shaped by it, the individual, concrete man, begins to emerge with traits of life and spirit that proclaim his commitment to another style of life and differentiate him basically from men of the previous age. Historically, there is an intrinsic correlation between the essential characteristics of a determined age and the typical traits of the individuals who belong to it. In these individuals appears a scale model of the structural characteristics of their age.

When there comes a change such as the one of which we are a part, there is also the formation of a new concept, of another image of man that begins to stand out and proclaim its own dynamics, to outline its life-spirit content on the horizon of the age under consideration.

Future days will be responsible for filling out the new idea of man, whose existential profile is already emerging from the convulsing present. Man is a pilgrim who through all the incarnations of his precarious and ephemeral humanity searches for man, anticipating the exultation of the full affirmation of himself. For man never *is,* in the sense of something finished and formed in the ideal mold of a goal that he proposed to reach; rather he is an eternal *coming to be,* suspended in the effort in which he projects himself toward historical concretions and temporal fulfillment of his *humanitas,* a *desideratum* never reached nor possessed in its total fullness.

Impelled by his temporal destiny, by his intrinsic making of himself, which is consubstantial with and even defines his being, his "essence" as *humanitas*,[4] he tempers and refines his soul in the uncertainties of becoming. According to the temper of the times, man's pilgrimage goes through calm and sunny regions or those that are stormy and dark. Sometimes to live is to be confident and serene; but at other times historical development is torrential, and to live is a dramatic mission to force destiny and hasten the rhythm of the march one's heart feels in a burning fever.

In the present man travels a dangerous stretch to the true crossroads of his destiny. And if vision and will are lacking, he may lose the way and forsake the task that history proposes for him: to remodel his essence, to give new form to being, a being both constant and changing, in whose successive thrusts of historic accomplishment his exhausted humanity is restated.

In turning toward a new image of himself, man seeks above all to rescue the meaning of his essential humanity from the prison of dead forms and from styles of life that are already perishing. After being formed by the Greek *logos,* after being deluded in the Christian netherworld and getting lost in the rationalist impasse of the modern period, man aspires to raise his humanity to a lordly height.

Man, Sketched by Reason

The Christian image of man reaches its culmination and end in the Middle Ages and with it the possibility that this man, fearful of everything terrestrial, should continue considering himself a candidate for peaceful existence in the life beyond. From the Renaissance comes the so-called idea of modern man. With the dawn of the Renaissance comes nothing less than the rediscovery of man himself, he who like a *terra incognita* offers himself to the obscured vision of that age. Thus, when the unifying norm of the Middle Ages was broken there emerged from its midst, as Jacob Burckhardt so aptly stated, the imponderable world of the human personality. The geographical horizon had already been expanded with the discovery of the New World.

European man therefore begins to feel himself the master of his destiny. Obstacles that hindered the free development of his vital forces were eliminated and he turned toward the Earth, dedicated to the unfolding of immanent possibilities. Stirred by new passion, he searches through nature, looking for a pattern that would harmonize with his own designs.

Through this exercise of his intellect new scientific disciplines took form. New discoveries fed his increasing curiosity and, filled with faith in the power of the instruments he was making, he dreamed of being lord of the material universe. One more step toward the dawn of the Enlightenment and "science now becomes an idol, a myth," says Paul Hazard. "There is a tendency to confuse science and well-being, material progress and moral progress."

With the apogee of the Enlightenment spirit, the image of man begins to bear the highly schematic seal of rationalism. Later there emerges the conception of History as a unified process, whose stages, oriented toward a predetermined end, must conform to the demands and modes of an all-powerful reason. Thus, for Hegel, the philosopher to whom the spiritual hegemony belongs in the first half of the nineteenth century, History is the dialectical process of the *Idea*. The conception of History as progress emerges as a skillfully drawn system in Hegel. Its first manifestation is found in Pascal, who imagines humanity as "a single man who always subsists and continuously learns through the course of the centuries."

The perspective holds that man as a rational being is not a psychological given, but a being in process turned toward becoming, who emerges as a historical task. He participates in universal reason and in the universality of reason only as a historical being (Hegel's correction of the Enlightenment concept of man); that is to say, man is conceived specifically and individually as developing, as in a process tending toward actualizing his essence, which as *humanitas* is a possibility that is achieved only in the concrete singular man and apart from him lacks meaning.

In these stages, the image of man becomes an image that is entirely schematized by reason, conforming to the demands of its postulated universality. This is the man who comes from nowhere, who has neither blood nor earthly roots, an anonymous being of utopian political constructions. Given this idea as the goal of his self-realization, man is constrained to imprison his essence, to shrink it into a simplistic rational scheme from which his vitality and intrinsic possibilities of historic progression are eliminated. This man, with no biological roots or temporal dimension, to the extent that he is an atomic element and a supposed constant, rational factor of a type of civilization, is dissolved into an entirely impersonal entity.

Toward a New Image of Man

The rationalist concept of man is dogmatically constructed on the peripheries of concrete humanity, of individual historic man, and of vital reality. Over against this rationalist concept, a real, living image of man is being raised, an image with blood and viscera, with earthly fluids and air to breathe.

A new image of man, man conceived according to other necessities and purposes, necessarily presupposes a new social order, a new hierarchical order of values to which the historical sensitivity of the age gives allegiance. The concept of man of rationalist humanism with its parallel postulate of progressivism is embedded in all the instances and sectors wherein it was able to gain preeminence, but even now, it is dead, though still hauled around on a declining verbal rather than mental plane on which are placed all the survivors of individual liberalism and its residual doctrinaire expressions.

This type of man, purely rational, antihistorical, and anonymous, is a ghostlike entity that eludes reality and struggles along a retreating front against the great events the future is preparing. It cannot be ignored, however, that this image of man has reigned for almost three centuries in the cultural and political life of the West, having shown that in the past it was an efficient reagent in the multiple aspects of this life. However, for the past three decades, this image of man is in obvious decline. It is barely a vanishing shadow that those adrift in the historical present vainly attempt to seize.

The completed man, conceptually constructed by rationalist humanism, that is to say, the isolated, completed, purely ideal man, without roots in a specific soil, with no vital ties to a nationality, with no connections to an instinctive and emotional repertoire of historically conditioned preferences— such a man does not exist. Neither is there an essential equality of all men based solely on universal reason as a constant and unalterable factor that would act independently in the psycho-vital, historical reality of national communities, classes, and racial constellations.

Having surpassed it, we are also far beyond the pseudoantinomy of *individualism* and *collectivism*. Our age no longer knows the individual as a social atom nor over against him the collectivity, considered as an aggregation of such atoms and billed as the leading actor of social and political history. It does recognize, however, opposing classes whose struggle, undoubtedly, is the crux of the economic-social process. There is also a growing awareness of the concrete historical man, the man who, without turning loose the bonds and surroundings in which he is implicated, stands out as a personal, psycho-vital unit, who affirms and gives life to his humanity as a function of his real goals, which are immanent in his particular becoming.

The Extinction of Modern Man

The unbalanced society of our age, especially the capitalist and mercantile commanders who are the possessors of political power, attempt in vain to live off the remains of the rationalist idea of man embodied in so-called "modern man," an image already in a state of dessication. These commanders are the crusty bark oppressing and retarding the buds of a new idea of man of great historical significance that have been germinating rapidly in the deeper levels of contemporary life. Suppressed forces that are emotionally and historically articulated by a generation destined to place its seal on the future give added thrust and life to this idea of man with which the coming generation will impose a new *ethos,* affirming a particular political will and instituting also a different scale of evaluation for the culture, economy, and society.

Modern man is a cadaver that senescent human groups, adrift in the storm of these days, attempt vainly to galvanize, appealing to slogans and incantations that no longer have meaning. In a letter to Dilthey, Count

Yorck von Wartenburg said: "Modern man, the man who began with the Renaissance and has endured until our time, is ready to be buried."

This type man, the man of individualistic liberalism, the ultimate, valedictory expression of "modern man," imbued with vestiges of the rationalist ideals of the nineteenth century is the corpse to be buried. The present age is responsible for carrying out this task so the new man can cover the whole surface of history and thus affirm and give full meaning to the spiritual and political orders now germinating.

History has no compassion for values in decline nor for human types that are repositories of endangered sensibilities and ideals, inanimate modules of a destiny that has made its rounds and can no longer swell history with new hope or give it new impetus. History takes into its flow only the vital ascending force, the *ethos* in which a new message for men is given form, the promise of accomplishment that is the incentive for renewed effort. History—the matrix of all possibilities—yields itself only to those generations capable of engendering the fullness of a new age, that is, to that type of man capable of implanting an ascending meaning in history and of proposing to it new and valuable goals.

Historical Becoming and Objective Goals

According to Dilthey, ages differ from each other in their structure. Each age contains a nexus, a correlation of similar, related ideas that govern the different realms of cultural life, the so-called objective spirit. It is the common repertoire that defines the character of an age. However, the ultimate foundation of this organic repertoire of ideas is constituted by the powers of the historical life, in whose nourishing soil all the objective spiritual structures, all the forms of culture take root. "The facticity of race, of space, of the relationships among powers constitute everywhere the foundation which can never be spiritualized. It was a mere dream of Hegel that different ages represent stages in the development of reason."

The remains of this dream, sifted through liberal rationalism of the nineteenth century, were thought to be unending sources of life and strength for the order of things that today is drawing near to its dissolution because its foundation has been undermined.

To affirm the spiritual personality and uniqueness of each age does not imply dissolution into a historical relativism concerned only with the pure, autonomous flow of these disconnected spiritual worlds. Such a relativism would never see in history anything firm that would serve as a point of reference, nothing that would tie these spiritual worlds together so they could establish an objective and transcendent nexus as a norm for change, as the goal of the historical process itself. Ranke saw this perfectly well, when in formulating his concept of the meaning of historical ages and in criticizing the idea of linear progress, he said "each age has its own particular tendency and its own ideal. . . . Its value does not reside in what emerges from it, but in its own existence, its own selfhood"; that is, in its identity with itself.

Neither does Ranke allow any given generation to be reduced in rank for the sake of successive generations, since "all generations of humanity appear with equal rights." Contemplating universal history as a whole, as a supreme process that includes every individuality and all spiritual realms, he considers States "as individualities, analogous to each other, but essentially independent of one another . . . original creations of the human spirit."

The same can be said of the individual, who in his historicity is not given to a bare flowing, a becoming with no meaning, that recognizes nothing firm in the midst of mutation and does not transcend toward anything objective, such as ideals, goals, and values, though such an objectivity would be functional and not ontologico-hypostatic. Objective truth as well as objective structures do not reside in a transcending moment nor in a transcending world of reason that has no tie with human historical becoming, rather they belong to such becoming, to its primary existential temporality, since they have been formed by its flowing.

Sameness, Otherness, and *Humanitas*

To be sure, there is a realm of ends, norms, and values structured on an objective plane that transcends individual consciousness. One may also conceive and accept the effectiveness of an objective spirit as a structured whole that has emerged from the historical process, but this process is a far cry from being the domain of pure contingency and subjective irrationality. For it is precisely man's ability to establish an objective realm of the spirit that permits him, in each moment of his becoming, to be himself, to apprehend his own self-sameness.

While man aspires to fulfill himself in his being, to affirm himself in his humanity, to feel identical with himself in each moment of temporal transition, the personal identity to which he aspires leads him to postulate time, a transcendence in the sense of otherness, as a guarantee of his identity and as the goal of his efforts. Stating this problem as a function of the finite-infinite, historicity-eternity antinomy, Kierkegaard tells us that man in his sameness, in his desired self-existence, always finds something, the Absolute, before which he is his own self-sameness.

While the sameness of man lives and exists, in the proper sense of these terms, through his becoming this sameness is bound to a concrete self-consciousness that, because it is expressed in temporality, is also becoming and thus never crystallizes, since there is no crystallizing in the existing man. This concrete-self-consciousness gathers man into the lived experience of its own identity, anchored to the temporal structures of existence. This is because man, in everything (ideals, values, objective norms of life) toward which he transcends and projects himself from his concrete historicity—which is the ineradicable moment of his being, of his being made in time—in all this transcending, man searches only for himself, he attempts only to seal his identity in the midst of mutations and change, shaping it into a consistent and stable image of himself, into an idea of his "humanitas."

He now strives toward a new actualization of his being, a new image of himself. He aspires to actualize and conceive himself in all his immanent possibilities, to integrate himself with his potentialities, to reencounter himself, at last, in the full concretion of his essential humanity.

Magnetizing its thrust, which is historically conditioned and limited, the ideal of the *full man*—as proposed by Max Scheler—is lifted up as the goal that at the same time that it transcends pure becoming, receives from it its meaning, which is latent, to the degree it is *existential,* in the immanence of the temporal structure. Although "this full-man, in an absolute sense, is far from us,. . .a relatively whole-man, a maximum of full humanity, is accessible to each age."

For the concrete, existing man, this ideal of the whole-man as a goal and model is an index of transcendence, a mediating synthesis of all objective structures. These structures represent *the other,* not in the sense of the naturalist idea of being or of an absolute conceived as a personal God, but of an *other* that, as a transcending instance toward which what is human is projected, permits man in each moment and stage of his temporal passing to know his concrete sameness. It is the apparently fixed limit that as an ideal point of reference hovers above historical becoming. Ultimately, however, existence activates and gives meaning to historical becoming, for existence historically determines and actualizes the humanity in man.

Conclusion (After a Decade)[5]

Within the structure of bourgeois philosophy and with respect to its doctrinal perspectives, the ontology of existence and existentialism have had a revolutionary impact, laying open the false suppositions and the state of crisis to which this philosophy had come. This ontology of existence and existentialism have served as true antidotes to the usual emphases of a sterile *Erkenntnistheorie* and of an absolutist axiology of Platonic heritage. At the same time, however, Heideggerian existential ontology and Sartrean existentialism—the latter derived erroneously from the former—in their encounter with the doctrines of bourgeois philosophy have revealed their own insufficiency and are implicated, as opponents of that philosophy, in its crisis and decadence.

We have, therefore, on the one hand an existential ontology [Heidegger] anchored in an irrationalist solipsism, and on the other hand an existentialism [Sartre] reduced to a phenomenalist ontologism with no foundation.

Above all, the first, with its solipsistic *Dasein* and its "onto-theology," has shown its own frustration, its lack of authenticity in the analysis of historicity. In its own formulation and development, it has been incapable of surpassing the radical, solipsistic individualism of Kierkegaard. Both positions, the ontologico-existential and the existentialist, have actualized, though without saying so, the vigorous and radical problematic of dialectical materialism within Western classical philosophy, accentuating by contrast the immense foresight of Marx's philosophy.

Earlier we pointed out that existentialism, although it is a "philosophy of crisis," is fundamentally the proclamation of *the crisis of philosophy*. It is such in that it sums up the breakdown of the ideological structures of bourgeois philosophy. Further, it is crisis on a deeper level, since the type man that is dominant—the bourgeios and the petit bourgeois—is involved in the actual decadent stage of Western capitalist civilization. Aside from this, the ecumenical man, struggling to rescue himself, from above and at the cost of concrete life, from the alienation in all the socially superstructured forms—from the fetish of consumerism to supposed eternal values and essences—this universal man searches for himself, searches for his own humanity along a path different from the one designated by historical humanisms, which up to the present, as ideas that have dominated successively, express only the ideas of the ruling classes, which gave to these humanisms their philosophical imprint. Thus, the crisis of one type of man—the so-called modern man who dates from the Renaissance—stems from the historical situation of the civilization in which he finds himself, which gives rise to the crisis of bourgeois philosophy and of its ideological structures. Basically, our concern here is not a temporary "philosophy of crisis" but the crisis of a particular philosophy, a superstructural expression of the crisis of a whole economic system, that inevitably follows the descending curve of its decadence to its dissolution and fall.

NOTES

1. Martin Heidegger, *Sein und Zeit*, 151.
2. Ibid.
3. Heidegger, *Sein und Zeit*, 38.
4. We can speak of the essence of man (with absolute exclusion of the "realist" presupposition of the doctrine of "universals") conceiving it only as an idea of a living individual, a specific individual, who is precisely the one who has or actualizes the idea. This essence or idea does not constitute an independent being that has primacy with respect to the concrete existing man, but as *humanitas;* it is realized only in individuals, in specific men. Outside of them, it does not occur nor does it have meaning. Hence we must avoid all absolutizing of the

concept of "man," of hypostasizing the idea of man as well as the idea of "humanity," as if we had under consideration something distinct and above the totality of men. Since the idea of man is constituted in the existing individual, this idea, *humanitas,* is subject to the mutation that is imposed upon it by historical becoming, by the very historicity of concrete man.

5. This is part of a section added by Astrada to the last edition of this work.—ED.

Francisco Miró Quesada
(b. 1918)

Born in Lima in 1918, Miró Quesada attended elementary school in Peru and France and completed secondary education at the Italian School in Lima. He received doctorates in mathematics and philosophy from the University of San Marcos, in Lima, where he also received a degree in law. At twenty-one years of age, he was appointed to the chair of contemporary philosophy at the University of San Marcos and subsequently to the chair of the philosophy of mathematics and to that of political science. He has given lectures in several Latin American universities—Buenos Aires, La Plata, Córdoba, México, Chile, Central Venezuela, and others—in European universities—Oxford, Cambridge, London, Rome, the Sorbonne, and the College de France—as well as the University of New York at Buffalo.

He is a member of the Peruvian Academy of Language as well as a corresponding member of the Royal Spanish Academy of Language. In 1942 he was one of the founders of the Peruvian Philosophical Society and has been its president several times.

Miró Quesada's principal interest has been in the theory of knowledge, but this interest has assumed a variety of expressions. He worked first of all in the phenomenology of Husserl as is reflected in his work *El sentido del movimiento fenomenológico* (1941). Later he became interested in mathematical logic and wrote the first book in this field published in Spanish America, *Lógica* (1946). Later he turned to juridical logic and wrote *Problemas fundamentales de la lógica jurídica* (1956) and *Apuntes para una teoría de la razón* (1963), in addition to many essays and books.

His principal aim has been to achieve a systematic perspective of the principles that govern rational knowledge. He claims that classical positions such as rationalism, positivism, pragmatism, dialectical philosophy, and historicism have been surpassed by advances in scientific knowledge. Miró Quesada uses the methodological procedures of modern logic and recent metatheory to formulate a design of the structure and dynamism of rational thought that enables one to account for the result and the modalities of the formal sciences as a first step for a general theory of rational knowledge. More recently he has worked on the problem of synthetic *a priori* judgments and has used Gödel's theorem to prove the existence of this type of judgment in mathematical knowledge.

135

In the last twenty years Miró Quesada's attention has turned toward political theory. In 1959 he published *La otra mitad del mundo,* the diary of a long trip through the USSR and continental China. In 1970 he published *Humanismo y revolución* in addition to many other essays.

In political philosophy, Miró Quesada seeks to find a foundation for political praxis that is more rigorous than that offered by Marxism, Christian socialism, and other contemporary views. In order to do this, he attempts to formulate a concept of humanism independent of every metaphysical position.

If one wished to characterize Miró Quesada's view as developed in his books, essays, and lectures, one would have to affirm that his is a neorationalism or "dynamic rationalism" that is different from classical, Hegelian, and phenomenological rationalism. This difference is due to the methodology employed to establish conclusions as well as the views he has developed, such as his theory of synthetic *a priori* judgments and his theory of evidence and intellectual intuition.

R. F.

Man Without Theory*

[THE FAILURE OF ALL THEORIES OF MAN]

Man cannot live without theory, for he is the theoretical animal par excellence. Ancient wisdom characterized him as "rational animal," because theories were formulated by reason. No longer does anyone hold that there are theoretical men and practical men, men dedicated to thought and others dedicated to action. All men are theoretical, only some know it and are distinguished by their determination to develop theoretical perspectives, whereas others are satisfied to live submerged in the theory and to use it to obtain pressing needs. Our life, however, is surrounded by theory. From our confidence in the firmness of the earth we walk on, all is the fruit of theory, of scientific thought, of our capacity to think about events and to interpret them. Thanks to theory we are able to confront the world, to have a world, to predict events, manage them, direct them, and take advantage of them. It is because there have been men dedicated to discovering how the world is that the "practical men" can dedicate themselves to modifying it through technology, a late and secondary product of theory.

Theory, the knowledge of things and events, emerges as a necessity in man's defense against the assault of the world. Theory is born as a function of man and for man to find a perspective within the endless labyrinth of events as he orders his world. He structures the world so he can reach his self-proposed goals. He must know himself to know what he pursues and what the true relationships to his world are. This is to say that every theory concerning the world, concerning the things that surround him, necessarily implies a theory concerning himself, for to think about the world is to think about one's self, since the world is only the terminus of action. Furthermore, it is to think that thought has particular possibilities, that it is capable of dominating specified situations. It is to think about what is going to be done with the knowledge acquired about the world, and to think about one's own destiny.

*From Francisco Miró Quesada, *El hombre sin teoría* (Lima: Universidad Mayor de San Marcos, 1959), 14-31.

However, at this point by their very nature things begin to be quite different, because the reality of man is infinitely more complex than that of the world. To theorize about the world is much easier than to theorize about man. In the surrounding world, simple patterns are more or less common, like the successions of various cyclical states such as day and night, tides, and movements of the stars. Given this simplicity and regularity, all theory can be verified, elaborate as it may be. One need only deduce the various consequences implicit in the presuppositions. As long as the consequences coincide with the facts one can continue to accept the theory as true, but if the facts contradict it, then one will have to reject, modify, or adapt the theory; otherwise it becomes untenable. This process of verification is the foundation of all possible knowledge of realities and is what has permitted man to evolve from the most primitive and infantile theories to the present elaborate systems of physics, astronomy, and biology.

The more complicated a segment of reality, the more difficult it is to elaborate a theory that will account for it and allow man to know it. It is more probable, also, that one will find a theoretical consequence that does not coincide with the facts and will make the theory fail. However, by means of corrections and reelaborations, it is always possible to improve it and to adapt it to the new demands of the facts, achieving thereby a knowledge of nature that is more or less uniform and progressive. When we are concerned with human beings, however, this procedure is practically impossible. Because man's complexity is such and the intertwining of the facts that characterize him is so great that to elaborate a reasonably acceptable theory concerning his nature, it becomes necessary to rely on a dense skein of concepts and hypotheses. From this theoretical mire an endless series of consequences unfold that must be correlated with the facts about man. And in the long run the facts ruin the theory because, unfortunately, some and often many of the consequences of the theory contradict the facts. In addition to this insuperable difficulty, there is another that is perhaps even greater, the phenomenon of freedom. Human freedom is not a theory, it is a fact—the fact of the unpredictability of our actions. Whereas in nature the smooth, simple recurrences of phenomena permit astounding predictions, the possibility of man making decisions that go counter to what is foreseen makes it impossible to achieve rigorous knowledge of what we are. In principle, every man can show any theory concerning man to be inadequate. All he has to do is act so as to contradict what the theory permits one to predict concerning his actions. In some cases, of course, the predictions are fulfilled, but it is on a superficial or pathological level. Ultimately, no one can predict anything concerning what a human being will do. Yet, the essence of theory consists in deriving consequences, that is, making predictions.

However, if formulating theories about man is such a difficult and demanding task, all our other theories concerning the world and life also incur a subtle, grave danger. For, as we have seen, to formulate a theory concerning nature one must presuppose something about man himself, about his capacity to formulate theories and about life's purpose that is his lot to pursue. Every radical change in the theory of man leads inevitably to change in our way of seeing the world, and this produces insecurity and distress. For, to change a theory concerning the world forces us to recognize that what we believed is not so certain, that the earth we walk on has suddenly become moving sand in which we may sink. Further, to have to change our perspective on ourselves forces us to recognize that we were in error, that what we believed was eternally true about our possibilities and destiny has been seriously questioned. Suddenly, as with the psychopath, we are strangers to ourselves, we no longer recognize ourselves. Nothing is more terrifying to man than to discover that he is not what he believed he was. For years, centuries, perhaps even millennia, he struggled for security only to have it dissolved in a gust of mysterious theoretical wind. Hence the furor, the resentment, and the hatred toward those who dare attack this security, for without it we are not able to live. . . .

The process in which theories concerning man dissolve is inflexible and its successive stages are easily describable. The first step is the general elaboration of the theory. In a majority of cultures this step has been simple and spontaneous. In the modern world it is conscious and has scientific and philosophical pretensions, as for example in Nazism, fascism, and Marxism. In all cases, however, the point of departure is the same: a tangled mass of extremely complicated hypotheses that are taken to be the sublime, incontrovertible, and definitive truth. For some people this truth is of a divine origin and in some cases these hypotheses seem quite simple when first proposed. . . .

In order to understand these issues, it is important to have a clear concept of what a theory is, especially of the relationship between a theory and its logical implications. As we have seen, a theory is a series of hypotheses about some aspect of reality, and it may be restricted or broad and encompassing. Once the hypotheses have been formulated a series of consequences can be derived logically. The fundamental aspect of this logical derivability is the immensity of its range, since, beginning with a small number of hypotheses one can derive innumerable consequences, so many, in fact, that they are practically infinite. This is the main characteristic of any theory whatever, constituting its greatness as well as its limitation, its usefulness as well as its terrible danger. Through the power of derivation, atomic energy has been developed, so that it will be possible within a few years to improve the world in unforeseen ways or to destroy it by pressing a button. Through this strange and almost magical power we have made airplanes fly, we have burned witches, invented the telescope and the microscope, committed atrocious genocides, saved millions of lives, and made martyrs of millions of human beings.

A theory's power of derivation is so immense that it is difficult to understand without a concrete example. If we take arithmetic as an example, it will be sufficient to clarify what we want to say. Those who know what mathematical theories are and how they are organized know that all, absolutely all arithmetical knowledge can be derived from the seven postulates of Peano. These hypotheses are extraordinarily simple and can be understood by a child. However, in spite of being only seven, an immense number of conclusions is derived from them, a number so great that, although our knowledge of arithmetic has been increasing for 2500 years, it still continues to increase, and will continue to increase in the coming centuries. Aside from being numerous, the consequences are so complicated that no one can foresee where they will eventually lead. This example permits us to see clearly the incalculable power of a theory, for, once hypotheses are formulated, we can deduce an incalculable number of conclusions from them by means of logic.

This example demonstrates that from a few, simple hypotheses one can derive an infinite number of consequences that because they are so rich and numerous are unforeseeable, for once the hypotheses are formulated, no one can foresee what the future consequences will be. These consequences follow a rigorous, logical line and as the investigators continue to deduce them, their derivation follows necessarily from the hypotheses. However, no one can foresee what the consequences will be or where they will lead. If this is true in the case of a theory that has only seven, very simple hypotheses, what would happen with a theory concerning man that, as we have seen, consists of a great number of complicated hypotheses?

Let us turn now to a third dimension of all theories about man, their strange quality and inevitable failure. To obtain security in the world and to make headway through life's complexities, man elaborates a complicated theory concerning himself. The complication is inevitable because man, the subject of the theory, is the most complicated being in the universe. Due to the inextricable complications of being human, every theory concerning man, in spite of its inevitable complication, is incomplete. In spite of this incompleteness but because the theory is so complicated, the consequences derived from it are numerically overwhelming. The liability, however, is not found in the number of the consequences, but in their unpredictability. Thus, in the case of arithmetic or for that matter, all mathematical theories, the hypotheses are few and simple, the consequences are so numerous that they become unforeseeable and leave the most perceptive minds stupefied. In the case of a theory as complicated as theories concerned with man, however, this impressive array of consequences must be multiplied by infinity. And this has always been true. Due to the complexity of the theories he has elaborated concerning himself, man has drawn very odd, strange, and stupefying conclusions concerning his own being. Beginning with hypotheses that for him were more or less evident, man has come to conclusions that in the beginning were quite foreign to his thought. We only need to review history to support the claim that the doctrines man has elaborated concerning himself have carried him to unanticipated extremes. Calvinism, for example, begins with ascetic principles but comes to the inevitable conclusion that wealth is a sign of having been chosen by God for salvation. From this perspective to modern colonialism is only a small step, a step that naturally was taken in the most sincere conviction of its being just. Think for example of the strange character of funeral rituals, of human sacrifices, of the auto-da-fé, of the differences of sexual morality that exist in diverse cultures, of religious wars. One must recognize that all these actions that seem so foreign to the points of departure are only their inevitable consequences. They lead to the failure of the theory, because given their great quantity, there comes a point at which the theory is obviously opposed to the facts. And then man ceases to believe in them or he tries to adapt them, if he can, to new demands. We must recognize that every theory concerning man is incomplete and thus has inherent limitations. However, because the theory is so complex it allows for the derivation of unexpected consequences, and in the long run one of the consequences will be evidence in support of the limitation or imperfection of the theory. Since man is such a complex reality, in the first theorizing efforts consequences usually coincide with the facts, but even if they do not one can pretend they do. The theory however, like Pandora's box, continues producing consequences that are added to the initial hypothesis, in turn leading to other more complex and wondrous consequences until it would seem the whole theoretical machinery had gone wild. A theory, however, is inflexible, the most inflexible thing in the world, much more so than machines or the will of man, and once placed in motion it has a terrifying force, like a monster that devours everything and can be detained by nothing. In a spontaneous manner as generally happens, or in a conscious manner, once the primitive hypotheses have been formulated, the consequences unfold and continue to do so without stopping, falling like grenades on a battlefield with increasing precision and explosive potential. It is as if man were a spider and the theory were his web, but a web that continued to expand unceasingly until it had imprisoned him in its own strands and slowly, inevitably asphyxiated him. When this happens, he realizes for the first time that the complicated theory that he created concerning himself is betraying him. Man does not create theories for his pleasure. He creates theories as a fundamental way of life, for it is his method of overcoming the chaos of existence. When consciously and often implicitly in secular pursuits, he elaborates a theory concerning himself, his nature, his relationship to the universe, or his ultimate destiny, it is in order to handle in a more adequate fashion the dangerous complexity of his existence, in order to feel more secure and well grounded. However, if the contrary occurs, it means that this theory is inadequate, that it must be amplified, restructured, or perhaps radically changed. . . .

The history of humanity is an impressive succession of complicated, yet false theories that man has woven around himself. Along the millennial pathway of history, theories lay semidestroyed and rusted like military equipment left behind by an army in retreat. Each great theoretical crisis, each great change, each new development marks the shift from one culture to another, from one age to another. In earlier days men were not sufficiently aware of what was happening, although they were aware that something was happening and expectantly waited the new. At times their desires were implemented in a conscious, more or less rapid manner. At other times, however, the restructuring process lasted centuries. Intuitively men grasped the significance of the situation, but the mechanism for restructuring was not grasped for two reasons: the lack of historical consciousness, that is, awareness of the relationship between their world view and historic era, and the lack of understanding of what a theory is. In the nineteenth century a great movement began that culminated in our day and overcame both limitations. For this reason, in the present, in this modern, troubled atomic era, the era of the machine and technology, we are aware nevertheless of what is really happening. We have a clear understanding that history is a succession of ways of conceiving the world and man, of ways considered absolute by men of different ages but that today are no more than vague shadows, difficult to understand. Our civilization, therefore, is the most philosophical of all, because none has had as clear an awareness of its limitation and relativity. In truth, our age is characteristically an age of search, of disorientation, and of acute consciousness of its negative traits. Contemporary man is one who experiences in his own flesh the failure of a great theory concerning himself: European rationalism, in all its facets, from the liberalism of "laissez faire" to Nazism and Marxism. Ortega has said of our age that it is an "age of disillusioned living," but to be more precise we should say, "an age of disillusioned theorizing." Scheler begins one of his books, perhaps his best, with the celebrated phrase, "Never has man been such an enigma to himself."

Given this situation the inevitable question is "What shall we do?" The depth of the question does permit a dogmatic answer. Indeed, perhaps this essay should end here. However, to be human means to try unceasingly to overcome every "non plus ultra" and since we do not wish to deny our human condition, we have no alternative but to forge ahead. Yet, before continuing we wish to emphasize that what follows is no more than the point of view of a particular individual who, along with all other individuals in this age, is faced with an immense problem that by its very nature transcends any purely individual response.

The first thought that might come to mind, and perhaps a majority already favors it, is to commit our efforts to the reconstruction of the old theory, making it more comprehensive and adapting it to the demands of our modern circumstance. Or, should this not be possible, to elaborate a new theory that may or may not be related to the old or to earlier theories, but would constitute an organic system, capable of providing answers to the most pressing questions and have the scope and flexibility necessary to permit men of our day to work with the total range of their problems. In actual experience, the normal or spontaneous attitude always develops a theory. So we, although disillusioned by theories, in seeing ourselves in a bind, think of amplifying or creating theories, like men of other ages. In this day, however, there is a difference: men of previous ages were not aware of the relativity or limits of their theories, nor of the horrible dangers implicit in creating a complicated theory concerning man from which unforeseeable and mortal consequences were derived. Furthermore, they did not suspect that their theories ran the same risks as all preceding theories. Therefore they created under illusion, but in faith, and so their theories had "vital force" and served to resolve human problems since men believed in them and were convinced that all previous ages had been in error whereas they were in the truth. In this day, however, we are not convinced our position is unique, true, or definitive. Indeed, we know that whatever we do, our theory about man will suffer the same end as the others.

Yet, instead of searching for a new theory and instinctively following the destiny of Sisyphus, what if we assume a completely different attitude? Instead of inventing a new and dangerous theory, why not simply give up formulating theories about ourselves? Now this proposal may well produce a scandal and for two good reasons. First, because man is so accustomed to formulating theories about himself, to taking for granted that he knows what he is, to feeling himself at the helm of a world of structures and hierarchies, to renounce theory leaves him with the impression that he is giving up the possibility of finding solutions, that he is spineless and morally decadent, that he has given up the struggle for good and against evil. Second, because it is believed, more for theoretical than practical considerations, that no matter what man does he is condemned to theorize and that he can give up everything except formulating a complete concept of the world, of things, and of himself. It is believed that man needs theory to live, that without it he flounders and does not know what to hold on to, he is a lost soul on a ship without a rudder. For, although he may deny theory, implicitly he is always constructing a system of concepts for clarifying the meaning of his life.

To be sure, this second argument is much more powerful than the first. Its strength, however, lies in its inclusive breadth, for its detailed analysis of situations is slipshod. For example, if one analyzes all the elements constituting the world within which man includes himself, one sees there are various dimensions. One dimension is the surrounding world. This dimension, naturally, is undeniable. If man does not possess a well-formulated theory concerning the surrounding world he is not even able to walk down the street. The simple act of dodging an automobile indicates the possession of a rather clear concept of the principles of causality and the laws of dynamics. Further, our cultural crisis is not a crisis in knowledge of the natural world. The cosmic world, our surrounding environment is known with increasingly greater certainty and vigor. It is perhaps the only part of our general vision of the world that at present follows a linear evolution. We have reached such a comprehension of what physical theory is, that the elaboration of that type theory is carried out in the awareness that in time it will be surpassed, and that it will be necessary to amplify it to include new facts. For this reason, it is possible that the nuclear emphasis of the old theory may be preserved intact and that it may be possible to consider it as a special case of a new theory. Some might believe that this procedure is applicable to the theory about the nature of man. However, given the complexity of all anthropological theory, this is not possible. Physical as well as mathematical theories are very simple, since they are based on broad abstractive processes. Therefore, this approach is not adequate for anthropological theory. But if we do not make use of it, we encounter the earlier objection, namely, that every theory concerning the surrounding world presupposes an integrated theory of the human being. And here we come to the crux of the issue. For, if this affirmation is true, then we will never be able to free ourselves from a theory concerning ourselves and we will always return to that monotonous, well-beaten path. This, however, we believe to be false, because even though it is undeniable that every theory concerning the cosmos presupposes a theory concerning man, it does not presuppose necessarily that the theory of the cosmos os complete. In order to grant validity to a theory about the cosmos, we must presuppose certain epistemological postulates, certain beliefs concerning the structure and organization of our consciousness, but in no way does such a theory necessarily include hypotheses about the moral life or destiny of man. The most to be said is that from these epistemological presuppositions, one can derive many consequences as to the possibilities of knowing the world in general and even ourselves and that these consequences may be positive or negative in some or in many aspects. However, this does not invalidate our point of view because what we are specifically trying to do is place brackets around our cognitive faculties insofar as these are applied to ourselves.

However, man is so accustomed to living on the theoretical level that he does not conceive the possibility of refraining from decisions about his own nature and fundamental relationships with the surrounding world. Thus he alway finds arguments that justify his use of theories. In the present case, those who deny the possibility of avoiding theory about man adduce that this avoidance is impossible because determining one's orientation in the world without language is impossible. To establish interhuman communication, whatever it may be, is impossible without speech, but speech is in itself a theory. The philosophical analysis of language shows unequivocally that every expressive system acquires its ultimate meaning from theoretical presuppositions about the nature of the world and of man. Thus the very possibility of language implies the immersion of the human being in a complete theory concerning himself, a theory that refers not only to his objective relationship with the environing world, but also to his norms of action and destiny. Philological analysis of the most trivial words reveals, in a surprising way at times, the immense background of cosmological, metaphysical, and ethical theory upon which all possible language rests. The argument, then, would seem to be definitive: man cannot live without an orientation in the world and to seek an orientation in the world requires a specific theory concerning the physical structure of the cosmos. This theory, however, cannot be elaborated without language, but language is the great, universal theory, the expression of what in the ultimate, collective, anonymous, and therefore inevitable sense man believes about the world and himself. Thus, it is impossible to live as a human being without presupposing certain theoretical axioms concerning our nature and our destiny.

The inference from this last bulwark of the theory is sound. The error, however, is not found in the conclusion but in the point of departure. The error is found in the lack of theory as to what a theory is. For if one analyzes what a theory really is one sees immediately that it is always possible to do without it. Better said, there are two classes of theories, one that is implicit and spontaneous, formulated by the primitive collective mind that creates language, and the other is conscious, elaborated and created for specific purposes of knowledge. *The first cannot be avoided, but the second can* and this is our concern. The first cannot be avoided because it is implicit in language and it is impossible to do without language. Even if it is a theory that decisively influences our manner of seeing the world and of being ourselves, it is an implicit, practically unconscious theory, a theory so remote that we have forgotten its true meaning. Words that in a primitive beginning embodied terrifying revelations about nature, about the world, and about ourselves are now applied mechanically to specific, concrete objects. "To exist" signifies etymologically, "to place oneself outside himself." Enormous theoretical ranges are implicit in this meaning. Nevertheless, for the man who is not specialized, who does not meditate philosophically on the meanings of words, "to exist" means simply "to live" if he refers to a human being and "to be real" if he refers to things. "Devil" meant "slanderer" for the primitive man. Much feeling is wrapped up in this meaning. However, in modern Western languages when speaking of the devil, one does not think specifically of a slanderer in spite of the biblical passage in which the devil tempts Eve, slandering God. In pursuing the analysis of the primitive meaning of language, one comes to the following conclusion: as constituted, language is an original theory about the world and ourselves, a theory containing ethical and metaphysical principles. In an indirect and inevitable manner it influences our manner of being. This influence, however, is weakened by distance and by forgetting the primitive meanings. With the passage of time, with the progress of expressive flexibility, in the coming of the scientific spirit words acquire a new seal, a precise meaning of associative reference to things, persons, and actions over their primitive, vague, and metaphorical meaning. Therefore, in spite of the theoretical "pressure" of language, we are quite capable of overcoming the primitive world view. Thus, any of our Western languages of Indo-European origin presupposes in its beginning a theological vision of the world, a special conception of "being" and a specified taxonomy of moral values and disvalues centered in a paternalistically organized society. However, these meanings are so worn by time and so covered with semantic accumulations that it is perfectly possible for a Western man to see the world in a completely different manner. To be sure, the liberation can never be complete, although it is sufficiently radical that the Indo-European origin of our languages does not oblige us to consider a man a scoundrel who does not believe in God or who believes, with respect to sexual morality, that men and women have equal rights. This shift is the focus of our concern.

Let us now take a look at the other type of theory, *conscious theory* or if one prefers "scientific-philosophical" theory in a very broad sense. *Every theory formulated by man about the world, life, and its destiny, belongs to this type of theory.* Every human being, in addition to the theoretical background imposed by language, lives subsumed in some scientific-philosophical theory. However, an analysis of the human situation shows quite readily that it is also possible to avoid this type theory. To do this only a clear concept of the epistemological significance of the word "theory" is needed. Every theory presupposes the existence of "facts" and although facts cannot be interpreted without a theory, this does not prevent them from existing as such. A completely convincing example is that in spite of the change in theories, facts remain the same. Thus, the orbital path of Jupiter can be explained by Newton's theory as well as by Einstein's theory of generalized relativity. Nevertheless, in spite of the difference between these two theories, Jupiter's orbital path, as fact, remains the same. It can be explained also by primitive concepts, for example, as the movement of a lamp carried by a nocturnal god as he travels his circular path through the firmament. Still, all men will inevitably see Jupiter in the same manner. And seeing it they will consciously or unconsciously formulate some theory about it. The facts are nevertheless undeniably there; the blue of the sky, the white of the clouds, the brilliance of the light, the green of the fields are facts that are seen alike by all men in spite of the theories.

And just as in nature, in spite of the change of theories or perhaps precisely because of this change, one can clearly identify the facts, so in the human realm the facts remain stable over against the changes in the understanding of life. Between the theory whose consequences lead to the sacrifice of human lives and the theory that interprets such action as intolerable there is, to be sure, a significant distance. Nevertheless, all men who lived with these theories have undeniable characteristics in common. All were capable of suffering and rejoicing, all wept and laughed at least once in their life. All spoke, all felt emotions, all loved and hated at one time or another. One might object that in these affirmations we are formulating a theory, for to affirm that all were men is to universalize a concept of man. For among savages there are many groups that do not consider others to be human, but see them as animals, and some tribes even see themselves as dispossessed of the human condition. To this, however, we respond that what presupposes a theory is not the description of the facts, but dividing men into men and other things. For one must have a theory that is thoroughly elaborated and proclaimed with zealous fanaticism in order to come to believe that a person that speaks as we speak and communicates with us is not equal to us. In such interpretations of the facts, complicated ethico-metaphysical theories of the totem and the taboo are at play. However, if one insists that the universal application of the word "man" is the direct or indirect implication of some theory, we can dispense with the term. We only need observe the facts directly: there is something animated that laughs and cries, sings and shouts, hates and loves, suffers and rejoices, and above all speaks and communicates with others by means of symbols. And this type of animated something we decide to call "man." We presuppose nothing concerning its nature, origin, destiny, or obligations. There it is before us with curious demeanor, mysterious gestures, and different looks. Its history develops through the centuries, elaborating strange theories for which it has strong attraction, an attraction that is so strong that in support of their truth it is capable of anything, even of killing and torturing a fellow man. However, just as some men are capable of killing and torturing to support a theory, others are incapable of doing so in spite of all theories, in spite of all the demands and pressures of their environment. There are men who love other men and there are others that do not feel any special love but nevertheless rebel and draw back in the face of suffering and injustice. Within the range of these attitudes of cruelty and brotherhood man displays all his possibilities. All human life is tinted with these two attitudes that are like the two ultimate but opposing colors of an infinite spectrum. When man takes hold of a theory to justify his desire to make others suffer, he descends to the level of the demonic. When he rises to the level of self-sacrifice in order to prevent the suffering of others, he attains sainthood. Between these two extremes are all other men. This is the great fact, the formidable fact of the human condition down through history. Through all changes and ages, all cultural cycles and crises, all great achievements and catastrophes, we find the same fact: there are men who make others suffer and there are men capable of suffering so that others will not suffer. There are men who struggle against man and there are men who struggle for man. This fact follows two possibilities, *two ways from which to choose:* One can decide either to exploit man or to defend him. These are the fundamental attitudes. All others belong in some degree to these two, for even indifference is the zero point at which one attitude shifts into the other. The course of history is guided by the way men have organized to implement some gradation of these two activities.

Part Two

Values

Introduction

Toward the end of the last century, the problem of values acquired special prominence. Since then, this importance has continued to increase because of the impact the problem of values has had on other areas of philosophy, especially ethics and aesthetics.

In Latin America, interest in the problem of values emerged from the impact of works by French and German authors. The earliest influences came through the French sociologism of Durkheim and Bouglé and led eventually to social subjectivism. However, with the rejection of positivism, which came to be associated with the French sociologism of Durkheim and Levy-Bruhl, social subjectivism suffered a gradual decline, and new philosophical currents from Germany—Husserl, Scheler, N. Hartmann—replaced it. The *Revista de Occidente* and in particular its editor, José Ortega y Gasset, exercised an influential role in this change. "What are Values?" an article by Ortega published in the *Revista* in 1923, is the point of departure for the objectivist, absolutist conception of value in the Hispanic world. With insight and enthusiasm Ortega summarized and supported Scheler's position. Scheler was heavily influenced by Husserl's phenomenology and in particular by his doctrine of essences. However, whereas Husserl maintained that essences are grasped through intellectual intuition *(Wesenschau),* Scheler emphasized the role of emotional intuition in grasping essences.

Ortega maintains that values, like triangles, "are *transparent* natures. We see them immediately and as a whole. . . . For this reason, mathematics is an *a priori* science of absolute truths. Therefore, "evaluation or the science of values, also will be a system of evident and invariable truths, of a type similar to mathematics."[1]

Ortega's support of a theory of immutable essences and *a priori,* absolute forms of knowledge is surprising. When writing this article on values, existentialist and historicist thinkers were already important for him, and he had begun to elaborate his "perspectivism," which led eventually to his notion of "vital reason." And "vital reason" necessitates the rejection of immutable and absolute essences in favor of concrete dimensions of human existence, as these are conceived by historicism and existentialism.

151

Even at this early stage, Ortega enjoyed an enviable reputation in Latin America and his views on axiological issues were not taken to constitute a mere theory among others but rather were taken as the indisputable truth. That value was an essence that could be grasped through emotional intuition was accepted as fact and very few questioned its *a priori* and absolute nature. A similar attitude was taken toward the hierarchy of values espoused by Ortega that had been derived from Scheler's *a priori,* absolute stance. There were a few isolated instances of rebellion, as in the case of Korn and Caso, but they did not have significant influence. Absolute objectivism was the accepted truth in university courses and textbooks.

Husserl's criticism of psychologism and of John Stuart Mill in particular made a profound impression on Latin American thought, particularly since positivism was being rejected in all its forms.

In addition to the above, another important development supported the interest in values and their objective interpretation. Positivism tried to separate values from human reality in order to apply freely the methods of natural science to the study of mankind. Thus, the German philosopher R. H. Lotze (1817-1881) maintained that values are independent of nature and summarized his views in a proposition that maintained its influence for many years, namely, "values do not exist, rather they are valuable." This separation prepared the ground in Germany for insisting on the radical distinction between the sciences of nature *(Naturwissenschaften)* and those of the spirit *(Geisteswissenschaften).* Windelband, Rickert, Dilthey, and other German philosophers insisted on this distinction that was accepted and taught in Latin America without major opposition or criticism. The sciences of nature are value-free whereas those of the spirit are value-oriented. In this way, the theory of values or axiology is converted into one of the principal instruments for understanding the human world. Axiological typologies such as that of E. Spranger emerge and value becomes indispensable in cultural anthropology, sociology, law, philosophy of religion, and history, in addition to aesthetics and ethics.

It is not too difficult to state the problem of the nature of value. Complication emerges, however, when solutions are proposed since all solutions seem to be open to insurmountable objections. Do we desire things because they have value or do they have value because we desire them? This is the principal problem. In addition, other problems arise out of this one. For example, do we confer value on things because we like them, desire them, or have some interest in them, or do all our reactions arise from qualities found in the object that we perceive—as occurs with primary qualities in visual perception? When we do not look at an object, we suppose that its qualities remain in it, ready to be seen as soon as we look again at the object. So-called "axiological objectivism" supports this principle, i.e., values depend on the object and the subject merely grasps the value. Subjectivism, on the other hand, claims that values are the result of our individual and collective responses.

The subjectivist asks, Can something have value if no one has perceived it nor can perceive it? Real or potential valuation seems to be an indispensable element in the concept of value, for in any case value is for man or for living things. It is unthinkable that something should have value without reference to any kind of subject.

Objectivism recognizes that valuation is subjective, but this does not imply that value is also. In the same way that perception is subjective whereas the object perceived is not, since the primary qualities remain intact when no one perceives the object, so it is with value. We do not confuse the perception of the object with the object.

Between the extremes of a radical subjectivism and an *a priori,* absolute objectivism that converts values into entities similar to mathematical entities, there are many different views. Among them is the social subjectivism of Durkheim that had its origin in France toward the beginning of the century. According to this view the isolated individual does not confer value on an object, since this is the task of a specific community or society. Individuals acqure valuations from their cultural environment. Bouglé, Levy-Bruhl, and other French sociologists amplified Durkheim's ideas in order to establish the social character of morality that for them is rooted neither in *a priori* forms nor in individual caprice. This view is represented in Latin America by Antonio Caso, who preferred to call it social objectivism because the value is objectified in the collective consciousness. The truth is that it is a form of subjectivism that is social rather than individual. Objectivism presupposes the recognition of qualities that are found in the objects.

Axiology had its beginnings toward the end of the last century in Austria and Germany. At that time, Meinong and von Ehrenfels, supported by the psychologism of the day, gave axiology a decided subjectivist bent. However, their axiological studies did not have great influence in Latin America. The first influence is that of the French sociologism referred to above, the work of Durkheim, Bouglé, and Levy-Bruhl.

As psychologism lost its predominant role in Europe, and Husserl "refuted" it in his *Logical Investigations (Logische Untersuchungen,* 1900, 1913), philosophical views with a phenomenological orientation, which considered values as essences, came to the fore. Max Scheler was the first to present this view in *Der Formalismus in der Ethik und die materiale Wertethik.* The first part was published in 1913 in the *Jahrbuch* edited by Husserl and the second part was published in 1916. This lengthy, important work was translated into Spanish in 1941 under the title *Ética,* making absolute objectivism more widely known. Scheler's perspective found additional support in Nicolai Hartmann's *Ethik,* published in 1926. Although the latter was not translated into Spanish, it was influential in Latin American university circles.

The views of these two German philosophers created the environment in which the problem of values is discussed in Latin America.

However, through the influence of Heidegger's historicism and Sartre's existentialism, the absolutist and *a priori* conceptions of value based on the views of Scheler and Hartmann began to lose their prestige. The Argentine Carlos Astrada was one of the first Latin American followers of the existentialism of Heidegger, under whom he studied at Freiburg. He formulated an incisive criticism of Scheler's axiology in his book *La ética formal y los valores* (1938). The Uruguayan Juan Llambías de Acevedo, however, defended Scheler (1952) in an article that reflects both a sound grasp of Scheler's position and enthusiastic adherence to it. The supposed refutation of axiological objectivism by existentialism was one of the main themes of the Third Inter-American Congress of Philosophy held in Mexico in 1950.

Since then, the discussion has become less intense and the problem is approached from other perspectives. Logical empiricism and subsequently analytical philosophy have become more prevalent, although both traditions are contrary to an objective, absolute understanding of value and are oriented toward semantic analysis.

Other orientations such as the axiological orientations of R. B. Perry and John Dewey have had minimal influence. The former published his *General Theory of Value* in 1926, and it was all but ignored in Latin America for three decades and has even yet to be translated. These decades were a time of strong objectivist influence in axiology and there was little sympathy for Perry's interpretation of value as the object of any interest or for Dewey's work on value.

At present there is no major predominating view in axiological thought in Latin America. The objectivism of Scheler prevails in some circles and that of Hartmann in others, while social subjectivism characterizes the views of some groups that are not strictly philosophical. Extreme subjectivism, on the other hand, never has taken root. In recent years philosophical analysis has acquired serious adherents. And, although the objectivist position resting on Thomistic foundations has endured, it borders on the routine and is weak in significant creative developments. The work of Monsignor Derisi is an example of this position.

Axiology is of importance in Latin America and in other areas as well not only because of its intrinsic theoretical worth, but also because of its possible applications to other complex philosophical problems. Scheler and Hartmann developed axiological positions as a foundation for ethics, even though for Scheler there were no ethical values, since he measured the morality of an act by the hierarchy of the preferred and achieved value.

Ethics and aesthetics are the two major areas of application for axiology. Nevertheless, they have not developed significantly in Latin America. However, the theory of values has been important in the philosophy of law and in philosophical anthropology.

Francisco Romero, for example, studies the problem of value in his *Theory of Man*. In this work he focuses on man's place in the total range of existence, pointing out that the levels of being can be hierarchically ordered according to their degree of transcendence, since "value is the degree of transcedence" (Buenos Aires, 1965, ed., p. 171). Spiritual values are absolute because absolute transcendence occurs only in the spirit (p. 172). He gives special attention to cognitive and ethical values.

Law has been the major field of application for axiology as reflected in the works of García Máynez, Reale, Llambías de Acevedo, Carlos Cossio, and other well-known philosophers of law. García Máynez expresses a widespread opinion when he writes, "Subsequent developments will demonstrate that the problem both of the validity of the isolated juridical precept and of the validity of the total order may be solved only in terms of a theory of value."[2] He dedicates the remainder of his essay to axiology (chap. 3) and its application to the problem of the validity of law (chap. 4).

In order to complete this brief discussion of axiology in Latin America, let us summarize briefly the views of the authors included in the anthology.

ALEJANDRO KORN

Korn is the only Hispanic American philosopher who openly defends a subjectivist position. He maintains that "value is the object of valuation" and "valuation is the reaction to an event" and an event is "a manifestation of the will." In his discussion aesthetic values, among others, are not considered.

Korn affirms that absolute, universal values exist only in an act of thought or imagination, since the only values we actually have are historical, changing, and relative. The same fact is evaluated differently by different subjects, and it is natural that this should be the case since each person responds in his own way. Valuations are therefore individual and vary with the changing stages and circumstances of life. There are also social, communal, and national evaluations.

He claims that the historical transmutation and the differences among contemporary values prove there are no fixed values. The supposed immutable values are no more than projections of one's ideals and desires or those of our society or historical age.

Since values are subjective, the hierarchy of values is also. Throughout history the supreme value has changed from time to time. "In reality, no objective hierarchy exists, although we have the right to establish one on our own," that is, arbitrarily.

One might object to Korn's thesis by pointing out that what he has described is true as a psychological or sociological description of valuation. However, there are erroneous evaluations and, if this is the case, one cannot reduce value to valuation. Inevitably one must consider the qualities of the valued object, since the adequacy of the evaluation depends on these qualities.

ALEJANDRO DEÚSTUA

The Peruvian Alejandro Deústua did not develop a theory of value, but chose to analyze a specific axiological experience, in this case, aesthetic experience. In *La idea de orden y libertad en la historia del pensamiento humano* as well as in *Estética general,* from which the selection in this collection has been taken, Deústua evaluates human activity on the basis of the fundamental concepts of liberty and order. He sees aesthetic activity as free creation in which one achieves the highest degree of freedom. Freedom, however, does not exclude order, for it is an ideal order. Furthermore, there can be no beauty if there is no freedom. Art thus becomes the highest expression of the activity of man. In man's other activities, such as economics, science, and religion, freedom is subordinate to principles, norms, or laws. As an intrinsic value, aesthetic value is "essentially disinterested" and is, therefore, the highest of all values. Its freedom rests in the emancipation from ends that might restrict it. Aesthetic activity embodies the "value of values."

CARLOS VAZ FERREIRA

The extensive work of Vaz Ferreira, the leading Uruguayan philosopher, does not provide a systematic analysis of fundamental problems in axiology. In the reprinted passages from the *Fermentario* he refers indirectly to moral value under the name of "optimism of value" that is opposed to the "optimism of success." His approach is a condemnation of moral pessimism. For Vaz Ferreira there is an undeniable moral progress. The view that negates such progress stems from an erroneous evaluation in which the past is idealized by the imagination and purified through forgetting all that is objectionable.

With the passage of time humanity has multiplied its ideals and dissatisfaction with some of them creates a pessimistic outlook in the present. On the other hand, the conflict of ideals is often difficult to reconcile. Therefore, according to Vaz Ferreira, at the present we are confronted with conflicting moral demands. We might go on to point out that this stems from a conflict in values.

MIGUEL REALE

A Brazilian philosopher of law, Reale comes to axiology by way of the law. In his *Filosofia do direito* (1953) he distinguishes between judgments of existence and judgments of value. The former refer to being and the latter to what ought to be. He rejects Hartmann's interpretation that value is an ideal object. Ideal objects are independent of space and time whereas values are linked to valuable things. In addition the former are quantifiable and the latter are not. He believes that value, like being, cannot be defined because it is a fundamental category and he repeats with Lotze that "value is what is valuable." According to Reale, the characteristics of value are: bipolarity, implication, referrability, preferability, incommensurability, and hierarchical ordering.

R. F.

NOTES

1. Jose Ortega y Gasset, "¿Qué son los valores?" *Obras completas* (Madrid: Revista de Occidente, 1947), 6:333.
2. García Máynez, *The Philosophical-Juridical Problem of the Validity of Law in Latin American Legal Philosophy* (Cambridge: Harvard University Press, 1948), 483.

Alejandro Korn
(1860-1936)

In spite of having written relatively little, Korn was the philosopher of the greatest prestige in Argentina during the first half of the twentieth century. His influence was personal and Socratic. He made his impact not only in the world of ideas but also in that of action. Pedro Henríquez Ureña referred to him correctly as "a teacher of knowledge and virtue."

Korn was born in San Vincente, in the province of Buenos Aires in 1860, the son of a German doctor who had emigrated for political reasons. He died in La Plata in 1936 in his house on Avenue 60, surrounded by friends and disciples. He received a degree in medicine at the age of twenty-three in Buenos Aires. After practicing medicine in several towns, he settled in the city of La Plata, which had recently been founded. He limited his practice to psychiatry and became the director of the State Hospital of the Alienated in Melchor Romero. In 1916 he resigned this position and retired, setting aside his medical career.

In 1906 he had been designated assistant professor of history of philosophy in the College of Philosophy and Letters at the University of Buenos Aires. In 1909 he was named full professor. Some years later he also was appointed to the chair of epistemology and metaphysics, and after the university reform of 1918 he was elected dean of the faculty. He retired from these responsibilities in 1930.

Although Korn's early orientation was positivistic, he soon overcame this perspective through his interest in literature and metaphysics and his reading of the works of German and Spanish mystics. *The Critique of Pure Reason* convinced him of the impossibility of any knowledge of metaphysics, but he remained torn by a deep inclination toward metaphysics that he knew he could not satisfy. His theoretical caution and his critical spirit prevented his falling into philosophical utopias and hypostasis, as can be seen in his theory of knowledge and in the passages from his axiology that are incorporated here. This attitude also gave an ironic quality to his terse, limpid prose.

His principal works are *Influencias filosóficas en la evolución nacional* (1912-14); *La libertad creadora* (1920-22); his fundamental work, *Axiología* (1930); and *Apuntes filosóficos* (1935), where he summarizes his thought in a clear form and in a simple style. He wrote many articles and bibliographical reviews that were published in several journals, principally in *Valoraciones* of La Plata.

159

Korn was a major influence in overcoming the theoretical limitations of positivism, the predominant philosophy in Argentina at the beginning of the century. However, he did not limit himself to criticizing it, as was the case with many others; rather, he developed a theory that went beyond it.

The problem of freedom attracted him not only for its theoretical importance, but also because of its impact in ethics and politics. The influence of Kant is evident at this point. Korn affirms that the objective world obeys necessary laws, whereas the subjective world lacks such laws and is free, hence the desires and resolutions of the subjective world cannot be foreseen. But the freedom of the self is that of wanting, not that of doing. The self aspires to actualize freedom, with science and technology as the instruments of that liberation. Korn refers to this process of liberation as "economic freedom." Man must also free himself from his own impulses, appetites, and passions and he does this by means of the moral law that he imposes upon himself in free choice. For Korn, there is no possibility of ethics without freedom. Economic liberty and ethical liberty are not opposed to each other, rather they interpenetrate. Nevertheless, one must distinguish between them because the useful is not always good nor is the good always useful. United, however, they constitute human liberty. "To actualize absolute freedom through economic dominion's conquest of nature and through ethical self-dominion and therefore submit necessity to freedom" is the goal of the process of liberation that is creative. Hence, this can be called a "creative freedom."

In axiology he was the main representative of subjectivism, to which he adhered when the absolute and *a priori* objectivism of Scheler was predominant, since Scheler's view had been introduced into the Spanish-speaking world by Ortega y Gasset. Korn's position can be summarized in his affirmation: "Value is the object of an evaluation." He refers to the existence of absolute and universal values in an ironic tone, since he believed that they have only a changing, historical existence.

Korn's influence remains alive through his writings and his followers. The greatest of these, without a doubt, was Francisco Romero, who succeeded to Korn's chairs in epistemology and metaphysics at the University of Buenos Aires. Romero wrote, "In Argentine philosophy, the significance of Korn is exceptional and allows for no comparisons."

R. F.

Philosophical Notes*

[VALUE AS THE OBJECT OF A VALUATION]

Valuation is the human reaction to a fact or an event. This subjective reaction, which grants or denies value, is the manifestation of the will: it says, "I want it" or "I do not want it." *Value is the object—real or ideal—of an affirmative valuation.*

We use the term 'will' to designate a psychological function, without hypostasizing it. It is not an autonomous faculty, and still less is it a metaphysical entity. It is the outcome of the psychic process and should, more properly, be called volition. And it would be better yet to use only the verb 'to want' or 'to desire', in referring to the final act of affirming or denying. Psychological analysis shows us, though not completely, the multiplicity of elements that take part, consciously or unconsciously and more or less strongly, in the act of volition: biological needs, inherited atavisms, acquired habits or prejudices, persistent memories, emotive, ethical, or aesthetic impulses, weighty reflections, odd suggestions, practical interests, and the like. But the final synthesis is not so much the mechanical addition of such various factors, as it is the culmination of a vital process, in which individual personality is revealed in its unprecedented and unrepeatable uniqueness. Once achieved, this synthesis comes to dominate and direct the whole complex of psychical activity. Thus we have a vicious circle. Wanting or desiring emerges from the psychical complex, not as a servant, but as a master. It is like the way a historical personality arises from the nameless mass, on which he imposes his authority, at the same time that he represents collective tendencies. The will—which disintegrates under analysis—grasps the elements that make it up so as to give them structure, unity, and meaning.

Volition is explained as much by its causes as by its aims. It is supported by the past but is directed toward the future. It is not moved by the facts

---

*From Alejandro Korn, *Apuntes filosóficos,* in *Obras* (La Plata: Universidad Nacional de La Plata, 1938), 1:244-34.

themselves but by the valuation of them. The will can override the claims of instincts and interests; it can counteract violent passions or set aside wise, rational counsel. It postulates its own values—that is, its own ends—and requires logical operations to provide it with appropriate theory and suitable means. This is when it is strong, since when it is weak it goes begging. Masterworks of fiction and drama serve better than psychological treatises to reveal these happenings. And history, in offering concrete and lively examples of the rule of will, shows us how it triumphs or fails.

Will is neither the complete master of judgment nor the slave of external forces. Here we leave the realm of theory to confront practical problems of life. There are still those who dispute whether the act of volition is compelled or spontaneous. It is the old quarrel over determinism and indeterminism, necessity and freedom. Too much time has been wasted on it. In each case we certainly know in what way our will feels restrained or free. We know when an oppression binds us and when we follow our own impulses. *Coercion and freedom are subjective states. If we were to speak objectively, it would be of necessity and contingency.* We only create confusion when we use these terms where they do not belong; to give them absolute value is to exceed the limits of experience.

Coercion is the basic fact; liberty is the absence of coercion. In an act—rare, to be sure—in which coercion is reduced to zero, we experience the full delight of liberation. When, on the contrary, the act is entirely compelled and opposed to our desires, it pains and oppresses us, until we suffer the consciousness of servitude. We find an intermediate condition in the normal course of life in which the degree of freedom one can acquire is the measure of personal dignity. When an energetic will strives to fulfill itself completely, it is overtaken by tragic conflicts.

It is only when people are conscious of coercion that they strike out for freedom. Coercion does not pain us when it does not bother us or we are not conscious of it or do not even feel it, or when we tolerate or even approve it. Human beings have often tolerated, and still tolerate, coercions that arouse protests, whether successful or not, in others. Coercion means different things to different people. Great numbers of people may agree at times, while at others a solitary voice hears no echo. A cave dweller may well feel himself coerced if he has to exchange his cave for a hut. The survival of troglodytic atavisms at least permits us to imagine this. Even now, many millions of the most oppressed and disinherited people do not feel the weight of their chains. They have neither consciousness of servitude nor desire for freedom. Their reaction is the same as that of the person who, not experiencing the tyranny of his instincts, follows them like an animal. Our tightest bonds are those within us.

One encounters coercion in all areas of human activity—whether those areas be physical or biological, political or economical, emotional or spiritual. Thus, man has to conquer freedom in combat with nature, with his fellowmen, and with himself. But this assumes the goals of mastery of the physical world, adequate organization of human coexistence, and personal autonomy. In each concrete case, the will has an affirmative or negative attitude, explicitly or implicitly, thoughtfully or impulsively, and well or badly advised.

We need general concepts to examine, classify, and systematize the indefinite number of valuations arising from all the shadings of individual reactions. This is the mission of the theory of values—or axiology. Various such efforts have been made with different criteria; they come to be evaluations of valuations and, like them, have a personal character. Evaluations necessarily differ, since each subject reacts in his own way. Different subjects value the same fact in unexpected and contradictory ways; what is good for one is bad for another. The fact itself is innocent of any such bickering. It is hard to argue over the empirical reality of things: one observes, one proves. But people dispute their valuations interminably, without agreement. There is great wisdom in the bumpkin's remark: "You can't convince me with reasons." A psychiatrist would be mad to try to cure madness with arguments. And the same rule applies to those who are sane: each to his own tastes. People are always confusing the fact and the valuation of it. Political economy is not concerned with the physical and chemical properties of gold as they are scientifically determined; it just endlessly discusses the value of gold. So it is with all axiological theories: law, ethics, and aesthetics—above all history. Philosophy itself, the theory of subjective action, is nothing other than axiology, once we separate it from science and metaphysics. Thus there is no way to reduce philosophy to a single expression.

Valuations are above all individual; each person is free to accept or reject them. But the gregarious community of the species, the community of psychological structure, the community of interests, the community of historical antecedents—all these, more or less extensively, determine collective valuations. One finds local, guild, and national valuations, just as one finds personal valuations. But valuations also change in the same person at different stages of his life and under different circumstances. It is useless to recall historical mutations, not to mention that fads change the current valuations every six months. Fads are not limited to clothes.

Are there then no absolute, universal, obligatory, and unchanging values? They seem to exist, but as creations of naive idealism. They exist insofar as we think them or imagine them. But in spatiotemporal reality, there are only perpetually changing, relative, historical values. The abstract concepts, which we use to put the world of values in order, are always double: they set an unreal fact against a real fact. They imagine in the distance the illusion of an end that is pursued but not reached; they suppose that we have already fulfilled our desire. Let us take a concrete example of what we see as an injustice. We immediately try to correct it. If we generalize the case, we begin the process of mental abstraction, at the limits of which we encounter the dualism of injustice and justice. But the first term is abstracted from reality, and the second is only its negation. The just state would be one in which there were no injustices. Is there anyone not eager for that? But we live in disagreement about what is just and what is unjust. Only the will decides; only historical power establishes the legal formula. And that for little time.

Humanity expresses its highest values in symbolic concepts; we do not have to defame them with a contemptuous epithet. It is not fair to deny satisfaction to the demands of feeling and faith, to deprive rhetoric of its preferred expressions. They are not tall tales; they are myths. The effective elimination of but one concrete injustice is worth more than all digressions about the perfect state. And yet, myth is an emotive factor that helps guide the historical process, when it is not used to avoid modest daily chores.

In the following table of values there are nine pairs of basic valuations, each of which has a historical fulfillment and an ideal concept. The table is only an attempt; the number of fundamental valuations can be increased or decreased.

	VALUATIONS	BASIC CONCEPTS	HISTORICAL FULFILLMENT	IDEAL GOAL
Biological	I Economic	Useful-Useless	Technical Skill	Well-Being
	II Instinctive	Agreeable-Disagreeable	Pleasure	Happiness
	III Erotic	Lovable-Hateful	Family	Love
Social	IV Vital	Select-Common	Discipline	Power
	V Social	Permitted-Prohibited	Law	Justice
Cultural	VI Religious	Sacred-Profane	Worship	Holiness
	VII Ethical	Good-Bad	Morality	Good
	VIII Logical	True-False	Knowledge	Truth
	IX Aesthetic	Beautiful-Ugly	Art	Beauty

It has been assumed that values form a hierarchy in which some are subordinated to others, and all of them, perhaps, to a supreme value. Of the nine basic affirmative values, there is not one that has not been put in first place by some thinker. Economic, historical, vital, religious, logical, ethical, and aesthetic values have been and still are the crux of certain philosophical systems. Utilitarianism, hedonism, empiricism, rationalism, mysticism, stoicism, aestheticism are all philosophical positions under the hegemony of a value. There has never been a truly uniform evaluation in the history of philosophy; they are all one-sided. There really is no objective hierarchy, although each of us has the right to decree one on his own account.

Historically speaking, biological values have been the most urgent for primitive man, when not the only ones. This is obvious. Other kinds of values have been added—shall we say, superimposed?—little by little. Nothing prevents us, if we like, from rating them higher. When man is freed from economic servitude, higher values will probably impose themselves. But as each day dawns, people nowadays, exactly like their remote ancestors, find themselves in the presence of the problem, not of existence, but of subsistence; economic value retains its rights. The anguish of life is real, although it sets us empirical, rather than metaphysical problems. It requires us to act. . . .

Action is will set to work in proportion to our power. The complex process of psychic activity ends in a material goal. The arm carries out the volition. By action man breaks his isolation, takes part in his world, conquers his well-being, repels aggression, and traces the limits of his authority. Action is communion of subject and object, conjunction of the ideal and the real. Action reestablishes psychophysical unity.

Theoretical examination of our knowledge of reality leaves us perplexed: we never hit upon certainty. Empirical facts, pure concepts, poetic myths—all these, alike, dissipate under analysis. The ultimate nature of things eludes us. Faith is a subjective conviction; logic ends in antinomies; evaluations are contradictory. Neither the secret of the cosmos, nor the secret of the soul, surrenders itself to us. Instead of solutions, we are offered problems; doubt is our intellectual inheritance.

But action cuts the Gordian knot. It cuts it after meditative reflection or by violent impulses, but in any case as a matter of life and death. Thus the problems evaporate. Action does not take place in a fictitious world; it confronts what is present and concrete. Our space-time environment is real: it both resists us and gives way to our effort. Because action is efficacious, we do not argue in limbo. Existence is real because we conquer it day by day. Conflict with our neighbor is real because it constrains and threatens us. The unknown is real because it limits us at each step. The fist that knocks down the obstacle is also real.

Action is justified by success, condemned by failure, and judged by its goal. It is subject to our valuation. Heroic actions have been carried out in the name of superstition, and base actions in the name of high ideals. Life does not depend on a theorem or creed; life is action. But action depends on will; man is responsible for his acts; he is on target or misses, triumphs or yields. If he accepts life, he accepts its risks bravely or pusillanimously, clearheadedly or stupidly. His sovereign will decides. Once done the act is irrevocable; no god can erase it; it happened once and for all; it is woven into the future for all eternity. One must accept and endure its inexorable consequences.

Action is unavoidable. We have not sought the gift of existence. It is by chance that we are born in a certain time and place, in a bare and fluffy cradle, into hardship or luxury. We choose none of it. For better or worse we find ourselves in our world. Those who are responsible for us redeem the sin by helping us get started. Then we are abandoned to our efforts. We have scarcely sensed the happiness of living when we feel its pain. He who takes account of it can reject his ambiguous destiny, or resign himself to it, or confront it boldly. There is an appropriate theory for each of these attitudes, but the problem can only be resolved, negatively or affirmatively, by action. Not to do anything is an action as heroic as to do something. How can we escape the dilemma? The animal, and thus the animal wilfulness in each of us, chooses life at all costs. Perhaps man discovers higher values in his consciousness or in the work of his predecessors than those that are merely biological, perhaps the life for fulfilling higher purposes. The values a man chooses express his personality, his own value. And then perhaps his own life acquires worthwhile contents, is justified, and comes to be appreciated.

Both history and personal experience prove that the instinct of self-preservation requires one to affirm life, in spite of pain, and in spite of the sentence we receive in bitter hours. Not even pessimistic negation spares us action. We have no alternative but to choose our place in the contest. We can do without theories, but not without action. "In the beginning was action." Not at the beginning of things, but at the beginning of human redemption. The species has forged its technical, human, and spiritual culture though action; and it is culture that enables us to pursue our emancipation from all servitude. Culture is the work of will; will desires liberty. Be it: *Creative Liberty.*[1]

NOTES

1. Reference to his own work, "La libertad creadora," *Verbum* (1920), revised and reedited several times.—ED.

Axiology*

*From Alejandro Korn, *Axiología*, in *Obras* (La Plata: Universidad Nacional de La Plata, 1938), 1:129-44.

[VALUATION]

Valuation is a complex process in which all psychical activities participate in various proportions, as part of a whole, until they are synthesized in a volition. Psychological analysis can identify the confluence of the most elemental biological impulses, the most instinctive appetites, the most refined sensibility, the most prudent reflection, the most remote memories, the most headstrong faith, the most idealistic or mystical vision—all of which come together in the act of valuation, in the movement of will that approves or repudiates. The genesis of valuation is influenced by the historical moment in which we live, the collective atmosphere—cultural, ethnic, and associational—that envelops us, and the more or less social features of our character. In short, there is a slippery, personal dimension to valuation, which eludes all logical coercion. Although psychological analysis, armed with the intuition of a Dostoyevski, may penetrate to the murkiest depths of the human soul, there will always remain something, an undecipherable *x*. And this is to say nothing of those professional psychologists who are condemned to skim the surface.

If we judge another person's valuation to be naive or stupid, wise or brilliant, this is a valuation in its own right. Even valuations that are personally repugnant to us—that strike us as paradoxical, cynical, or extravagant—originate in a conscience that can declare them whenever it assumes the responsibility. They do not bind us, to be sure; they cannot even command our respect since we accept or reject them according to our own judgment. A universal conscience can deny the most pampered valuation, however attired in dogmatic authority. So many valuations, originally scorned and vilified, come to win general assent. Many others become silent, without echo, because they were isolated occurrences. We should realize not only that the valuations of our contemporaries disagree among themselves to infinity, but also that there is a continuing transformation of values throughout successive generations. How strange, indeed, if even in the course of our own brief existence we change our minds as we do!

We should not be led into error by the apparent existence of valuations that seem to be supported by indisputable evidence, as well as by our own assent. They would vanish as soon as one barely squeezed them. There is no need to choose a trivial example. Let us take the fifth of the Ten Commandments, but with its tacit qualifications: you shall not kill, if you are not a warrior, judge, or priest; you shall not kill, except for members of another tribe; you shall not kill but those who profess a different creed; you shall not kill, except in defense of your life, your honor, or your property; you shall not openly kill, although you may exploit the life of your neighbor; you shall not kill, as long as you have no motive for it. The author of this commandment was never concerned with living up to it; he must have been a very word-minded person. History is the history of human slaughter. Thinkers have justified it; poets have glorified it.

There is no need to multiply examples; they all lead to the same conclusion. Normative valuations may assume airs of universality, but that claim can be, and is, converted into a lie by historical reality. Effective valuation dwells in our inner authority; there is no judge outside the conscious will. We insist: it is impossible to point out a universal, permanent, or constant valuation that is esteemed by all people in all times. Conscience always reserves the right to choose or refuse the presumed obligation. I like it when someone else agrees with my evaluation; but I am not disposed to submit mine to an extraneous authority, whether that of the overwhelming majority of men or that of the highest magistrate. The decision is in the last resort that of the autonomous person. This is the common root of the infinite number of concrete valuations, and also the reason for their divergence.

Well, someone may say, these conclusions reflect historical and empirical reality, and in this sense they are beyond attack. And yet, valuations are not arbitrary: the will does not adopt them capriciously, nor can it ignore the existence of values independent of human whim—indeed, of human valuation. In other words, we do not create value, we are limited to discovering it, and the concept of it is independent of the psychological or historical process. Let us now examine this new problem.

Value, we have said, is the object of an affirmative valuation. It has to do with real or ideal objects. No one should attribute intrinsic value to real objects. Neither natural nor made objects have value if no one appreciates them, if they are unrelated to human interest. There are no values for science; there are only equally interesting or equally indifferent facts. When we attribute value to a thing, it is a shaky title; it is not the same for me as for another, nor the same today as yesterday. The Arab who was lost in the desert found what he took to be a sack of dates in the track of a caravan. He looked inside, and threw it away in disgust. They're only pearls, he said. The conditional value of real objects depends on our estimation of them. But let us leave the case of real objects: it is too simple.

We have examined the historical creations that pertain to the different order of valuations. The value of these creations depends on our evaluation. We can withhold it. The religious dogma, the work of art, the judicial formula, the practical advice, the philosophical truth—what other value should they have than what they receive from our assent? Has not the protest of the martyr or of the reforming genius always come under the scrutiny of the dominant valuation, armed perhaps with material power? When a secular value ceases to rule, first in one conscience and then in many, it ends by disappearing or by being replaced. Each person can bring this about, individually, within the jurisdiction of his own conscience, and he will do it if the dominant value strikes him as coercive. Historical, like material values, remain subject to our personal valuation.

Let us, then, get down to a discussion of the most important concepts: the great ideal values. Positivism manages to convert them into subjective postulates derived from the cosmic mechanism. The current metaphysical reaction classifies them as absolutes. In either case they are regarded as constant and immutable values, set apart from any act of will. They would continue to exist, whether or not any human mind conceived or esteemed them. Their own authority is enough to establish them; they cannot be denied: who would dare deny justice, beauty, truth?

It is commonsensical that such values do not exist. One does not find them in spatiotemporal reality. In what superreality or in what unreal limbo can one place them? They are the abstract name for still unrealized ultimate aspirations, and they put us in contact with the transcendent as we think about their fulfillment. They are pure ideas; they come to be but are not. Word on our lips, ideal concept in consciousness, they only become effective and efficacious when, through action, they are objectivized in concrete, relative, and deficient form, destined to be a historical episode in the evolution of human culture. These creations of will symbolize its ultimate aims. We cannot conceive of purposes as part of the mechanical process of nature as it is interpreted by science; only will proclaims them. Causal and teleological conceptions cannot be reconciled; they constitute a basic antinomy that is deepened, rather than avoided, by rational anaysis. Let this be said for the naturalists.

Those axiological theories that make use of objective, unreal, and atemporal values represent a shamefaced metaphysics scarcely disguised by its mask of logic. We are by no means denying metaphysical need. Man keeps trying new roads to escape the greatest of his anxieties. Unfortunately, reason is no help. We deny the possibility of a logical and rational metaphysics and we require philosophies to set a neat boundary between empirical reality and metaphysical poetry. The "Great Demolisher" did his work to give the neo-rationalists a chance to hide amid the ruins of their miserable shacks. Any rational metaphysics is a sin against logic. We have no words—hardly even metaphors—to express the eternal—that is, the ineffable. There is no scholastic technique for finding the *coincidentia oppositorum*[1] of irreducible antinomies. That can come only from the great creations of art and mystical vision, aesthetic and religious emotion.

The authors who are committed to discovering absolute values, valid *a priori,* have already invented an *ad hoc* gnoseology. They will not discuss the historical and psychological consequences of valuations; they will maintain, however, that this process arises from values and does not create them. This assumes that our axiological knowledge transcends empirical reality and arrives at the notion of timeless values. In effect, they rely on a theory according to which spatiotemporal objects are only one kind of object within a multiplicity of objective orders. The unreal as well as the real can be an object. This is another effort to open the royal road to metaphysical truth.

It affirms, first, the autonomy of logical values, and then the autonomy of ethical values. They are objective and not subjective. They are born following a psychological gestation but, once the umbilical cord is cut, they have their own destiny. We know the offspring: the "substantial forms" of scholasticism, the old "rational entities," which prudent criticism, not daring to hypostasize, deprives of "being" and reduces to vague nonsense in a kingdom where they neither are, exist, nor act. If this paradox does not captivate us, it is, according to Rickert, because our mental habits are deficient.

We are dealing with wordplay, in which talented men waste their great erudition in byzantine discourse, a marvelous mixture of logical subtlety and essential intuitions *(Wesenschau)*. They claim to have captured the unreal object, but they have only lost contact with reality. . . .

But now some terrified soul will break in: "In this case we are without fixed and binding values!" And indeed, we never had them; they do not exist. Is not the historical change of values an obvious fact, along with the incompatibility of contemporary values? One finds different values at each geographical latitude, in each ethnic group, in each political alliance, and with each social interest. Within each group, however homogeneous it may seem, we find persons who resist the current valuation. There is always some dissent on the way to triumph or failure. Is it not amusing how the satisfied bourgeoisie try to turn their profit into a timeless value, or how the true believer hawks the promptings of his fanaticism like dogmas?

Philosophers are no better; indeed, they provide the most disconcerting spectacle. It is the very nature of philosophy, they say, to aspire to universality. Philosophical truth must be one. It is impossible to conceive it as circumscribed by geographical limits, or determined by the historical moment, or by the interests of a social level. Nevertheless, this is what happens. As in so many cases, the paradox is the real. We know of a Western philosophy and of another that is Eastern; of a Greek philosophy and of another that is modern, of an empirical position opposed to rationalism, skepticism to dogmatism, realism to idealism. All systems are logical, but their pied multiplicity simply shows how ineffective logical argumentation is. Each different philosophy is the expression of a different valuation. Thus it has to run the same risks as all valuations. Each philosophy is systematized as a legal brief for the will that inspires it. Sometimes, though, in periods of decadence, the professor's poor and empty pedantry reveals a lack of will, a lack of vital conviction.

People should not be so afraid of subjective valuation. Humanity has not fallen into anarchy just because valuations have always been subjective. Aristotle alerts us, with his usual sagacity, by his observation that man is a gregarious animal. An isolated individual is a rare event; as a member of a group, his personal impulses are toned down by the rule of the gregarious instinct. Without feeling himself restrained, he will recite the liturgical formula that he has been taught, he will revere the established legal norms, he will respect the hallowed commonplaces, and will dress according to the current fad. No one rebels against an oppression he does not feel. Satisfied souls do not change collective values.

If rebellious evaluation appears, it will take its chances. Only a closed mind would object to it; while if many experience the same coercion, the rebellious judgment will be generalized. But a subjective valuation will be extinguished without consequences if, after a short or long conflict, it comes to have no historical dignity. Expressions of the general will, to be effective, should at least express the will of a more or less large group.

How, then, are we to choose from among the available valuations those that ought to prevail? The historical process does this; those that triumph prevail. It is not always the most just valuation—namely, ours—that triumphs. So, to conciliate them, we have recourse to argumentation, to persuasion, to the coincidence of interests, or to authority—if we have it. And yet, let us not forget that valuations represent our reaction to a physical or historical reality that is given to us, that common setting within which the individual and the collectivity act. . . .

NOTES

1. Scholastic term popularized by Nicholas of Cusa in the fifteenth century. The Mexican José Vasconcelos borrowed the term from Cusa and made it the foundation of his "Aesthetic Monism"; see Part 1 of this book.—ED.

Alejandro Octavio Deústua
(1849-1945)

Deústua belongs to the group of thinkers Francisco Romero has called the "founders" of Latin American philosophy. This group is characterized by its rejection of the dogmatic positivism in which its members were educated and by a turn toward a more spiritual perspective. The "founders" had long careers as educators and molders of a generation of young men dedicated to the serious study of philosophy. Deústua's merit rests more in his career of over fifty years as a dedicated teacher than in the originality and depth of his thought, which found its inspiration primarily in the idealism of Krause and the vitalism of Bergson.

Deústua was born in Huancayo, Peru, in 1849. At the age of twenty he received his degree in philosophy and was named assistant professor of history in the University of San Marcos. Three years later he received a doctorate in philosophy (1872) and a year later a degree in law and a doctorate in jurisprudence. In 1882 he was named associate professor of literature and aesthetics and in 1884 professor of philosophy in the same university. In addition to his teaching responsibilities he also held high offices within the university and in public life. Among his more important positions were director of justice, culture, instruction, and welfare in 1895, senator from Lima in 1901, dean of the faculty of philosophy and letters in 1915, and president of the university from 1928 to 1930. On three occasions, in 1898, 1909, and 1924, he visited Europe in order to study modern pedagogical methods to be incorporated into the Peruvian educational system. He was widely respected and appreciated in his country. He died in Lima on August 6, 1945.

Because of his interest in the education of Peruvian youth, Deústua dedicated a significant portion of his writings to pedagogical themes. Nevertheless, it was in the areas of ethics and in aesthetics that he made his more important contributions. The strength and originality of his own ideas are evident in his discussion of the thought of European authors, especially in the volume on aesthetics, *Estética general* (1923). To a lesser degree, one also finds elements of his personal philosophy in the last chapters of *Los sistemas de moral* (1938-40) and in one of his earlier works, *Las ideas de orden y de libertad en la historia del pensamiento humano* (1917-19). In this work he formulates the view that is developed more fully later on within the axiological context of his *Estética*. The thesis is that order as well as freedom are basic ideas in social development and although the first has dominated

173

in the history of human thought, the second has priority over it, since it constitutes the positive expression of the spirit. In addition, freedom is the necessary condition of all change of order.

In the chapter from the *Estética* reprinted here, Deústua develops the position that aesthetic value is the source of all value. This "value of all values" as he calls it is the product of free activity whose essential function consists in the creation and the contemplation of the ideal aside from any practical intent. In contrast to the essentially instrumental character of other values, aesthetic value constitutes its own end, generating a completely disinterested activity, the creation of beauty.

> Free activity never gives up its essential and supreme function: the creation and contemplation of the ideal with no practical intent whatever. This is pure aesthetic function, the production of beautiful art in which the spirit aspires to achieve its creative ambition which is capable of producing something that the coercion of the environment makes impossible. This function constitutes, therefore, the fount from which other values derive their aspirations.

J. G.

General Aesthetics*

AESTHETIC EXPERIENCE

Even if we grant that all creation has aesthetic value, this still does not settle the question of the nature of beauty: the creative imagination takes different forms, aside from those classified as beautiful or ugly; they make up orders of phenomena distinguished by their subjective and objective natures; and they aspire to be treated with the same respect as other human values. In fact, all the normative sciences have an independent end, which seeks to become a value created by imaginative intuition. Logic, economics, ethics, law, and religion strive to achieve the values or ideals of truth, utility, goodness, justice, and holiness. Imagination is active in each of those disciplines. It performs an aesthetic function, which is nevertheless different from the creation of the beautiful, since this last has to do exclusively with what would, strictly speaking, be called the aesthetic emotion. The phenomenon of the beautiful, fully understood to include the ugly as well as the beautiful, both in nature and in art, is based on free activity, whether or not the activity is conscious. And yet we find that same kind of activity in logical, economic, moral, legal, and religious creations. Like artistic creations, they take on both psychic and social aspects; they tend also to set norms for thinking and willing, criteria for distinguishing and judging, and motives for conscious actions.

It is often discussed whether truth and utility are final values, true values like the others mentioned, or whether they are merely means to attain human ends considered as supreme. We have to exclude them if we look only at the question of the end; and we must also exclude them if we consider them in relation to the feeling of liberty, whether pleasant or painful, which is a necessary element in value.

Logic, like economics, proceeds with the rigorous determinism of science, without feeling or freedom. We can think of the demonstration of truth

*From Alejandro Octavio Deústua, *Estética general* (Lima: Eduardo Rávago, 1923), pt. 2, chap. 2, 424-40.

and the calculation of interest as purely intellectual functions, as means to final values although distinct from them. But this is pure abstraction and it neglects the intuitions of imagination in the discovery of new truths that, here, have the character of true values, even when they do not have all their traits. As instrumental values they differ radically from other values, and especially from aesthetic value, which can be classified as the *value of values*.

The dichotomy set by contemporary philosophy between science and art—which is different from Aristotle's distinction between theory and practice or thought and action—is a distinction between two activities: the ordering activity and the free activity; and this marks the difference between truth, as instrumental value, and beauty, as final value. Orderly, logical activity, which eliminates freedom for the sake of science, is auxiliary to the free activity that shapes the work of art, or that results from its aesthetic contemplation. Unlike truth, the beautiful cannot be demonstrated. One understands its nature by intuiting or feeling it, because the inspiration that engenders it or results from it escapes the exclusively logical process of deduction. Neither the concrete origin of the work of art, nor the aesthetic state, suffused by freedom and feeling, can be explained logically.

Intelligence can indeed collaborate in both: it can prepare the elements of inspiration, and it can support the efforts involved in making them objective; but it can in no way substitute the imaginative and free function of the beautiful creation. To suppose otherwise is to include norms antagonistic to freedom within aesthetic activity; it is to disregard the nature of imagination; it is to assume arbitrarily that there are innate types of beauty that function like axioms in logic; or to attribute to the action of physical and social media a dominating power that psychology disproves by the infinite variety of artistic works and, also, by the infinite possibilities of aesthetic emotion. The great error of intellectualism has been to assign thought a contemplative, primordial, and theoretical function, like the aesthetic, while subordinating art to it by placing art in the realm of practical activity. But contemporary voluntarism has reduced thought to its proper role in the psychic synthesis: to be an instrument auxiliary to freedom in its effort to become effective. Such are the real relations between the true and the beautiful, between logical and aesthetic phenomena, between pure art and pure science.

These relations are analogous to those between economic and aesthetic phenomena, and between the useful and the beautiful. So it is seen by those who have rejected the hedonistic or eudaemonistic theory of the beautiful, according to which aesthetic value is based on human happiness which, in turn, is based on pleasure. The aesthetic phenomenon is essentially disinterested. It pursues no end exterior to itself, whether economic, moral, or religious; its end is within itself; this is its essential characteristic, on which both its disinterest and its freedom are based. Thus it is, as Kant says, a "purposiveness without purpose." The economic phenomenon is subject to the imperative of desire, which destroys its autonomy completely; the useful depends exclusively on desire. Even when desire is present in the development of aesthetic emotion, it is not there as a necessary element. Aesthetic emotion can and should exist apart from the desire to appropriate the contemplated work, the benefits that its author hopes to receive, or even those ends of artistic utility that are part of the work. Once desire is eliminated, the beautiful does not disappear, although the aesthetic emotion may lose or gain intensity. The so-called aesthetic congruity is an associated, but not necessary element. The freedom with which the artist produces his work can be limited by the need for congruity or fitness. Aesthetic feeling can be integrated with it without being dependent on it. On the other hand, if freedom is suppressed, the beautiful disappears, although the economic phenomenon persists.

Although the aesthetic phenomenon is radically different from logic and economics, it is analogous to the moral phenomenon. Freedom is essential in both. The moral ideal may indeed be regarded as an aesthetic creation, and, in the same sense, the actions to attain that ideal may be regarded as aesthetic. An action of great moral value becomes beautiful; beauty and goodness interpenetrate to such an extent that any effort to separate them would drastically change the nature of the action. For all their similarities, they are different, because freedom plays a different role in each. Moral phenomena involve the coercion of duty, imposed by a norm that moral consciousness finds superior to its will. There is no avoiding this imperative quality of law, whatever character we may attribute to it and whatever influence it may exercise over freedom. Whether categorical, hypothetical, or persuasive, it remains an imperative that imposes a duty, to which moral consciousness feels the need to submit, even when it rebels. The moral norm, like the logical norm, is an inescapable condition, which spirit ought to follow. Without fulfilling the first, the goodness of an action disappears; without obedience to the second, there is no truth in thinking. None of this applies to the aesthetic phenomenon, in which freedom is all and any norm is subordinate to it. Properly speaking, there are no norms in the aesthetic order, since the feeling of liberty can create or feel beauty within a unique and original psychic state. Originality is precisely the basic characteristic of the great work of art. A genius can alter or destroy existing norms, creating new ones, as he offers new models of artistic production. If he does not always do so, if he uses canons established by technical tradition, he does so freely because he considers them useful to the production and for the intelligibility of his work. Furthermore, since those canons are the results of the free activity of spirit, they can oppose it only when they come to set narrow limits to its expansion, by crystallizing forms that do not respond to freedom's greater ambitions. Unlike morality, aesthetic judgment is not content to establish absolute and eternal dogmas; nor does it feel the need to preserve them; nor is it troubled by substituting some ideals for others even when they are opposed. It is, on the contrary, eager for diversity as an essential condition for what it is and does. When the ideal, in the process of unification, takes the abstract form of universality—which is what ethical judgment constantly aspires to—aesthetic judgment rejects unity as anti-aesthetic.

Although aesthetic emotions are closely related to moral emotions, they spring from different causes in their contemplation of beautiful actions. Aesthetic consciousness enjoys what it has of free action, while moral consciousness enjoys what is appropriate to the norm. The moral act is based essentially on the power to inhibit consciousness, and even in regard to positive acts it supposes the absolute inhibition of opposing acts. Not so with the aesthetic act, which is essentially expansive. Aesthetic enjoyment is based on intuition of the ideal; moral appreciation, on the comparison of the deed with the precept, in such a way that reflection surpasses intuition to the extent of rendering it useless. Thus moral beauty has intuition and reflection at the same time; one feels its beauty and its morality can be demonstrated as a logical consequence of the universal and abstract precept.

Such demonstration presupposes an invariable principle, a dogma, an imperative norm that is superior to the will. But as I have said, there is no such norm in aesthetic activity, however much the aesthetic sociology of Lalo may want to claim it for technique. Whatever influence one may attribute to traditional rules, they cannot go beyond the freedom of spirit that creates the artistic work, nor can they condemn passive aesthetic feeling to a particular form of pleasure, nor can they explain its existence and evolution without reference to freedom, which is its source.

On the other hand, the idea of order performs a different role in each area. In morals it is the transcendent end of freedom, which ought to submit to it. The norm here creates an order in its own likeness. Such order is imperative, necessary, absolute, eternal. It is the very perfection of human life, which the individual does not create, although he freely accepts it as an ideal; it constitutes, even in the hedonistic concept of the moral law, an external and superior end for the will. Freedom does not create that order, because if it did the norm would no longer be external and superior; it would no longer impose a system of duties on conduct. The morality of the act is, at bottom, just such a submission to the norm. Freedom is connected with it at all only as the postulate for the sanction of the act, and because, in a spiritualist conception of man, only free actions are human, whether freedom be understood in an intellectualist or voluntarist sense. With the aesthetic phenomenon everything is the other way around: freedom creates its own order; it is an end in itself; it has no transcendent goal. The aesthetic order is that which best satisfies the expansion of spirit, and which best eliminates the coercion that is opposed to its nature. The whole aspiration of the aesthetic will is to achieve that order and ideal. The moral order and the aesthetic order thus have very different characteristics. The moral order, at its best, is a system of relations, of concepts, established by a normative law, even when it may originally have been an order of images. The second has been and always is a system of images. Systematization in the first is a logical process, which pursues the unity of the ideal and of the norm external to the individual, as in science. In the second, systematization is an intuitive process that finds unity and variety simultaneously in the individual's imaginative activity. In the first, one seeks universality in the extension of the norm, while in the second one finds it in the extension of aesthetic activity and in the depth of its intuition. The moral order presupposes the existence of an ideal of perfection, which it dogmatizes and imposes on the will in its relation with other wills; the aesthetic order is the ideal that is created by the spirit in the exercise of its freedom. Without that creation there would be no other than the biological imperatives; the moral imperative could not be explained. The moral order is thus based on the aesthetic order, because only the latter is a creation.

The religious phenomenon is even more closely analogous to the aesthetic phenomenon. They were born together in the creation of myth, as Wundt says, and they have never been completely separated. The religious phenomenon has always sought its most effective and complete expression in aesthetic form. But their difference is clear, when we consider the role that freedom plays in each. The religious state is one of liberation or emancipation from the world, but of absolute submission to divinity. The aesthetic state is absolute freedom. In the religious phenomenon, the norm, dictated by the divine will and known by revelation, is all. In the aesthetic phenomenon, whether in the work of art or in aesthetic enjoyment, inspiration is not subject to any norm. The work of art does not suffer its imposition, and aesthetic enjoyment does not adjust to it. The feeling of liberation is profound in both, but their causes and tendencies differ radically. They coexist in the original myth, but myth is above all the work of the creative imagination and is therefore an aesthetic phenomenon par excellence. Revelation is either aesthetic inspiration or an inexplicable mystery. Without that inspiration myth would never have existed. Within the limits of philosophical investigation, we must presuppose the primacy of aesthetic activity in religion as in the moral order.

But the differences we have noted between aesthetic value and other values do not permit us to deduce that the aesthetic phenomenon exists in a pure state, isolated from other social events, with which it is obviously closely related.

Such parity would be another mere abstraction. In living reality, to the contrary, the different phenomena are so closely associated that the effort to analyze them gives rise to different theories of the beautiful—and of art, which is its most perfect expression.

The assumption that there is a directing *Idea*—which guides spirit in the slow process of artistic execution, or which permits aesthetic contemplation to discriminate beauty already achieved, whether to enjoy it or to criticize it—has given logical value a great importance in aesthetic evaluation, to the point that the very nature of the beautiful and the basis of our judgment of it depend on the realization of the *Idea*. To know that idea and to realize it, or to appreciate it after realizing it, has been the fundamental problem for those who have confused the aesthetic phenomenon of the beautiful with the logical phenomenon of the true. They have attributed to reason what properly belongs to imagination. They have erroneously supposed that the aesthetic function is reflective rather than intuitive, that reason has a dynamogenic power that it lacks, and that the aesthetic problem is solved by knowing the beautiful, rather than by feeling it and producing it freely.

The influence of intellectualism in the development of aesthetic ideas has led to the dispute between idealists, who emphasize *content,* and realists, who emphasize *form* in the aesthetic phenomenon. Idealists are dominated by panlogism, which hinges its doctrine on the idea of *order,* in spite of their sympathies for the principle of liberty. The realists are subject to the powerful influence of artistic technique, which looks for the laws of its execution in scientific methods. Since both groups are more logicians than aestheticians, they have looked at the problem of the beautiful in terms of truth, as a theory of knowledge, as a logical explanation of harmony, taking it to be the essential characteristic of the beautiful and therefore subject to the methods of discursive knowledge.

This mistaken point of view derives from the systematic orientation of all philosophy toward the central idea of order, which is essentially a matter of logic, and from the reduction of all knowledge to that exclusive form and of all logic to the logic of thought. It ignores the intuitive activity of imagination, although it is intuition that penetrates into reality with all the energies of spirit, discovering what there is of the essential that exists through the forms accessible to sensory experience and in the very depth of the ideas elaborated by thought. The "divining sympathy" that Bergson speaks of, which explains aesthetic inspiration, is not an idea in the Platonic or Aristotelian sense, nor is it the fruit of a fragmentary consciousness that mutilates or eliminates reality; it comes from the whole consciousness, freely projecting itself toward an ideal that it has formed and tries to fulfill, or toward an ideal already gained that satisfies the drive for creative expansion. We cannot do without logic in this activity; it has a necessary role, but as a means, not as an end. Instead of imposing unity and direction on aesthetic life, logic is subordinated to the *élan* of spirit, which pursues a freer reality in a world forged by imagination, as a result of which it can guide the intellectual efforts that are directed toward practical matters. It is at this point that the directing idea, already an aesthetic creation, gives importance to logic—to conscious reflection—as it develops effective means to the established practical end.

Economics, too, in spite of its external goal, has an auxiliary role in aesthetic activity. Aesthetic activity does not altogether exclude the idea of utility, derived from the feeling of sensory pleasure, which is the basis of economics. Utility does not, to be sure, enter into aesthetic activity with the overwhelming force of human egoism, which destroys all solidarity in the name of a false liberty. This liberty is false because, concentrating entirely on effects, it ignores the slavery of the passion that causes it. To be sure, the economic phenomenon can be openly opposed to the aesthetic phenomenon. A disinterested activity having an end in itself is not conceived in a state of consciousness reduced to egoism, following a unilateral direction, and excluding any affective element that might sidetrack it or attenuate its destructive force. But of course, such a purely economic state would be abnormal, just as pure avarice would be; it would have no value, except as a pure abstraction; it loses its extreme character in normal experience. The useful and the disinterested are combined in ways that demonstrate possible harmony between the aesthetic and the extra-aesthetic. Useful coordination can favor aesthetic value by placing or disposing of beautiful objects effectively—as, for example, when different artistic objects come together in architecture, in drama, and in beautiful objects in nature. Even a simple, useful coordination of coexistence or succession can produce aesthetic emotion, if it can also present to the spirit the appearance or symbol of freedom. The useful, then, offers the illusion of a free life. It no longer seems to be an external goal to the person who contemplates it. It has the appearance of fertile spontaneity, from which it borrows an illusory aesthetic value—as illusory as the spontaneity on which it is founded. Guyau, unlike Spencer, finds an aesthetic element in the useful. Instead of destroying the disinterested character of the beautiful by assimilating the aesthetic phenomenon to the economic, it deprives utility of its special character in order to relate it to aesthetic form. Guyau thus confirms the belief that the useful and the beautiful can help each other without losing their own natures: thus utility conserves its practical end, while the beautiful preserves its intrinsic liberty from any objective end. Architecture and oratory give proof of how beauty and utility compenetrate, so that utility attains beauty, while beauty makes utility more efficacious.

The cooperation of moral experience is still closer. And it is necessary when the aesthetic object is a human action, whether it is now being carried out, or has been, or will be; or whether the imagination invents it, reproduces it, or intrudes only to make the action plausible. In each case the beautiful is inseparable from the good; they tend to fuse, so that aesthetic judgment becomes moral; there is a tendency to alter the nature of art, imposing a pedagogical end on it as an essential ingredient. The theories of *didactic art* and of *art for art's sake,* which are equally exclusivist and inexact, arise from that confusion. As they do so, they affirm these two theses, respectively: the powerful influence of moral value in the appreciation of aesthetic value, and the autonomy of art. Yet, far from being mutually exclusive, the theses complement each other, theoretically and practically: the moral phenomenon, for all its concern with order, supports aesthetic freedom; and aesthetic activity, for all its freedom, favors moral order. The full integrity and depth of the ideal feeling of both factors come together. Even when the feeling of moral value is extra-aesthetic and merely associated with what is aesthetic, it participates so much in the phenomenon of the beautiful that, without it, beauty would lose objectivity, leaving only aesthetic representations that are very different from those expressed by conscious acts of will. All poetry, especially dramatic poetry, would become merely sculpturesque, picturesque, and musical if moral value were excluded from aesthetic content. Even outside of art, human action would be beautiful only because of its practical form. In the other arts, with the exception of architecture, the exclusion of moral value would alter the nature of that beautiful action as long as the feelings that arouse expressions of the human spirit do not always enter the domain of moral value. This explains why immoral symbolism hurts the efficacy of aesthetic emotion, working against it and weakening it, and why the opposite happens when the symbol is not contrary to the moral beliefs of the aesthetic spectator, but is changed into a symbol of those same beliefs. And yet that fusion does not prevent one from feeling the hegemony of beauty, even finding and feeling it in the symbol as it expresses a powerful freedom that resolutely opposes morality and perishes in the struggle or remains in opposition as the aesthetic principle of freedom.

Religious values are related to aesthetic values in providing content for the feeling produced by the work of art. The highest aesthetic forms of art have sought to express the principle of divinity. The temple, the statue of the god, the religious painting, the mystic depth of music and lyric poetry—all of these, revealing what is divine in the human soul, have more or less directly and intensely expressed a religious content. The feeling of emancipation, which characterizes both aesthetic and religious values, relates them in the artistic expansions of spirit. On the other hand, religious feeling could not emerge from human consciousness if it did not clothe itself in forms produced by the imagination, and it would not purify itself if those forms were not idealized by art. Pure thought could never have understood the divine principle. Logic could never be a substitute for inspiration in creating religious ideas and feelings. God becomes man is the most perfect aesthetic symbol of the religious idea.

But just as we can analytically distinguish aesthetic from moral value in experience, so can we also distinguish it from religious value. Symbols opposed to art have had and still have a great religious value for mystical contemplation, while art may express the divine principle in aesthetic forms that leave religious sentiment inactive. The only aesthetic forms that are generally influential amid the many types of worship are those that are in harmony with the beliefs that people actually hold. It is only aesthetically that they can be admired by those who hold different religious beliefs. On the contrary, among people of the same religion, the religious symbol, united to religious form, can be adored as a symbol of divinity, even though it is not understood, or even judged, as an expression of the beautiful. Aesthetic form can even be condemned if it is opposed to religious belief—and in this respect, too, the situation is comparable to that between aesthetic and moral value.

In reality, then, the aesthetic phenomenon is not isolated, but is combined with other phenomena that are derived from the same creative activity and concur in attaining the aesthetic ideal of freedom. It is the nature of spirit to act and to be limitlessly fertile. But if free activity is so conceived as, logically, to eliminate all resistance, we would find that we could not create, or even subsist, without that coercive reality that helps produce consciousness of the self in our psychological development. It has been said that birds would believe that they might fly more freely if there were no atmospheric resistance, because they do not know that they could not fly without that resistance. The same is true of the flight of spirit. If there were no external coercion to provide resistance that one must take account of and control for the sake of greater freedom, a wider and more effective creation, psychic potentiality would be exhausted in an instant; it would stop being activity and would become merely inertia; it would not be spirit but matter—as Bergson holds.

Free activity fights the obstacles set by its surroundings. It can conquer the opposition of external nature by using intelligence to obtain the material means necessary to its ideal. Thus is born the close partnership of logic and economics. This is also why science was born: to destroy our slavery to physical reality and to enhance the production of riches. But it is all too easy for this utilitarian ideal at last to absorb inner freedom, so as to make egoism the exclusive criterion of happiness.

But free activity has another battle: it triumphs over the social medium pervaded by egoism by means of the moral solidarity that abandons the biological process of conquest. In doing so, it finds in the free association of free beings a network of unlimited flexibility, which organizes the function of will, together with the pure expansiveness of freedom. The ideal of expansion without norm, which is the essence of the creative imagination, becomes the ideal of joint activity; it creates morality in human coexistence, in the service of interior freedom; and legal and political values, which are values of the same sort, grow out of morality.

Free activity finally makes the aesthetic ideal, which is beyond human morality, incarnate in a divine personality. It erases the limits of all human work and raises creation to an infinite and absolutely free power, located in the region of the mysterious and inexplicable, wherein it generates religion, which feeds on supernatural inspiration.

Notwithstanding these expressions, free activity never renounces its essential and supreme function, the creation of the ideal and its contemplation without practical purpose, its pure aesthetic function, the production of beautiful art, in which spirit aspires to attain that creative ambition capable of producing what cannot be done by coercing the medium. This function is the spring from which the other values drink their inspirations. There is therefore no exaggeration in calling this disinterested activity the "value of all values."

Carlos Vaz Ferreira
(1872-1958)

Vaz Ferreira is the teacher par excellence in twentieth-century Latin American philosophy. The biographical note that introduces the publication of his complete works reads, "The professor prevailed over all other forms of expression of his creative spirit," and we might add, even at the expense of the originality and philosophical depth of his thought. He possessed a spirit that was eminently antisystematic, preventing him from accepting any school of thought and leading him to fight against all philosophical dogmatism, beginning with the positivist perspective in which he was educated. As a result of this iconoclastic attitude and the germinal character of his thought, his views are best expressed in short essays and in aphoristic notes based on concrete experience. Theoretical analyses are not suitable to his approach.

Vaz Ferreira was born in Montevideo, Uruguay, in 1872. He enrolled at the School of Law in the University of the Republic and graduated as a lawyer in 1903. He began teaching in 1897 when he obtained a position teaching philosophy in the University of the Republic. Due to his success as a professor and to the unprecedented reputation he acquired, a special position was created for him, "Maestro de Conferencias," which permitted him to express his ideas with complete freedom (1913-57). From 1924 until 1929 he also assumed a professorship in the philosophy of law. In addition to his teaching responsibilities he held important positions as dean of preparatory schools (1904-06), president of the university on three occasions, (1929-30, 1925-38, 1938-43), director of the College of Humanities and Sciences (1946-49), and later (1952) dean of that college until his death. Shortly before his death on January 3, 1958, the House of Representatives of Uruguay authorized a complete edition of his works in special honor of his life's work.

Vaz Ferreira's extensive publications reflect ethical, social, and educational concerns grounded in a pervasive humanism. Beginning with his first works, *Conocimiento y acción* (1907) and *Lógica viva* (1910), and continuing through his more mature works, such as *La actual crisis del mundo desde el punto de vista racional* (1940) and *Racionalidad y genialidad* (1947), Vaz Ferreira consistently attacks the narrow, purely rational concept of knowledge that excludes the dynamic vitality of reality. This "philosophy of experience," as described by Ardao, is based on the analysis of the concrete human situation, and finds its most adequate expression in *Fermentario* (1938). This work is a collection of aphorisms and short philosophical

185

essays touching on a variety of human themes that were of concern to Vaz Ferreira from his youth. One finds topics such as "Men of Thought and Men of Action," "Reason and Experience," "To Search for the Truth," "Concerning Systems," and many others. As might be expected, this is the final statement of his moral perspective that, according to him, stems from the conflict of ideals, an irreconcilable conflict that leads to an uneasiness in man but does not condemn him to philosophical pessimism. On the contrary, the awareness of this conflict opens the way to an axiological optimism.

J. G.

Fermentary*

WHAT IS THE MORAL SIGN OF HUMAN ANXIETY?

There are two meanings to "optimism" and "pessimism": optimism (or pessimism) of success, and optimism (or pessimism) of value.

The optimism or pessimism of success and the optimism or pessimism of value: better than a definition is an example. In evaluating an adventure of Don Quixote, we could be, and in many instances reasonably will be, pessimists of success, but optimists (in the other sense) with respect to moral value, with respect to the sign "good" or "bad." And we would declare that adventure generous or noble, we will judge that it is good. This optimism concerning the moral sign is the optimism of value.

The optimism or pessimism of value is intertwined with the moral sign: good or bad.

To continue: as to a certain great adventure, begun and carried on, with all its efforts and aspirations, by a certain species on a given planet, the optimism of success could be risky and one might even say illusory. (We shall see, in addition, that this is an unfortunate way of stating the problem, for insofar as partial success is concerned, optimism is adequate. And to be truthful, a reasonable discussion would focus on the particular cases and the degree.) However, the optimism that seems to me should be upheld against the superficiality of some of the theories and states of spirit predominant today is the optimism of value, even though these theories and states of spirit have held fast in times of pain and hopelessness. I say this because perhaps they have engendered and reinforced the pain and lack of hope.

By way of preparation I need to summarize something that I have attempted to demonstrate for many years and in a long series of lectures: Generally it is thought and said that intellectual progress has not accompanied or is not correlated with moral progress. The claim is even made that

---

*From Carlos Vaz Ferreira, *Fermentario*, in *Obras* (Montevideo: Homenaje Cámara de Representantes, 1957), 10:196-207, 41-44.

there is no such thing as moral progress and again, some say this is an age of decadence. I have tried to maintain that this is not the case.

Let us set aside to begin with whether progress is or is not necessary. In fact, with respect to progress, one can question whether intellectual progress occurs. Moral progress, however, cannot be questioned.

Intellectual progress can be debated. It has been said and perhaps correctly, with respect to progress, that what differentiates man's present from his beginning is the mere accumulation of intellectual acquisitions, for it has not been established that the discoverer of the theory of gravity was more of a genius than the one who invented the wheel or fire . . . perhaps, but that other progress, moral progress, cannot be questioned. . . .

Now the primary question is why does the contrary seem to be the case? Why does it appear that there is moral degeneration in human history? For reasons that only go on to create more illusions.

Some of these illusions are historical. For example, history isolates events and schematizes them. I was going to say that it turns these events into heroic acts and makes men heroic, but that is not the truth either since real heroism is something more than this fictitious heroism. Real heroism, the valuable heroism always comes with pain, it conquers cowardliness, and is accompanied by hesitation and moral doubt. But what History does is to make these acts appear more sensational and it gives men this same appearance. And then on top of all comes the educational process that goes to work on all of this. . . . Hence the first illusion of ancient supermorality. The effect is such that even in the multiple cases in which History itself reveals the inferiority of men, the historico-pedagogical cliches continue to act. The typical case, for example, is that of Cato, whose name is cited in multiple examples, and in great numbers of speeches even when history teaches us that he was cruel and avaricious, that he mistreated his slaves, and that he changed wives in order to obtain the wealth of the dowries. . . .

Furthermore, the men who carried out these acts were specialists, if we may use the expression. For example, there were specialists in patriotism who were capable of nothing else and even the specialists in saintliness or love may have lacked the relevant feeling for their country, family, work. . . .

But none of this is essential, because there is something much more important for which I ask special attention. And this, indeed, is essential: *in the human adventure, ideals are continually added.*

You have heard speak of the problem of the three bodies. Celestial mechanics calculates with ease the reciprocal attraction of two bodies, but when a third is introduced, the problem becomes so complicated that it is very difficult to solve satisfactorily. Nevertheless what has been introduced is only one body. If others, many more, were added the solution to the problem could not even be attempted.

This, then, is what had to happen and what has happened in morals. It is difficult to recognize what the addition of a single ideal could have meant, of what it had to mean in human moral evolution. We speak of adding, not substituting.

Let us look at the societies of Greece and Rome that were based on slavery, an institution natural for them and to which, to tell the truth, all other institutions were bound. Now let us consider the effects of the suppression of this institution alone, namely, the addition of only one idea, that of freedom for all men.

However, in resolving this situation, humanity, as if it were one, was not satisfied. It wanted a hundred, a thousand, indeed everything. Not only was slavery suppressed but humanity was not even satisfied that there should be less fortunate classes. It wanted to equalize and lift up all men. . . .

Given this perspective two conclusions are to be drawn:

The first is *the conflict of ideals.* These ideals can be reconciled only in part, in part they conflict. As to affections and feelings, the ideals of personal life, of the family, and of humanity are in part harmonious but in part conflicting, in part they have to be sacrificed to one another. Scientific ideals and artistic ideals conflict in part with one another. The ideals of work and those of the benefits of work, the ideals of material well-being and the ideals of spiritual perfection conflict with each other in part and in part are reconcilable. The ideals of reason and those of feeling, the good of the majority as an ideal and the conservation and preservation of superior beings . . . In part, these ideals struggle with one another and are not reconciled.

There are the ideals of love, but also ideals of justice. We have ideals of a positive, earthly life but also those of a transcendent afterlife.

Furthermore, correlative with those conflicts of ideals there is another fact upon which we do not insist sufficiently nor reflect adequately and which is not discussed in treatises and books on morals, namely, that humanity has thus been creating a type of *conflictual morality.* This is to say, that few moral problems can be resolved in a completely satisfactory manner and if one senses all the ideals, generally one will have to sacrifice some in part, or perhaps even all of them.

On this issue I have been accustomed to refer in a special sense to possible "obscure Christs." One could conceive of a man that had as much love as the saints of old, as much patriotism as ancient heroes, as much love for science as the martyrs had for truth, indeed, had all the feelings in their historic maximum and, in addition, the nonhistorical feelings in their maximum also, that is, the feelings for family, friendship, and all the rest. Only with great difficulty could such an attitude be of importance to history. After all, what goes into history is what certain great men did. It does not record what others, perhaps even greater, were inhibited from doing. And above all the conflicting dimensions do not go into history or, if they do, they go in as "contradictory" or as a "weakness." Humanity, however, will nevertheless receive the warmth of these obscure Christs. . . .

In fact, no one will be this perfect, but what is coming to be a specialty in modern life *is the increase in the number of men who, although they do not have every feeling to the highest degree, have them all.* This is not sensationalism, for there it is—if you please, in this *our mediocrity*—there is our moral superiority as well as the cause of the illusion of our inferiority. This is essential, my friends: *what was added was not evil, but the increasing resistance, although yet small and poor, still a growing resistance to evil. This is essential* with respect to moral progress. What has been added, for example, is not war but an increased suffering because there is war and because one has to make war, there is more psychological resistance to it. What has been added is not that the less-favored classes should suffer, but the increasing suffering of humanity because of their suffering with the consequent reforms at least partially effective, leading to their betterment or relief.

When one takes this point of view, and these are only two examples to which many others could be added, one perceives the moral betterment of mankind down through history.

This remembering of ideas that I have defended so stoutly suggests an attitude of spirit I have always wanted to suggest as the most truthful and the most just and, it is, indeed, an optimistic attitude. But let us take a look at its two meanings.

The optimism of success can only be relative. Human pretension taken as a whole exceeds by far what is possible, namely, to reconcile all ideals yet let each develop to its fullness. . . . Adding more and more ideals before satisfying those at hand cannot be resolved even in the imagination. . . . But there is always some optimism for obtaining something and then a bit more, in each case and in each of the different directions.

The above can be stated objectively. However, with respect to value, the moral sign of our human adventure, there is no need for restrictions.

Yet, to be fair in our discussion, there is one possible restriction. If there is a transcendent power that works in support of what is good, as is proposed by some religious and metaphysical hypotheses, then all evil is conquered. However, I set aside and in reasoning with me I ask that you also set aside these possibilities that are part of one's personal beliefs.

So, on such an adventure, the rash and absurd and touching human adventure that is all these adventures taken together though individually each is no longer possible . . . perhaps I might repeat and say, in this rash and absurd and touching human adventure which is all the adventures taken together though individually each is no longer possible, deflection would only be natural: it would be "human," if it were not precisely the human that is so heroic!

Here we need to point to a possible error. Someone may have in mind the horrors of today, the horror of war and the terrible character that war has taken on. However, that there has been a change for war is merely the means, the technique, but this change is not of a moral nature, for had the ancients had access to this technique they would have exterminated each other more ferociously than we, for they did it right well with the elemental "putting to the sword." . . . No, the technique is not *what is added, it is not the new*. The added is the increase of our horror of war; that there should be more moral resistance, more repugnance, so much feeling, so much effort. It may be little as yet, weak and overcome thus far, but it is growing and it is more intense and present in more people. The same thing happens in other orders of events: the technology of modern economy may have provoked new sufferings for the worker but what is *morally* added is the suffering, the sympathy, and the growing effort to alleviate or suppress these evils. And this is what determines the moral direction of progress. . . .

So let me repeat more clearly and simply, without any complicating hypothesis or interpretation. The direction of moral progress is seen in the course of human history.

What is surprising is that man's adventure becomes increasingly impossible, but to his own honor. Don Quixote had only one adventure at a time, but for us all occur at the same time and they are ever more far-reaching. With each new dimension new ideals are added and in every case we want to fulfill each ideal more completely.

We have referred to those ideals added as we left the ancient world, when slavery was suppressed. But humanity was not satisfied, since it wanted the well-being of all classes and of all men. This humanitarian tendency and the concern for poverty has become increasingly intensified.

In other ages patriotism was a narrow sentiment. Now humanity, its better part at least, increasingly wants to reconcile patriotism with humanitarianism.

Furthermore, one must incorporate happiness and progress into the ideal, although they are in part contradictory, since progress brings with it an element of suffering. One must also incorporate happiness and culture that are also in part contradictory. One must include religious feeling and practice, consolation and hope, but reason as well. The afterlife with all its possibilities and its hopes along with life on this our earth must be woven in, along with feeling and logic, art and science. And one might say, in passing, that it is easy to rail against science and reason and logic, but even those who do, know that science, reason, and logic continue to work through them and for them.

Another enormous conflict and one of the most tragic is the ideal of goodness, yet one must struggle against evil.

"Reconciliation" in the common sense, "reconciliation" in the sense of satisfying all ideals is impossible. These ideals struggle against each other in part but we want to satisfy them all.

Another conflict: the health of the human race and compassion for the sick person. They are in part contradictory.

And yet, another conflict: intellectual and moral perfection, along with preservation of those that are inferior. To develop the elite, even to the level of a "superman," but also to raise the general level.

And all this together! Each one of these ideals is impossible, but even more impossible when all are taken together and more yet because of their interference with each other since in part they are contradictory!

From this perspective then *comes the optimism of value.*

There are many sincere human beings, whether among them fanatics for an ideal such as nationalists or humanitarians, sages or saints, practical men or mystics, yet all of them are "specialists."

Above all, however, *what grandeur for him who feels all these ideals, which in part contradict each other, and gives himself to all, or to many, without being able to satisfy any one of them completely and even less his own conscience!*

To summarize then, there are two ways of approaching history and the human adventure:

One can emphasize the evil or sad aspect, the impossibility of realizing everything, the impotence, the proportion of evil, and those that fall by the wayside.

Or one can measure the grandeur of the adventure and of the effort precisely because of the inferiority of the point of departure and because of the noble exaggeration of the whole group of ideals that we pursue.

I am not going to add more examples. I do not even have time to develop those that I have chosen. This is no more than a direction of ideas and feelings that I commend to you in every case as a spiritual exercise.

And now do these ideas and feelings bring some consolation?

Perhaps none but perhaps it is not a good thing that humanity console itself. But even though they may bring none, they should teach us and in teaching us to interpret the true feeling of human anxiety, they should teach us not to add to the pain and the inevitable horrors, the pain and the supreme horror of moral pessimism.

ON MORAL CONSCIOUSNESS

It has been observed and written that remorse is not inseparable from immorality nor proportionate to the immorality of the person or his acts. However, there are other errors and even some mystification concerning moral consciousness; for example, to believe, to make another believe or make oneself believe that peace of mind is a natural possession of good people, that it is their normal state, and even that it is a criterion or measure of their moral superiority. Here is a mixture of error and mystification, that pedagogical mystification in which at times it is so difficult to distinguish the sincere from the hypocritical, although the latter is more or less unconscious.

To be able to live with an undisturbed conscience, far from being a criterion of moral superiority, normally reflects some inferiority, usually an insensitivity, except in some cases of mental simplicity, in which case the inferiority would be intellectual.

There is more than one reason for this.

In the first place, the option, as made available for our action by the real circumstances of life, is ordinarily between acts or rules of conduct, each of which contains some evil. Only in exceptional cases, exceptions from real life, does one have the choice between good acts and one or more evil acts. In any case it is quite frequent that the only option we have is among acts, all of which are in part evil and of which, if one can say that one is better than the others, it is only because one produces or contains less evil.

Thus, even in the life of the most refined and pure man, evil is achieved, damage is caused, and pain is produced. And although logically or intellectually this should not give rise to suffering and even less to remorse, as a matter of fact, in the sensitive man it does.

And further, there is moral doubt. Even supposing a man who had resolved all the moral difficulties of his life in what we might call an objectively good fashion, if his moral psychological perspective is refined, he will have doubts: moral doubts about the past, about the present, and concerning the future. Now moral doubt is suffering and it is also an unpeaceful mind. So the absence of moral doubt, except in the case of singular mental simplicity, is not a criterion of moral superiority but of inferiority.

The illusion of peace of mind can be produced from the outside also, as with some historical types in which, even though one supposes they had the peace of mind attributed to them in their biographies or that the historians have ascribed to them, we still find some insensitivity or deficiency even in the most noble characters. To take a prime example: if Marcus Aurelius had the peace of mind described in his *Memoirs,* we still feel that there was in him a deficiency akin to insensitivity in the soul of a man responsible for the persecution and death of many Christians. The insensitivity to which I refer would be twofold: insensitivity to the evil actually done and insensitivity to scruples and moral doubt.

Another absurd state or attitude related to "moral consciousness" is the pretense to "console" through appeal to peace of mind, to console a man in some specific circumstance or to console the human soul in the midst of evil, injustice, or suffering. For example, some employee, a man of action who has completed a good project and then sees it destroyed, is a man who suffers. He feels and suffers because he loved the project not through vanity or not so much through vanity but because good was accomplished through the project. To pretend, then, to console him with peace of mind would be as absurd as pretending to console a father who had lost his son by reminding the father that he had done everything possible, such as calling the doctor in plenty of time and giving his son all required aid.

It is true that the father would suffer if he had not done what should have been done, but that is all that suffering has to do with "peace of mind."

However, on this foundation certain pedagogical mystifications, more or less well intentioned, are organized, but their effects in the end are counterproductive, even from a pragmatic point of view. For that mystification is precisely the unfortunate aspect of a certain kind of book that in preaching truth and justice promises happiness as an automatic reward. There is no need to name authors since any one of them can be substituted for another, for the tendency is the same in them all. Those who write this kind of book are either insensitive or pretenders or perhaps they do not feel the pain of inevitable evil and injustice, of inevitable moral doubt and remorse. Perhaps they are hypocrites or write with mere words.

Furthermore and even more important, these books show a lack of respect for suffering and for the victims of the injustices of nature and of men. For if it has been possible to write these books, books for which peace of mind always accompanies the good, so that good finds its prize and recompense, again, if it has been possible for these books to be written (in the sense intended here, but not on the much more profound level in which it is all true, but in another sense), it is because their authors do not have a proper fellow feeling or sufficient understanding of human suffering. Their mental state proves they have not adequately experienced the pain of those who suffer unjustly or the pain of evil and injustice itself. The true books on moral issues, the good books had to be written by those capable of feeling pain and injustice and of recognizing its partial inevitability.

As for those phrases such as "to have no guide or judge other than one's conscience," and with its approval to live satisfied and happy, let us not forget that the conscience adjusts to situations. If there is any kind of man to be feared in this life, it is that kind who has managed to train his conscience and at the same time has no judge other than his conscience.

Miguel Reale
(b. 1910)

The continuing labor as educator and as supporter of philosophical activity that Reale has carried out in his country for more than fifty years, together with voluminous published works in philosophy, has gained for him an outstanding reputation among Brazilian thinkers in the second quarter of this century. His interests are focused primarily on the philosophy of law, the field in which he has made his contributions. However, this has not prevented him from making important contributions to axiology and philosophical anthropology from the general historicist perspective that he calls "cultural realism."

Born in 1910 in São Bento do Sapucai, in the state of São Paulo, he concluded his secondary studies in the Dante Alighieri Institute in that city. He placed first in a class of over a thousand members with an essay entitled "O valor da previdência na formação do carater," in which he formulates themes that were basic to his later work. He entered the faculty of law the year after his graduation from high school and received his degree in 1934. In the same year he published his first book, *O estado moderno*. He decided to give teaching his major attention and taught Latin, Portuguese, law, and psychology. In 1940 he obtained the chair of philosophy of law in the University of São Paulo on the basis of *Fundamentos do direito*, his first important theoretical work, in which he lays the foundation for his well-known "tridimensional theory of law." From this moment on he began his tireless efforts to promote philosophical thought. With the assistance of a distinguished group of Brazilian philosophers, among whom were Ferreira da Silva, Washington Vita, Euríalo Canabrava, and others, he established the "Instituto Brasileiro de Filosofia" in 1949 and the following year the *Revista Brasileira de Filosofia*, one of the most important philosophical journals in Latin America. As president of the institute he assisted in organizing several national and international congresses of philosophy (São Paulo, 1950-56, 1959, 1972; Fortaleza, 1962), and in 1954 he assisted in founding the Inter-American Society of Philosophy, of which he has been president. In addition he has had other important administrative positions in academic and political institutions, holding the position of president of the University of São Paulo in 1949 and on two occasions secretary of justice. In more recent years, concerned about the destiny of his country, he joined the opposition to the leftist government of President João Goulart, playing an important role in the revolution of March, 1964. In 1969 he again assumed the presidency of the University of São Paulo.

Reale's work is extensive, including more than twenty books and numerous articles and essays. Among the books, the most outstanding are *Horizontes do direito e da historia* (1966), *Teoria tridimensional do direito* (1968), and *O direito como experiência* (1968). However, it is in his *Filosofia do direito* (1953), which has been translated into Italian, and *Pluralismo y liberdade* (1963) that his thought acquires a greater maturity and strength and his conception of the person as "the value-source of all values" is formulated. He states,

what is certain is that man . . . the more he sounds the depths of the mysteries of the cosmos, the more he feels the urgency to turn toward himself, toward the inwardness of his consciousness, in toward the *deep self,* whose *being* is its *ought to be,* where freedom and value, *being* and *ought to be,* individual and society, existence and transcendence are interwoven, only when this occurs does man experience plenitude of being as a person, as a value-source of all values, aside from which the most rigorous and verifiable conquests of the sciences would have no meaning.

Philosophy of Law*

VALUES AND THE REALM OF OUGHT TO BE

Some authors acknowledge only the sphere of objects or determinations of reality seen thus far, namely, that of natural and ideal objects, because they include within the latter what seem to me ought to constitute a third fundamental category under the designation of values. They maintain that values also are ideal objects.

I disagree with that point of view, because, although there are elements of contact and similarity between values and ideal objects, there is no lack of other essential elements of difference. Values as such possess a reality that is also aspatial and atemporal—in other words, they display a mode of "being" that is not bound to space and time. But already here a great difference arises. Insofar as ideal objects have value independently of what happens in space or time, values can only be conceived in terms of something existing, that is, of valuable things. Furthermore, ideal objects are quantifiable; values allow no possibility of quantification whatsoever. We cannot say that Michelangelo's *David* is five or ten times more valuable than Bernini's *David*. The idea of numeration or quantification is completely alien to the valuative or axiological element. It is not a matter, then, of mere absence of temporality and spatiality, but rather of *absolute impossibility of measurement*. The valuable cannot be numbered or quantified. Sometimes we measure it by indirect, empirical, and pragmatic methods, as happens, for example, when we express the "utility" of economic goods in terms of price; but these are mere references for practical life. Values as such are immensurable and not subject to comparison in terms of a unit or common denominator.

At first sight, it seems that we have started out with a definition of value. In fact, however, it is impossible to define value according to the logico-formal requirements of proximate genus and specific difference. In this sense, however legitimate the purpose of a rigorous definition might be,

*From Miguel Reale, *Filosofia do direito*, 4th ed. (São Paulo: Saraiva, 1965), pt. 1, chap. 12, 167-72; pt. 1, chap. 16, 213-15; pt. 2, chap. 27, 332-34.

we agree with Lotze that about value we can only say that it has value. Its "being" is its "having value." In the same way that we say that "being is what is," we must say that "value is what has value." Why so? Because *"being"* and *"having value"* are two fundamental categories, two primordial positions of spirit in the face of reality. Either we see things insofar as they *are* or we see them insofar as they have value; and because they have value, they *ought to be.* No equivalent third alternative exists. All other possible alternatives are reducible to those two or are governed by them. When we say, for example, that things "evolve," the "evolving" is nothing more than an unfolding or modality of "being"—it is being unfolding in time. We often say, using a metaphor, that *to be* and *ought to be* are somewhat like the left and right eyes, which together allow us "to see" reality, discerning it in its regions and structures, which are explained in terms of two fundamental principles: *causality* and *purpose.*

The distinction between *to be* and *ought to be* is an old one in philosophy, but it begins to take on a more pronounced importance with Kant's *Critique of Pure Reason.* It is in this major work that the distinction between *to be* and *ought to be,* between *Sein* and *Sollen,* is established with clarity and with the full weight of its significance.

Reality—the consistency of which in itself constitutes a problem that transcends the particular area of ontognoseology to find its place in metaphysics—reality unfolds, thus, into a multiplicity of "objects," according to a double perspective corresponding to the distinction between *judgments of fact* and *judgments of value.*[1] If, as we have said, *an object is anything that can be the object of a judgment,* then we can distinguish two orders of objects according to the two prisms cited, as follows:

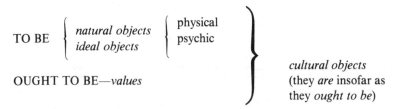

As we shall see in the following pages, values are not to be confused with *cultural objects.* The latter are derived and complex objects, representing a form of integration of *to be* and *ought to be,* which means that we do not conceive *culture* as "value" in the way that Windelband, Rickert, or Radbruch do. Rather, *culture* is first and foremost an integrating element, inconceivable without the *to be-ought to be* correlation; and if culture marks a perennial reference of what is natural to the world of values, it is no less true that without it nature would have no meaning and values would not even be possible. . . .

CHARACTERISTICS OF VALUE

Value is always bipolar. The *bipolarity* possible in the realm of ideal objects is only *essential* in values; this alone would be sufficient not to confuse the two. A triangle or a circumference *are,* and nothing is opposed to this manner of being. On the contrary, bipolarity is inseparable from the realm of values, because a negative value is opposed to each value: an evil to a good, the ugly to the beautiful, the vile to the noble; and the meaning of one demands that of the other. Positive and negative values contradict and imply each other in a single process.

The dynamics of right result, as a matter of fact, from estimative polarity, since right is the concretion of axiological elements: there is a "right" and a "wrong," a licit and an illicit. The contradictory force that characterizes juridical life in all its areas reflects the bipolarity of the values that shape it. It is not by mere coincidence that there always is a victim and a culprit, a contradiction in the revelation of right, since the juridical life develops in the tension between positive and negative values. Right promotes certain values that it regards as positive and suppresses certain acts that constitute negations of values. It could be said that to a certain extent right exists because there is the possibility that values regarded by society as essential to living together might be violated.

If values are bipolar, it must be added that they are also *reciprocally implied,* in the sense that they are not realized without influencing, directly or indirectly, the realization of the remaining values. Nicolai Hartmann makes very clear the expansive and exclusivist force of values, each one tending to subordinate the rest of its estimative schemes. The realm of culture is a realm of *solidarity,* in the sense of the necessary interdependence of its elements, but not in the sense of a pacific or harmonious coexistence of interest and values. In this light, the total ethical solidarity implied by objective justice is a living tension in the quadrants of history and, in that way, as we shall see, right represents the fundamental force of the ever-confined social composition of values. Although the characteristics of *polarity* and *implication* are observed in values considered in themselves, or in the relation of some to the rest, we must remember that they lend themselves to the same situation in reality. Every *value* is opposed to the *given,* that is, to that which is presented as a mere *fact* here and now, as pure phenomenal reality. Value, in short, is opposed to *fact;* it is never reduced to fact. At the same time, moreover, every value *implies* a fact as condition of its realization, although it always transcends it.

Bipolarity and *implication* are qualities of value that reflect or translate the very nature of human conditionality, of spirit that is only conscious of itself and realized insofar as it is inclined and objectifies itself "to be as it ought to be." This brings us to consider the third characteristic of value, namely, its *necessity of direction or reference.*

Besides bipolarity, value always implies a taking of position by man and, consequently, a direction, a reference in existence. All that has value, has value for something or in the *direction of something and for someone.* We usually say—and we find that expression also used by Wolfgang Köhler, although in a slightly different way[2]—that values are *vectorial entities,* because they always point toward a direction, they are directed toward a determinate, recognizable point as an end. It is precisely because values have a direction that they determine conduct. Our life is nothing spiritually but a perennial experience of values. To live is to take a position with respect to values and to integrate them in our "world," perfecting our personality in the measure that we give value to things, to other men, and to ourselves. Only man is capable of values, and only in virtue of man is axiological reality possible.[3]

Value involves, then, an orientation and, as such, presents a fourth characteristic, *preference.* It is for this reason that, for us, every theory of value has as a logical, not causal, consequence, a teleology or theory of ends. Thus we say that an *end is nothing but a value insofar as it is rationally recognized as a motive of conduct.*

Every society has a table of values, so that the physiognomy of an epoch depends on the way in which its values are distributed or ordered. It is there that we find another characteristic of value: *the possibility of its ordering or preferential* or hierarchical *gradation,* though such gradation is incommensurable, as we have already stated.

Bipolarity, implication, reference, preference, incommensurability, and *hierarchical gradation* are, clearly, characteristics that distinguish the realm of values.

There is a possible ordering of the valuable, not absolutely, but rather in the cultural cycles that represent human history, while it is also true that there is something *constant* in the realm of estimations, something that conditions the historical process as a fundamental axiological category. This is man himself seen as value or spiritual source of all axiological experience.

Values represent, consequently, *the realm of ought to be,* of ideal norms, according to which human existence is realized, reflecting itself in *acts* and *works,* in forms of behavior, and in the achievements of civilization and culture, that is, in *goods* that represent the object of cultural sciences.

We have already said that from *to be* one cannot pass to *ought to be,* but the reciprocal is not true; if values were never realized, at least relatively, they would mean nothing to man. There is a vast field of experience whose existence results from the historical objectification of values: it is the *historico-cultural realm,* or the realm of "cultural objects," which are distinguishable *"by being insofar as they ought to be."* This, then, is a distinct category of objects, whose special nature requires the solution of some problems raised above. . . .

Only then will it be possible to clarify other aspects of value, such as, for example, its *objectivity* and *absoluteness,* understanding it as a quality not susceptible of revealing itself without something on which to support itself and without one or more consciousnesses to which it may refer.

The characteristic of *objectivity* of value, by which is recognized the necessity of distinguishing between *value* and *valuation* or *value* and *interest,* that is, that values are objectively imposed upon our subjective experiences, requires that we make a reference, though short, to the principal doctrines on the origin and binding or normative force of values. Only then shall we be able to understand one of the fundamental characteristics of value, which consists in never coinciding entirely with the awareness that we may have of them, always superseding it in a dialectical process that involves the historical dimension of man. . . .

[CLASSIFICATION OF VALUES]

For our purposes, we shall prefer a simple distinction, from the point of view of content, generally accepted, with this or that variant, by writers on this subject matter:

VALUES	TRUE	Logic and Methodology Ontognoseology
	BEAUTIFUL—Art and Aesthetics	
	USEFUL—Economy and Economic Philosophy	
	HOLY—Religion and Philosophy of Religion	
	GOOD	individual—Moral
		social { Law, Custom } Ethics

This is more an illustration of values than a classification pretending to satisfy all logical requirements. We could say that, within the fundamental values, we emphasize the above mentioned, because it is around these that subordinate values are gathered, constituting true "axiological constellations," which control, at times completely, collective and individual behavior. However, we must repeat, all of these gravitate around the fundamental value, which is that of man as *person,* in virtue of which and through which all values have value.

In the first place, we have the value of the *true,* to which some authors refer purely and simply by the word *truth,* giving to this term an axiological meaning.

The truth, as such, is not properly a value, but rather an objective relation. The true is the axiological expression of truth, that is, the attitude of spirit or spiritual dimension in the face of truth. The true only concerns knowledge, whether its *structure*—and thus we have logic—or its method— and thus we have gnoseology or, to use a more comprehensive term, ontognoseology. . . .

The second value is that of the *beautiful,* which is the basic value of the arts and gives origin to aesthetics.

Is the beautiful an autonomous value or is it reducible to some other value? The Socratico-Platonic definition of the beautiful as the splendor of the true is well known. There are some who deny full significance to the beautiful, conceiving beauty as an instrument for the realization of something true, the good, the useful, or the economic—taking the last adjective in its broadest sense.

Thus arises the problem of the autonomy of art, the problem of knowing whether there is a possible realization of the beautiful in itself, in its full significance, or whether the beautiful should be considered merely as an instrument at the service of an ideology, of any social or individual end. We believe the beautiful to be irreducible to other estimative foci, and although it shines more in conjunction or harmony with the remaining values, it does not lose its specific nature for this reason.

The third value, better known as a result of already available studies of political economy, is the value of the *useful.* Political economy, in its broadest sense, is the science of the useful, that is, of goods that can satisfy the desires and needs of man in society and that, as a consequence, are destined for exchange and consumption.

The *useful* is the founding value of economic, commercial, industrial, or agricultural activity. It poses at the same time a series of problems that economic science tries to solve, involving itself in investigations that constitute the object of economic philosophy.

As is well known, there are many who attempt to transform the value of the useful in value *par excellence,* the value characterizing the dominant line of the historical process, to such an extent that all other values, including the ethical and religious, would be simple consequences of technical processes of production, dictated by the increasing needs of social life.[4]

In the fourth place, we have as fundamental value the value of the *holy* or *religious;* the value of the transcendent, of the human destiny to what is beyond existential contingency. This is the basic value of religion as well as the cause of the philosophy of religion.

We would have, in the fifth place, according to some authors, the value of *life,* which is not to be understood in the biological sense of the term, but rather as indicating the full realization of individual or social existence.

Life is even presented as the fundamental value, considering as science *par excellence* that which is concerned with the life of man in the totality of its expressions, whether psychical or sociological, spiritual or material. Our times feel, in fact, a very strong attraction for the problem of life or existence. This should not cause surprise in a historical moment in which nothing seems so endangered as life itself or so precarious as existence.

The appearance of the philosophy of existence, of which existentialism is one expression, as well as the flowering of the philosophy of life, is understandable in the present historical coordinates and circumstances, because philosophy is never a series of conjectures formulated by some men eradicated and separated from the social and historical medium to which they belong. In those trends there is a correct insistence on the thesis that all philosophical systems or thinking is conditioned by historical experience, being impossible to conceive the attitude of a thinker without taking into consideration his existence, according to Ortega's formula: "I am myself and my circumstances."[5]

We think, however, that *life* as such is not a fundamental value, except in the sense that it contains or can contain the condition of the material realization of all values. All values, in a certain sense, refer to life, the vehicle of estimatives.

On the other hand, the life value can be considered as reducible to the *useful*, taking the latter term in a broad sense, since the useful is such only in the measure in which it enters in harmony with the fundamental needs of existence. Under this aspect, one can speak of the *useful-vital*, pointing to a unique axiological integration.

It is still left for us to deal with the value of the *good*, whose consideration, however, involves the whole problem of the philosophy of law. . . .

ACT AND VALUE

Only man educates because only man conducts himself. The problem of education is linked to the problem of self-determination. I educate because I conduct myself—*"educo, quia duco"*: I educate because I am capable of conducting myself. If I were simply led, without awareness of the determinant motives of my acts, I would have no right to transfer or transmit values to others. Man, insofar as he is merely caused, is no different from other animals except for the awareness of his determination, due to which he carries out the same acts in which all other beings belonging to the same genus participate.

What is specific to man is to conduct himself, to choose ends and consequently means to ends. *End-directed action* (the *act* properly called or the *action* in its proper and specific sense) is something belonging only to man. One cannot speak, except metaphorically, of the action or the act of a dog or a horse. "Act" is something pertaining exclusively to the human being. Other animals move themselves; man alone acts. Action presupposes awareness of ends, possibility of option, singular projection in the seal of the species, excellence of attitudes, perfecting in the ways of being and acting. This problem is linked to that of culture, and, as the latter has its roots in freedom, in the *power of synthesis* that allows man to establish new processes while conscious of being integrated in nature and the vital complex conditioned by culture.

Let us emphasize now the problem of action in order to examine its constitutive elements.

Action in its strict sense, or *act,* is energy directed toward something that is always a *value.* Value, therefore, is that toward which human action tends, because it recognizes itself in a determined moment, to be motive, positive or negative, of action itself. We do not investigate here the nature or species of values, but only confirm that every time man acts he *objectifies or opposes something valuable.* To act without motive is proper to the alienated. The alienated is one who is alien to his conduct. It is one who loses the sense of his direction and dignity.

We posit here the problem of *alienation,* of the state of the man who finds himself divorced from his essence, an alien or stranger to himself, with all the consequences that are being pointed out from Hegel and Marx to Gabriel Marcel. These consequences should always be present to the spirit of the jurist or politician, whose main difficulty consists in conceiving and realizing a social order *in which men, groups, and classes do not become alienated.*

To say that man is a rational being is the same as saying that he is a being who directs himself. Action, therefore, always implies a valuation. Every value, consequently, is an opening to ought to be. When one speaks of value, one speaks always of a solicitation of behavior or of a direction for action.

Value and ought imply and need each other reciprocally. Without the idea of value, we have no understanding of ought. When ought originates in value and is rationally received and recognized as the motive of action or act, we have what is called an *end.*

End is the ought to be of value, rationally recognized as the motive of action.

This distinction between *value* and *end* is not made with precision in classical thought. Many times it is spoken merely of ends, but every doctrine of ends hides an axiological theory in its bosom.

Here is a very delicate problem: the relation between axiology and teleology. For us, every teleology presupposes a theory of values. It is possible to speak of ends because the problem of the valuable has been posed before. . . .

In our view, the notion of end is derived from the notion of value. End is value insofar as it can be rationally grasped and recognized as motive of action. We have already seen that we climb to the world of values through emotional roads, and that value always transcends our rational ways of understanding. Beauty, justice, and all other values are not exhausted in rational formulas or schemes. What we declare as *end* is but a moment of value comprehended by our limited rationality, while its realization involves a problem of adequate *means.*

The nexus or relation of *means* to *end* is, and cannot stop being, of a rational nature; but the reference or adherence to a value can be dictated by motives that reason does not explain. Human history is a dramatic process of conversion of values into ends, and of cultural crises resulting from the loss of axiological force verified in ends that new generations refuse "to recognize."

NOTES

1. A literal translation would be "judgments of reality" and "judgments of value."—TRANS.

2. See Wolfgang Köhler, *The Place of Value in a World of Fact* (New York: n.p., 1938).—TRANS.

3. Ibid., 104.—TRANS.

4. The reference is to Marxism, a strong movement at the time Reale's book was published.—TRANS.

5. Ortega y Gasset, *Obras completas* (Madrid: n.p., 1947), 2:19.—TRANS.

Part Three

The Search for
Philosophical Identity

Introduction*

One of the most pervasive and characteristic preoccupations of Latin American thinkers for the past one hundred years has been the search for philosophical identity. Discussions of this issue are frequently introduced with the question: Is there, or can there be, a Latin American philosophy? But this question is ambiguous, since it can be interpreted in various ways. For example, it may be taken as asking whether there are Latin American philosophers, or whether philosophical works have been and are being produced in Latin America. If the question is interpreted in this way, then its answer is quite clear, for there are many Latin Americans who practice philosophy and produce considerable philosophical writing; it is no more than an empirical question that is easily answered in terms of the empirical evidence available. As such, it lacks philosophical interest, belonging to the realm of history and not of philosophical speculation. In order for the question to have philosophical bearing, it must be concerned with something more than historical fact; it must address the issue of whether it is possible for there to be a peculiarly Latin American philosophy. Moreover, in order to resolve this matter, two things must be established first: the nature of philosophy, and the nature of what is purely Latin American. Once this is done, one can determine, first, whether the nature of philosophy allows for the acquisition of characteristics that may qualify it as Latin American and, second, the relationship that such characteristics may have with philosophy. This type of inquiry, in contrast with the former, is philosophical, for it implies an analysis of the notions of "philosophy" and "Latin American," and the establishment of their relationship. And this is, indeed, what has preoccupied those philosophers who have discussed the problem of the philosophical identity of Latin America.

*A longer version of this essay appeared in the *Inter-American Review of Bibliography* 34 (1984): 53–71. We would like to thank Fernando Salmerón, Ricardo Maliandi, and Ezequiel de Olazo for several corrections and criticisms that helped in the revision of the essay.

THE SOLUTIONS: UNIVERSALISM,
CULTURALISM, AND THE CRITICAL VIEW

In spite of the fact that Latin American philosophers have expressed many positions on this subject, their opinions can be classified under three basic views: universalist, culturalist, and critical. The first is inspired in a long tradition that goes back to the Greeks. According to this view, philosophy is a science (be it of concepts or of reality); as such, the principles and inferences that it establishes are meant to be universally valid and, consequently, it makes no sense to talk about a Latin American philosophy just as it does not make any sense to talk about Latin American chemistry or physics. Philosophy, as a discipline of learning, cannot acquire peculiar characteristics that may, in turn, make it Latin American, French, or Italian. Philosophy, strictly speaking, is simply philosophy, or philosophy "as such," to use an expression in vogue in the literature.[1] In spite of the fact that normally one may speak of "French" and "Italian" philosophy, this does not mean that philosophy as such is any different in these two cases. Categories like "French" and "Italian" are used as *historical* designations to refer to historical periods that include the thinking of the time or place one wishes to discuss. This does not mean that philosophy in a particular period is in itself any different from philosophy in another period. What may be considered peculiar to the philosophy of a given period is not an essential part of philosophy, but simply the product of circumstances surrounding the development of the discipline at the time. As a result, then, such peculiarities, which could also be called accidents, are not part of the discipline, and are not included in its study; they are only part of historical studies concerning the period in question, just as a mathematical error is not part of mathematics, and just as the study of Egyptian physical theories is not part of physics. Philosophy, like mathematics and other disciplines of human knowledge, consists of a series of truths and methods of inquiry that have no spatiotemporal characteristics. Its application and validity are universal and therefore independent of the historical conditions in which they are discovered. The conclusion, for instance, that rationality is part of human nature is true or false anywhere and at any time.

Consequently, the answer to the question of whether there is a Latin American philosophy is, from this perspective, negative. Furthermore, this view not only denies that there is a Latin American philosophy, but it also rejects that there could be one, for it sees an intrinsic incompatibility between the nature of philosophy as a universal discipline of learning and such particular products as culture.

To this, the culturalist responds by contending that the universalist makes a serious mistake. Philosophy, as everything else based on human experience, depends on specific spatiotemporal coordinates for its validity.

There are no universal and absolute truths. Truth is always concrete and the product of a viewpoint, an individual perspective. This can be applied even to mathematical truths, as Ortega, a philosopher followed by many culturalists, suggests.[2]

Orteguian perspectivism, introduced in Latin America by many of Ortega's disciples, particularly José Gaos, is to a great extent responsible for the popularity of the culturalist view in Latin America. A philosophy that emphasizes the value of the particular and idiosyncratic lends itself quite easily to support the views of culturalist thinkers.[3] Consequently, many of them adopted this view unhesitatingly, adapting it to their conceptual needs. This is how the idea of a Latin American philosophy as a philosophy peculiar to the continent came about, a philosophy different from that of other cultures, and particularly opposed to Anglo-Saxon philosophy. This philosophy is supposedly the product of Latin American culture, which is in turn the product of the perspective from which Latin Americans think. This view has given way to the search for an autochthonous philosophy that can unambiguously reflect the characteristics of Latin American culture.

From this perspective, it is not only possible to find a Latin American philosophy, but also one is led to conclude that any genuine philosophy produced in Latin America must be Latin American. If it is not, then it is simply a copy of philosophies produced elsewhere, imported and imposed on the continent. As such, these alien ways of thinking do not constitute a genuine philosophy when they are adopted in Latin America, since they do not have any relation to Latin American culture, being as they are the product of perspectives and conditions completely foreign to those of the continent.

Many of the thinkers who adopt this view conclude that, at present, there is no Latin American philosophy because the only philosophy that has been practiced in the region is imported. But at the same time, while accepting this, they trust in a different future. Others, on the contrary, point out that there are some Latin American philosophical perspectives that can be classified as Latin American, and although they may be few, they are sufficient to justify the use of the term "Latin American philosophy" with a culturalist connotation.

A third view adopted by Latin American philosophers in relation to this problem is critical; it has been put forward as a reaction against both universalism and culturalism, although it takes some elements from both. This view, as the universalist, rejects the existence of a Latin American philosophy not because "Latin American" can be seen as incompatible with "philosophy," but rather because until now philosophy in Latin America has had an ideological character, that is, it has not been a free pursuit. Philosophy has been used and is used in Latin America, according to the proponents of this view, to support ideas conducive to both the continuation of a *status quo* and the benefit of certain groups. Followers of this view point out as examples the cases of scholasticism and positivism. In relation to the former, they stress how the Spanish crown made use of scholastic philosophy to maintain its political and economic control over the New World. Scholastic philosophy, they suggest, became an instrument to sustain an otherwise ideologically untenable position. In the case of positivism, they emphasize how certain Latin American governments used this philosophical school to justify both their notion of social order and the supremacy of a ruling elite. The most frequently cited case is that of Porfirio Díaz's government in Mexico, which adopted positivism as the official doctrine of the regime. The inference drawn, on the basis of this and other examples, is that until now there has not been, and in the future there cannot be, a genuine Latin American philosophy so long as present social and economic conditions prevail. Only when this situation changes, and philosophy is no longer used ideologically to justify the *modus vivendi,* can there be an opportunity for a genuine Latin American philosophy to develop. Some of those who defend this view think that this Latin American philosophy will be the product of a peculiar Latin American perspective, adopting therefore a culturalist view with respect to the future. Others, on the contrary, take a universalist position, and suggest that this nonideological philosophy will be universally valid and purely scientific. They all coincide, however, in viewing the role of philosophy at present in a critical light.

HISTORICAL DEVELOPMENT OF THE PROBLEM

Explicit questions about the existence of a Latin American philosophy were first explored in the writings of Leopoldo Zea and Risieri Frondizi in th 1940s. The growth of philosophical literature until then seemed to justify, and perhaps even require, a meditation on the nature, themes, and limits of this philosophical activity. The proliferation of specialized journals, the creation of philosophy departments in various universities, and the foundation of international associations that had started to coordinate philosophical activity in the continent made possible the raising of an issue that continues to concern Latin American philosophers even today.[4]

Even before Zea and Frondizi, however, the Argentinian Juan Bautista Alberdi (1810-1884) had raised the problem of the character and future of Latin American philosophy.[5] As an outstanding member of the thriving liberal movement of his time, Alberti put forth his ideas under the influence of a liberalism very closely related to the philosophical rationalism, the anticlericalism, and the optimism about industrialization that are so characteristic of nineteenth-century Latin America. His view of philosophy, consequently, is not alien to the basic tenets of this movement. Alberdi, however, had a high degree of awareness with respect to the connection between philosophy and cultural identity that, for good reasons, has drawn the attention of many philosophers who have subsequently focused on the theme of Latin American philosophy.

According to Alberdi, a Latin American philosophy must have a social and political character intimately related to the most vital needs of the continent. Philosophy, to this thinker, is an instrument that can help to introduce an awareness about the social, political, and economic needs of the Latin American nations. This is why he categorically rejected metaphysics and other "pure and abstract" philosophical fields, for he viewed them as alien to urgent national needs.[6]

In spite of Alberdi's early reflections on the character of Latin American philosophy, as already mentioned it is not until the fifth decade of the twentieth century that the problem of the philosophical identity of Latin America is explicitly formulated and fully explored. The decade of the 1940s is a period in which intellectuals looked back on Latin American culture and attempted to use it as the basis for philosophical thinking. A generation of Mexican authors inspired in Orteguian perspectivism, introduced in Latin America by the *trasterrados,* or Spanish exiles, and particularly by José Gaos,[7] suggested that the cultural "circumstances" of the continent provided the basis for the development of an original Latin American philosophy. Leopoldo Zea, the leader of these intellectuals, asserted that any type of philosophical reflection emerging in the continent could be classified as a "Latin American philosophy" by virtue of the intimate relationship between philosophy and culture.[8] He also suggested that this Latin American philosophy had a historical foundation, owing to the fact that the Latin American man had always, in Zea's judgment, thought of his situation from a vitally Latin American perspective.[9] In this sense, even philosophical reflection lacking originality, resulting from mere imitation, could pass as "Latin American philosophy" by virtue of its historicity and of the fact that it emerged in the continent in response to peculiar vital circumstances. Therefore, Zea categorically affirms the existence of a Latin American philosophy. It is significant to note, however, that he does not proceed by formulating his theories on the basis of the peculiar *ethos* manifested by the region's culture. Rather, as many others of his generation, his views are based on an *a priori* conception—of Orteguian origin—of philosophy that sees this discipline as a historical product always emerging from particular perspectives.

The nationalistic sentiment that characterized the politics of most Latin American nations at the time, but particularly Mexico, helped to promote Zea's views concerning the existence and nature of Latin American philosophy. Advocates and detractors of this conception of philosophy made their voices heard quite quickly throughout the continent. Abelardo Villegas, Diego Domínguez Caballero, and Guillermo Francovich are but some of the advocates of Zea's culturalist perspective.[10] Among the detractors, Risieri

Frondizi counts as a leader. For him and those who opposed Zea and his followers, philosophy must be distinguished from cultural nationalism and should be considered independent from geographical boundaries. One should speak of philosophy *in* America rather than of a philosophy *of* America.[11] Philosophy, as Francisco Romero had pointed out earlier, has no last names, that is, it must be understood as a discipline of universal characteristics.[12]

Vasconcelos himself, whose work in many ways reflected a culturalist perspective, adopted a universalist position when discussing the nature of philosophical activity. He went so far as to deny explicitly the existence of a peculiarly Latin American philosophy on the grounds that the discipline was universal in character, although he conceded that it was the prerogative of each culture to reconsider the great themes of universal philosophy. Philosophical nationalism had no place in his thought.[13]

The polemic that suddenly surrounded the question of the existence of a Latin American philosophy in the forties had the effect, in many cases, of undermining the focus on cultural identity that had characterized Latin American philosophical thought prior to the dispute, and which in many respects had prompted it. The controversy set a precedent for discussions of culture that became increasingly separated from the actual analysis of cultural phenomena. The culturalists themselves, who base their conception of a Latin American philosophy on a cultural perspective, have left few detailed accounts of the continent's cultural *ethos,* and frequently refer to culture in very general terms.

The controversy continued to grow and attracted much attention among members of practically every philosophical tradition, with the exception of philosophical analysis. Existentialists, phenomenologists, Thomists, Kantians, Orteguians, etc., all felt compelled to explore this issue. But since none of the different interpretations of the cultural identity of the continent has become widely accepted, it has been impossible in turn to establish a consensus on the notion of Latin American philosophy. This is the reason why during the 1960s a number of authors re-addresssed this problem, although this time not in terms of either universalism or culturalism. It is at this time that the critical position arises. Augusto Salazar Bondy, for instance, viewed philosophy in Latin America as the province of intellectual elites. These elites have borrowed European cultural forms uncritically, lacking an identifiable and rigorous methodology and an awareness of the situation of other social groups. Viewed in this light, the problems of culture and philosophy have been the problems of only a small minority of intellectuals alienated from the rest of society, and from the economic, social, and political problems of the continent.[14] This position, which has also been shared by Juan Rivano and others, suggests that the history of the controversy concerning the existence and nature of a Latin American philosophy epitomizes the lack of concern with the most urgent problems of their respective communities on the part of the region's intellectuals.[15]

It is in this context that the so-called "philosophy of liberation" later appears. For philosophers like Enrique Dussel, Horacio Cerutti Guldberg, and Arturo Andrés Roig, the fundamental task of philosophy in Latin America consists in the social and national liberation from the unjust relations such as that of dominating-dominated that have traditionally characterized it. For Roig in particular, this implies an integration of the Latin American peoples based on the consciousness of the historicity of the American man and of the history of philosophy in Latin America. His position rejects the formalism and ontologism characteristic of traditional academic philosophy, favoring instead a philosophy of commitment that seeks integrating concepts in Latin America. The novelty of this philosophy will be founded in the political discourse of the marginal and exploited segments of society, developing an authentic thought that may serve to originate man's humanity.

There is more involved in the history of this controversy than a simple aggregation of themes and authors. For one thing, the relationship between philosophy and cultural identity in Latin America provides one of the constant topics of study since Alberdi's time. In many cases, definitions of philosophy and culture lack precision, but reveal an effort, on the part of the Latin American thinker, to handle cultural problems with the aid of the philosophical discipline. Indeed, in spite of the strong disagreement voiced by the various authors discussed, most of them would agree that philosophy has historically provided one of the most important vehicles for the expression of cultural concerns in Latin American society. Not always listened to, and at times suppressed by regimes of the right or the left, philosophy in many ways reflects the very situation of Latin American society today. Polemics on the nature of philosophy continue, and so do larger questions requiring the expertise of the philosopher. The incorporation of the area's nations into the political determinism that characterizes the current situation of the world, the collapse of many traditional models of organization and thought, the rise of extreme nationalism, militarism, political and religious persecution, the vulnerability of the political systems, the precarious nature of the institutions, the massive introduction of modern communication systems, and other technological innovations that coexist with poverty are all issues that bring to a cultural and philosophical level the types of problems and conflicts that characterize Latin American society today. However the polemic on the nature of philosophical activity in Latin America may be resolved, it is bound to have an impact on the society that nurtures it, and it accurately reflects the historical situation in which Latin America finds itself today.

J. G., I. J.

NOTES

1. Risieri Frondizi, "Is there an Ibero-American philosophy?" *Philosophy and Phenomenological Research* 9 (March 1949): 355. See also a slightly different use of the expression in Fernando Salmerón, "Los problemas de la cultura mexicana desde el punto de vista de la filosofía," in *Cuestiones educativas y páginas sobre México,* 137; originally published in *La Palabra y el Hombre* 6 (1958).

2. José Ortega y Gasset, *El hombre y la gente,* ch. 13, in *Obras completas,* vol. 3, 115.

3. See Samuel Ramos, *Historia de la filosofía mexicana* (Mexico: Imprenta Universitaria, 1943), 149.

4. One of the most useful bibliographical tools for the study of Latin American philosophy is the *Handbook of Latin American Studies,* which has been publishing a section on philosophy since 1939.

5. A prolific writer and one of the outstanding members of the generation of Argentinean intellectuals who criticized the regime of Juan Manuel de Rosas, Alberdi spent many years in exile in Uruguay, Chile, and Europe. The piece of writing that most specifically addresses our subject of concern here is "Ideas para presidir la confección del curso de filosofía contemporánea," in *Escritos póstumos de Juan Bautista Alberdi,* vol. 15 (Buenos Aires: Imprenta Europea, Moreno y Defensa, 1895-1901). This essay was originally published in 1842.

6. Alberdi, "Ideas," 613.

7. José Gaos, *En torno a la filosofía mexicana* (Mexico: Porrúa y Obregón, 1952), 53-54, 88. An excellent study of the impact and importance of the Spanish contributions to Latin American philosophy is provided by José Luis Abellan's *Filosofía española en América* (Madrid: Ediciones Guadarrama, 1967).

8. Zea, *Ensayos,* 166.

9. Zea, *Ensayos,* 201.

10. Abelardo Villegas, *Panorama de la filosofía iberoamericana actual* (Buenos Aires: Editorial Universitaria de Buenos Aires, 1963); Diego Domínguez Caballero, "Motivo y sentido de una investigación de lo panameño," in Zea, *Antología,* 157-169; Guillermo Francovich, *El pensamiento boliviano en el siglo 20* (Mexico: Fondo de Cultura Económica, 1956), and "Pachamama," in Zea, *Antología,* 79-87.

11. Frondizi, "¿Hay una filosofía iberoamericana?" 166.

12. Ibid., 167.

13. Vasconcelos, *Indología: una interpretación de la cultura iberoamericana* (Paris: Agencia Mundial de Librería, 1926), 109-110.

14. Augusto Salazar Bondy, *¿Existe una filosofía de nuestra América?* (Mexico: Siglo XXI, 1968), section 8, "Una interpretación."

15. Juan Rivano was born in Santiago, Chile, in 1926, and taught philosophy at the University of Chile until the Chilean military regime imprisoned him in 1975 and forced him into exile in 1976. Trained in logic, he has written mostly on the subjects of theory of knowledge and philosophy of science. Rivano addressed the problem of Latin American philosophy in his *El punto de vista de la miseria* (Santiago: Facultad de Filosofía y Educación, Universidad de Chile, 1965), 145-172. Some of his publications include *Entre Hegel y Marx: una meditación ante los nuevos horizontes del humanismo* (1962), *Lógica elemental* (1970), and *Introducción al pensamiento dialéctico* (1972).

Leopoldo Zea
(b. 1912)

Leopoldo Zea was born in Mexico City, where he studied with Antonio Caso, Samuel Ramos, and later with the Spanish exile José Gaos. He is currently a professor at the National Autonomous University in Mexico. Zea was the organizer of the philosophical group *Hiperión,* which had as its aim the establishment of a philosophy based on the examination of the Mexican man and his characteristics. Among the thinkers who took part in this group and who followed Zea's direction are Emilio Uranda, Ricardo Guerra, Joaquin McGregor, Jorge Portilla, Luis Villoro, and Fausto Vega.

Among Zea's major works are the following: *El positivismo en México* (1943), *Apogeo y decadencia del positivismo en México* (1944), *En torno a una filosofía americana* (1945), *Ensayos sobre filosofía en la historia* (1948), *La filosofía como compromiso y otros ensayos* (1952), *Conciencia y posibilidad del mexicano* (1952), *América como concienca* (1953), *La filosofía en México* (1955), and *La filosofía americana como filosofía sin más* (1969).

Zea's thought focuses on a very particular conception of philosophy. Philosophy for him is not a system of abstract and theoretical propositions, but the product of "men of flesh and bones struggling in their own circumstances " Every philosophy, according to this author, emerges from specific historical situations; that is why one must reflect on such circumstances in order to understand it. This attitude, which is inspired by Ortega, leads Zea to the study of the history of Mexican philosophy and the specific historical circumstances from which it emerged.

Zea was one of the first Latin American thinkers explicitly concerned with the issues explored in the third part of this book. The article that follows is one of the first he published on the subject; it opened the door for a multitude of other studies. His position, based on a culturalist point of view, categorically affirms the existence of a Latin American philosophy. Every form of thought emerging in Latin America is Latin American thought and every philosophy emerging in Latin America is Latin American philosophy, even when lacking originality. The reason is that Latin American thought and philosophy arise from specifically historical Latin American circumstances.

J. G.

Essays on Philosophy in History*

THE ACTUAL FUNCTION OF PHILOSOPHY IN LATIN AMERICA

1

Some years ago, a young Mexican teacher published a book that caused much sensation. This young teacher was Samuel Ramos and the book was *El perfil del hombre y la cultura en México*. This book was the first attempt at interpreting Mexican culture. In it Mexican culture became the subject of philosophical interpretation. Philosophy came down from the world of ideal entities to a world of concrete entities like Mexico, a symbol of men who live and die in their cities and farms. This daring attempt was derogatorily termed *literature*. Philosophy could not be anything other than a clever game of words taken from an alien culture. These words of course lacked meaning: the meaning they had for that alien culture.

Years later another teacher, this time the Argentinian Francisco Romero, emphasized Ibero-America's need to begin thinking about its own issues, and the need to delve into the history of its culture in order to take from it the issues needed for the development of a new type of philosophical concern. This time, however, Romero's call was based on a series of cultural phenomena that he identified in an essay entitled "Sobre la filosofía en Iberoamerica." In this article he showed how the interest in philosophical issues in Latin America was increasing on a daily basis. The public at large now follows and asks with interest for works of a philosophical character and nature. This has resulted in numerous publications—books, journals, newspaper articles, etc.—and also in the creation of institutes and centers for philosophical studies where philosophy is practiced. This interest in philosophy stands in sharp contrast with periods when such an activity was

---

*From Leopoldo Zea, *Ensayos sobre filosofía en la historia* (Mexico: Stylo 1948), 165-77. Originally published in *Cuadernos Americanos* (1942).

confined to a few misunderstood men. Their activity did not transcend literary or academic circles. Today, we have reached the level that Romero calls "the period of philosophical normalcy," that is, a period in which the practice of philosophy is seen as a function of culture just as is the case with any other activity of a cultural nature. The philosopher ceases to be an eccentric whom nobody cares to understand and becomes a member of his country's culture. There is what one may call a "philosophical environment," that is, a public opinion that judges philosophical production, thus forcing it to address the issues that concern those who are part of this so-called "public opinion."

Now, there is one particular issue that concerns not only a few men in our continent, but the Latin American man in general. This issue concerns the possibility or impossibility of Latin American culture, and, as an aspect of the same issue, the possibility or impossibility of Latin American philosophy. Latin American philosophy can exist if there is a Latin American culture from which this philosophy may take its issues. The existence of Latin American philosophy depends on whether or not there is Latin American culture. However, the formulation and attempt to solve this problem, apart from the affirmative or negative character of the answer, are already Latin American philosophy, since they are an attempt to answer affirmatively or negatively a Latin American question. Hence, the works of Ramos, Romero, and others on this issue, whatever their conclusions, are already Latin American philosophy.

The issue involved in the possibility of Latin American culture is one demanded by our time and the historical circumstances in which we find ourselves. The Latin American man had not thought much about this issue before because it did not worry him. A Latin American culture, a culture proper to the Latin American man, was considered to be an irrelevant issue; Latin America lived comfortably under the shadow of European culture. However, the latter culture has been shaken (or is in crisis) today, and it seems to have disappeared from the entire European continent. The Latin American man who had lived so comfortably found that the culture that supported him fails him, that he has no future, and that the ideas in which he believed have become useless artifacts, without sense, lacking value even for their own authors. The man who had lived with so much confidence under a tree he had not planted now finds himself in the open when the planter cuts down the tree and throws it into the fire as useless. The man now has to plant his own cultural tree, create his own ideas. But a culture does not emerge miraculously; the seed of that culture must be taken from somewhere, it must belong to someone. Now—and this is the issue that concerns the Latin American man—where is he going to find that seed? That is, what ideas is he going to develop? To what ideas is he going to give his faith? Will he continue to believe and develop the ideas inherited from

Europe? Or is there a group of ideas and issues to be developed that are proper to the Latin American circumstance? Or rather, will he have to invent those ideas? In a word, the problem of the existence, or lack of existence, of ideas that are proper to America, as well as the problem of the acceptance or rejection of ideas belonging to European culture that is now in crisis, comes to the fore. Specifically, the problem of the relationship between Latin America and European culture, and the problem of the possibility for a genuinely Latin American ideology.

2

In light of what has been said it is clear that one of the primary issues involved in Latin American philosophy concerns the relations between Latin America and European culture. Now, the first thing that needs to be asked has to do with the type of relations that Latin America has with that culture. There are some who have compared this relationship to that between Asia and European culture. It is said that Latin America, just as Asia, has assimilated only technology from Europe. But if this is so, what would belong to Latin American culture? For the Asian man, what he has adopted from European culture is regarded as something superimposed that he has had to assimilate owing to the change in his own circumstance caused in turn by European intervention. However, what he has adopted from European culture is not properly the culture, that is, a life-style, a world view, but only its instruments, its technology. Asians know that they have inherited an age-old culture that has been transmitted from generation to generation; they know that they have their own culture. Their view of the world is practically the opposite of the European. From Europeans they have only adopted their technology, and only because they have been forced to do so by the intervention of Europeans and their technology in a circumstance that is properly Asian. Our present day shows what Asians can do with their own world view while using European technology. Asians have little concern for the future of European culture, and they will try to destroy it if they feel that it gets in their way or continues to intervene in what they regard as their own culture. dNow, can we Latin Americans think in a similar way about European culture? To think so is to believe that we have our own culture, but that this culture has not perhaps reached full expression yet because Europe has prevented it. In light of this, one could think that this is a good time to achieve cultural liberation. If that were the case, the crisis of European culture would not concern us. More than a problem, such a crisis would be a solution. But this is not the case: we are deeply concerned about the crisis of European culture; we experience it as our own crisis.

This is due to the fact that our relationship with European culture as Latin Americans is different from that of the Asians. We do not feel, as

Asians do, the heirs of our own autochthonous culture. There was, yes, an indigenous culture—Aztec, Maya, Inca, etc.—but this culture does not represent, for us contemporary Latin Americans, the same thing that ancient Oriental culture represents for contemporary Asians. While Asians continue to view the world as their ancestors did, we Latin Americans do not view the world as the Aztecs or the Mayans did. If we did, we would have the same devotion for pre-Columbian temples and divinities that an Oriental has for his very ancient gods and temples. A Mayan temple is as alien and meaningless to us as a Hindu temple.

What belongs to us, what is properly Latin American, is not to be found in pre-Columbian culture. Is it to be found in European culture? Now, something strange happens to us in relation to European culture: we use it but we do not consider it ours; we feel *imitators* of it. Our way of thinking, our world view, is similar to the European. European culture has a meaning for us that we do not find in pre-Columbian culture. Still, we do not feel it to be our own. We feel as bastards who profit from goods to which they have no right. We feel as if we were wearing someone else's clothes: they are too big for our size. We assimilate their ideas but cannot live up to them. We feel that we should realize the ideals of European culture, but we also feel incapable of carrying out the task: we are content with admiring them and thinking that they are not made for us. This is the knot of our problem: we do not feel heirs of an autochthonous culture, because that culture has no meaning for us; and that which has meaning for us, like the European, does not feel as our own. There is something that makes us lean toward European culture while at the same time resists becoming part of that culture. Our view of the world is European but we perceive the achievements of that culture as alien. And when we try to realize its ideals in Latin America we feel as imitators.

What is properly ours, what is Latin American, makes us lean toward Europe and at the same time resists being Europe. Latin America leans toward Europe as a son to his father, but at the same time it resists becoming like his own father. This resistance is noticeable in that, despite leaning toward European culture, Latin America still feels like an imitator when it seeks to achieve what that culture does. It does not feel that it is realizing what is proper to it but only what Europe alone can achieve. That is why we feel inhibited by and inferior to Europeans. The malaise resides in that we perceive what is Latin American, that is, what is ours, as something inferior. The Latin American man's resistance to being like a European is felt as an incapacity. We think as Europeans, but we do not feel that this is enough; we also want to achieve the same things that Europe achieves. The malaise is that we want to adjust the Latin American circumstance to a conception of the world inherited from Europe, rather than adjusting that conception of the world to the Latin American circumstance. Hence the divorce between ideas and reality. We need the ideas of European culture, but when we bring them into our circumstance we find them to be too big because we do not dare to fit them to this circumstance. We find them big and are afraid to cut them down; we prefer to endure the ridicule of wearing an oversize suit. Indeed, until recently the Latin American man wanted to forget what he is for the sake of becoming another European. This is similar to the case of a son who wants to forget being a son in order to be his own father: the result has to be a gross imitation. This is what the Latin American man feels: that he has tried to imitate rather than to realize his own personality.

Alfonso Reyes portrays the Latin American man's resistance to being Latin American with great humor. The Latin American man felt "in addition to the misfortune of being human and modern, the very specific misfortune of being Latin American; that is, having been born and having roots in a land that was not the center of civilization, but rather a branch of it."[1] To be a Latin American was until very recently a great misfortune, because this did not allow us to be European. Today it is just the opposite: the inability to become European, in spite of our great efforts, allows us to have a personality; it allows us to learn, in this moment of crisis for European culture, that there is something of our own that can give us support. What this something is should be one of the issues that a Latin American philosophy must investigate.

3

Latin America is the daughter of European culture; it is the product of one of its major crises. The discovery of America[2] was not a matter of chance, but rather the product of necessity. Europe needed America: in every European mind there was the idea of America, the idea of a promised land. A land where the European man could place his ideas, since he could no longer continue to place them in the highest places. He could no longer place them in the heavens. Owing to the emergence of a new physics, the heavens were no longer the home of ideals but rather became something unlimited, a mechanical and therefore dead infinity. The idea of an ideal world came down from heaven and landed in America. Hence the European man came out in search of the land and he found it.

The European needed to rid himself of a world view of which he was tired. He needed to get rid of his past and begin a new life. He needed to build a new history, one that would be well planned and calculated, without excess or wanting. What the European was afraid of openly proposing in his own land, he took for granted in this land called America. America became the pretext for criticizing Europe. What he wanted Europe to be became imaginarily fulfilled in America. Fantastic cities and governments that corresponded to the ideals of the modern man were imagined in America. America was presented as the idea of what Europe should be. America became Europe's utopia. It became the ideal world that the old Western world was to follow to rebuild itself. In a word, America was the ideal creation of Europe.

America was born to history as a land of projects, as a land of the future, but of projects and a future that were not its own. Such projects and such future were Europe's. The European man who put his feet in this America—becoming part of the Latin American circumstance and giving rise to the Latin American man—has been unable to see what is properly American. He has only seen what Europe wanted America to be. When he did not find what European imagination had placed in the American continent, he was disappointed, and this produced the uprooting of the Latin American man from his own circumstance. The Latin American man feels European by origin, but he feels inferior to the European man by reason of his circumstance. He feels inadequate because he regards himself as superior to his circumstance, but inferior to the culture he comes from. He feels contempt for things Latin American, and resentment toward Europe.

Rather than attempting to achieve what is proper to Latin America, the Latin American man labors to achieve the European utopia and thus stumbles, as it could be expected, into a Latin American reality that resists being anything other than what it is: Latin America. This gives rise to the feeling of inferiority about which we already have spoken. The Latin American man considers his reality to be inferior to what he believes to be his destiny. In Anglo-Saxon America this feeling expresses itself in the desire to achieve what Europe has achieved in order to satisfy its own needs. North America has strived to become a second Europe, a magnified copy of it. Original creation does not matter, what matters is to achieve the European models in a big way and with the greatest perfection. Everything is reduced to numbers: so many dollars or so many meters. In the end, the only thing that is sought with this is to hide a feeling of inferiority. The North American tries to show that he is as capable as the European. And the way to show it is by doing the same things that Europeans have done, on a bigger scale and with greater technical perfection. But this only demonstrates technical, not cultural ability, because cultural ability is demonstrated in the solution one gives to the problems of man's existence, and not in the technical imitation of solutions that other men found for their own problems.

The Latin American man, however, feels inferior not only to the European, but also to the North American man. Not only does he no longer try to hide his feeling of inferiority, but he also exhibits it through self-denigration. The only thing that he has tried to do so far is to live comfortably under the shadow of ideas he knows are not his own. To him, ideas do not matter as much as the way to benefit from them. That is why our politics have turned into bureaucracy. Politics is no longer an end but an instrument to get a job in the bureaucracy. Banners and ideals do not matter anymore;

what matters is how these banners and ideals can help us get the job we want. Hence the miraculous and quick change of banners; whence also that we always plan and project but we never achieve definitive results. We are continually experimenting and projecting with always-changing ideologies. There is no single national plan because there is no sense of nation. And there is no sense of nation for the same reason that there is no sense of what is Latin American. He who feels inferior as Latin American also feels inferior as a national, that is, as a member of one of the Latin American nations. This is not to say that the fanatic nationalist who talks about a Mexican, Argentinian, Chilean, or any other Latin American nation's culture, to the exclusion of anything that smacks of foreign, has any better sense of what a nation is. No, in the end he would only try to eliminate what makes him feel inferior. This is the case of those who say that this is the appropriate time to eliminate everything European from our culture.

This position is wrong because, whether we want it or not, we are the children of European culture. From Europe we have received our cultural framework, what could be called our structure: language, religion, customs; in a word, our conception of life and world is European. To become disengaged from it would be to become disengaged from the heart of our personality. We can no more deny that culture than we can deny our parents. And just as we have a personality that makes us distinct from our parents without having to deny them, we should also be able to have a cultural personality without having to deny the culture of which we are children. To be aware of our true relations with European culture eliminates our sense of inferiority and gives us instead a *sense of responsibility*. This is the feeling that animates the Latin American man today. He feels that he has "come of age," and, as any other man who reaches maturity, he acknowledges that he has a past that he does not need to deny, just as no one is ashamed of having had a childhood. The Latin American man knows himself to be the heir of Western culture and now demands a place in it. The place that he demands is that of collaborator. As a son of that culture he no longer wants to live off it but to work for it. Alfonso Reyes, speaking on behalf of a Latin America that feels responsible, demanded from Europe "the right of universal citizenship that we have already conquered," because already "we have come of age."[3] Latin America is at a point in its history when it must realize its cultural mission. To determine this mission constitutes another issue that what we have called Latin American philosophy has to develop.

4

Once we know our cultural relations with Europe, another task for this possible Latin American philosophy would be to continue to develop the philosophical issues of that culture, but most especially the issues that European philosophy regards as universal. That is, issues whose level of abstraction allows them to be valid at any time and at any place. Among such issues are those of being, knowledge, space, time, God, life, death, etc. A Latin American philosophy can collaborate with Western culture by attempting to resolve the problems posed by the issues that European philosophy has not been able to resolve, or to which it has failed to find a satisfactory solution. Now, it could be said—particularly by those who are interested in building up a philosophy with a Latin American character—that this cannot be of interest to a philosophy concerned with what is properly Latin American. This is not true, however, because both the issues that we have called universal and the issues that are peculiar to the Latin American circumstance are very closely linked. When we discuss the former we need also to discuss the latter. The abstract issues will have to be seen from the Latin American man's own circumstance. Each man will see in such issues what is closest to his own circumstance. He will look at these issues from the standpoint of his own interests, and those interests will be determined by his way of life, his abilities and inabilities, in a word, by his own circumstance. In the case of Latin America, his contribution to the philosophy of such issues will be permeated by the Latin American circumstance. Hence, when we address abstract issues, we shall formulate them as issues of our own. Even though being, God, etc., are issues appropriate for every man, the solution to them will be given from a Latin American standpoint. We may not say what these issues mean for every man, but we can say what they mean for us Latin Americans. Being, God, death, etc., would be what these abstractions mean for us.

It should not be forgotten that all European philosophy has worked on these issues on the assumption that their solutions would be universal. However, the product has been an aggregate of philosophies very different from each other. Despite their universalistic goals, the product has been a Greek philosophy, a Christian philosophy, a French philosophy, a British philosophy, and a German philosophy. Likewise, independently of our attempts to realize a Latin American philosophy and despite our efforts to provide universal solutions, our solutions will bear the mark of our own circumstance.

Another type of issue to be addressed by our possible Latin American philosophy is related to our own circumstance. That is, our possible philosophy must try to resolve the problems posed by our circumstance. This point of view is as legitimate and valid a philosophical issue as the one we have just discussed. As Latin Americans we have a series of problems that arise only in the context of our circumstance and that therefore only we can resolve. The posing of such problems does in no way diminish the philosophical character of our philosophy, because philosophy attempts to solve the problems that man encounters during his existence. Hence the problems encountered by the Latin American man are the problems of the circumstance in which he lives.

Among such issues is that of our history. History is part of man's circumstance: it gives him a configuration and a profile, thus making him capable of some endeavors and incapable of others. Hence we must take our history into account, because it is there that we can find the source of our abilities and inabilities. We cannot continue to ignore our past and our experiences, because without knowing them we cannot claim to be mature. Maturity, age, is experience. He who ignores his history lacks experience, and he who lacks experience cannot be a mature, responsible man.

With respect to the history of our philosophy, one might think that nothing could be found in it other than bad copies of European philosophical systems. In effect, that is what one will find if one is looking for Latin American philosophical systems that have the same value as European ones. But this is a shortsighted attempt: we must approach the history of our philosophy from a different standpoint. This standpoint is provided by our denials, our inability to do much besides bad copies of European models. It is pertinent to ask the reason why we do not have our own philosophy: perhaps the very answer will be a Latin American philosophy. This may show us a way of thinking that is our own and that perhaps has not needed to express itself through the formulae used by European philosophy.

It is also pertinent to ask why our philosophy is a *bad copy* of European philosophy. Because being a bad copy may very well be part of our Latin American philosophy. To be a bad copy does not necessarily mean to be bad, but simply different. Perhaps our feeling of inferiority has made us consider bad anything that is our own just because it is not like, or equal, to its model. To acknowledge that we cannot create the same European philosophical systems is not to acknowledge that we are inferior to the authors of those philosophies, but simply that we are different. On the basis of this assumption we will not view our philosophers' production as an aggregate of bad copies of European philosophy, but as Latin American interpretations of that philosophy. The Latin American element will be present in spite of our philosophers' attempts at objectivity. It will be present despite our thinkers' attempt to depersonalize it.

5

Philosophy in its universal character has been concerned with one of the problems that has agitated men the most at all times: the problem of the relations between man and society. This problem has been posed as political, asking about the forms of organization of these relations, that is, the organization of human interaction. Since the institution in charge of such relations is the State, philosophy has asked by whom it should be established and who should govern. The State must take care to maintain the balance between individual and society; it must take care to avoid both anarchy and totalitarianism. Now, in order to achieve this balance a moral justification is necessary. Philosophy attempts to offer such a justification. Hence, every metaphysical abstraction ultimately leads to ethics and politics. Every metaphysical idea provides the foundation for a concrete fact, the justification for any proposed type of political organization.

There is a multitude of philosophical examples in which metaphysical abstractions have provided the basis for a political construct. One example is found in Plato's philosophy, whose theory of ideas provides the basis and the justification for *The Republic*. In Saint Augustine's *The City of God* we find another example: the Christian community, the Church, is supported by a metaphysical being that in this case is God. The *Utopias* of the Renaissance constitute yet other examples where rationalism justifies the forms of government that have given birth to our present democracy. One thinker has said that the French Revolution finds its justification in Descartes's *Discourse on Method*. The Marxist revision of Hegel's dialectics has given way to such forms of government as communism. Even totalitarianism has sought metaphysical justification in the ideas of Nietzsche, Sorel, and Pareto. Many other examples from the history of philosophy can be cited where metaphysical abstraction provides the basis for social and political practices.

What we have just discussed underlines how theory and practice must go together. It is necessary that man's material acts be justified by ideas, because this is what makes him different from animals. But our times are characterized by a schism between ideas and reality. European culture is in crisis because of this schism. Man is now lacking a moral theory to justify his acts and hence has been unable to resolve the problems of human interaction. All that he has achieved is the fall into the extremes of anarchy and totalitarianism.

The various crises of Western culture have been produced by a lack of ideas to justify human acts, man's existence. When some ideas have no longer justified this existence, it has been necessary to search for other sets of ideas. The history of Western culture is the history of the crises that man has endured when the harmony that should exist between ideas and reality has been broken. Western culture has gone from crisis to crisis, finding salvation sometimes in ideas, sometimes in God, other times in reason, up to the present time when it no longer has ideas, God, or reason. Culture is now asking for new foundations of support. But this is, from our point of view, practically impossible. However, this point of view belongs to men who are in a situation of crisis, and this could not be otherwise, since we would not be in a situation of crisis if the problem seemed to us to have an easy solution. The fact that we are in a crisis, and that we do not have the much-wanted solution, still does not mean that the solution does not exist. Men who like us have been in situations of crisis before have had a similar pessimism; however, a solution has always been found. We do not know which values will replace those that we see sinking, but what we do know for certain is that such values will emerge, and it is our task as Latin Americans to contribute to this process.

From this we can infer yet another goal for a possible Latin American philosophy. The Western culture of which we are children and heirs needs new values on which to rest. These new values will have to be derived from new human experiences, that is, from the experiences that result from men being in the new circumstances of today. Because of its particular situation, Latin America can contribute to culture with the novelty of untapped experiences. That is why it is necessary that it tell its truth to the world. But it must be a truth without pretensions, a sincere truth. Latin America should not pretend to be the director of Western culture; what it must aspire to do is to produce culture purely and simply. And that can be accomplished by attempting to resolve the problems that are posed to the Latin American man by his own Latin American perspective.

Latin America and Europe will find themselves in a similar situation after the crisis. Both will have to resolve the same problem: what will be the new way of life that they will have to adopt to deal with the new circumstances? Both will have to continue ahead with the interrupted task of universal culture. But the difference is that Latin America will no longer be under the shadow of Europe's accomplishments, because there is neither a shadow nor a place of support at this point. On the contrary, Latin America finds itself at a vantage point in time—which may not last long—but that must be used to initiate the task that belongs to it as an adult member of Western culture.

A Latin American philosophy must begin the task of searching for the values that will provide the basis for a future type of culture. And this task will be carried out with the purpose of safekeeping the human essence: that which makes a man a man. Now, man is essentially an individual who is at the same time engaged in interaction with others, and hence it is necessary to maintain a balance between these two components of his essence. This is the balance that has been upset to the point of leading man to extremes: individualism to the point of anarchy, and social existence to the point of massification. Hence it is imperative to find values that make social interaction possible without detriment to individuality.

This task, which is universal and not simply Latin American, will be the supreme goal of our possible philosophy. This philosophy of ours cannot be limited to purely Latin American problems, that is, the problems of Latin America's circumstance. It must be concerned with the larger circumstance called humanity, of which we are also a part. It is not enough to attempt to reach a Latin American truth, but we must also attempt to reach a truth that is valid for all men, even if this truth may not in fact be accomplished. What is Latin American cannot be regarded as an end in itself, but as a boundary of a larger goal. Hence the reason why every attempt to make a Latin American philosophy, guided by the sole purpose of being Latin American, is destined to fail. One must attempt to do purely and simply philosophy, because what is Latin American will arise by itself. Simply by being Latin American, philosophers will create a Latin American philosophy in spite of their own efforts at depersonalization. Any attempt to the contrary will be anything but philosophy.

When we attempt to resolve the problems of man in any spatiotemporal situation whatever, we will necessarily have to start with ourselves because we are men; we will have to start with our own circumstances, our limitations, and our being Latin Americans, just as the Greeks started with their own circumstance called Greece. But, just like them, we cannot limit ourselves to stay in our own circumstances. If we do that it will be in spite of ourselves, and we will produce Latin American philosophy, just as the Greeks produced Greek philosophy in spite of themselves.

It is only on the basis of these assumptions that we will accomplish our mission within universal culture, and collaborate with it fully aware of our abilities, and be aware also of our capacities as members of the cultural community called humanity, as well as of our limits as children of a circumstance that is our own and to which we owe our personality: Latin America.

NOTES

1. Alfonso Reyes, "Notas sobre la inteligencia americana," *Sur,* no. 24 (September 1936).
2. Zea consistently uses "America" and "Americanos" to refer to Latin America and its inhabitants. I use "Latin America" and "Latin Americans" respectively to render these terms throughout the paper, except in the present case, because here Zea is referring to the period of discovery, when there was no distinction between Anglo-Saxon and Latin America.—TRANS.
3. Reyes, "Notas."

Augusto Salazar Bondy
(1927-1974)

Salazar Bondy was born and educated in Lima, Peru. At the time of his death he was full professor at the Universidad Nacional Mayor de San Marcos and director of the Biblioteca Filosófica, a publication series of the mentioned university. Salazar Bondy was a prolific and active philosopher who traveled extensively throughout the American continent, giving lectures in Latin American and North American universities and attending many congresses of philosophy. The impact of his thought was strongly felt in Peru and in several other Latin American countries.

Among his many works we may mention *La filosofía en el Perú* (1954), *Irrealidad e idealidad* (1958), *Tendencias contemporáneas de la filosofía moral británica* (1962), *Historia de las ideas en el Perú contemporáneo* (1965), *Breve antología filosófica* (1967), *¿Existe una filosofía de nuestra América?* (1968), *Sentido y problema del pensamiento filosófico hispanoamericano* (1969), and *Para una filosofía del valor* (1971).

Salazar Bondy began his philosophical career from a phenomenological perspective inspired by Hartmann and Heidegger. Later he became interested in some Marxist ideas and in the last few years of his life adopted a more analytic approach, particularly with respect to value theory. This lack of rigid ideology was a direct result of his view of philosophy as a broad and integrating discipline.

As is clear from the titles of the works cited above, from the very beginning of his philosophical career this author was interested in the philosophy of his country and later in the philosophy of Latin America in general. His knowledge of Latin American philosophy and his contributions as critic and historian of it led him to an examination of the problem of philosophical identity in Latin America. The position he adopted, as already noted in the Introduction, is critical. According to him, the type of philosophy practiced in Latin America has been the product of the efforts of intellectual elites that, having no originality of their own, imitated the different philosophical currents fashionable in Europe. The result has been a nonauthentic philosophy, divorced from Latin American society and its needs; Latin American philosophy is a direct product of the alienation of Latin American society.

J. G.

The Meaning and Problem of Hispanic American Thought*

[CAN THERE BE A LATIN AMERICAN PHILOSOPHY?]

Following the direction of current Hispanic American thought, let us inquire about the quality and scope of the intellectual products of the philosophizing of four-hundred-years of evolution. . . . Our balance cannot fail to be negative, as has been that of practically all historians and interpreters of ideas in Hispanic America. In fact, it is impossible to extract clearly from this process an articulation of ideas, a well-structured dialectic of reflections and expositions, and of concepts and solutions nurtured by its historical and cultural circumstance. On the contrary, what we find in all our countries is a succession of imported doctrines, a procession of systems which follows European, or, in general, foreign unrest. It is almost a succession of intellectual fashions without roots in our spiritual life and, for this very reason, lacking the virtue of fertility. Just as scholastic colonial thought . . . was imposed by the interests of the mother country, so also the systems that replaced it responded to an historical logic that was foreign to the conscience of our peoples. For this reason these systems were abandoned as quickly and easily as they were embraced, having been chosen by the upper class and the intellectual sectors of Hispanic Americans according to their immediate preferences and momentary affinities. To review the process of Hispanic American philosophy is to relate the passing of Western philosophy *through* our countries, or to narrate European philosophy *in* Hispanic America. It is not to tell the history of a natural philosophy *of* Hispanic America. In our historical process there are Cartesians, Krausists, Spencerians, Bergsonians and other European *"isms."* But this is all; there are no creative figures to found and nurture their own peculiar tradition, nor native philosophic

---

*From Augusto Salazar Bondy, *The Meaning and Problem of Hispanic American Thought,* ed. John P. Augelli (Lawrence, Kans.: Center of Latin American Studies of the University of Kansas, 1969).

"isms." We search for the original contributions of our countries in answer to the Western challenge—or to that of other cultures—and we do not find them. At least we find nothing substantial, worthy of a positive historical appraisal. No one, I believe, can give testimony to its existence if he is moderately strict in his judgment.

The characteristics which, according to this balance, stand out in boldest relief in Hispanic American thought are the following:

1. *Imitative sense of thought.* Thinking is done according to theoretical molds already shaped in the pattern of Western thought—mainly European— imported in the form of currents, schools and systems totally defined in their content and orientation. To philosophize is to adopt a pre-existent foreign *"ism,"* to incorporate into one's thought theses adopted during the process of reading, and to repeat more or less faithfully the works of the most resounding figures of the period.

2. *Universal receptivity.* An indiscriminate disposition to accept all manner of theoretical product coming from the most diverse schools and national traditions, with extremely varied styles and spiritual purposes. This, of course, always provided that they will have obtained a certain reputation, a perceptible ascendancy in some important country of Europe. This receptivity, which betrays a lack of substance in ideas and convictions, has often been taken for an Hispanic American virtue.

3. *Absence of a characteristic, definitive tendency,* and of an ideological, conceptual proclivity capable of founding a tradition of thought, of sketching a profile in an intellectual manner. Notice the "empiricist" seal that Britannic thought has, perceptible even in the work of its speculative idealists. There is no solid basis upon which to define a similar style in Hispanic American philosophy. At times one speaks of a practical inclination in the Hispanic American, at others, of a speculative vein. Apart from the fact that these two traits are contradictory, their manifestations—weak and confusing—have disappeared rapidly and almost completely each time that contrary influences have prevailed. The only alternative is to count as a distinctive character precisely the absence of definition and the nebulous state of conceptions, which is merely to confirm the thesis.

4. *Correlative absence of original contributions,* capable of being incorporated into the tradition of world thought. There is no philosophic system of Hispanic American roots, or doctrine with meaning in the entirety of universal thought. Neither are there polemic reactions to the affirmations of our thinkers, nor sequels and doctrinary effects of them in other philosophies. All of this is an additional proof of the inexistence of our own ideas and theses. The most relevant philosophical figures of Hispanic America have been commentators or professors, but, no matter how fruitful their action in this field may have been for the educational process of our countries, it has not had an effect beyond our own cultural circle.

5. *Existence of a strong sense of intellectual frustration* among cultivators of philosophy. It is symptomatic that, throughout the history of our culture, its most lucid interpreters have planted time and again the question of the existence of their own philosophic thought. Responding to it, as we said, almost unanimously with a complete negation, they have formulated projects for the future construction of such thought. Significantly, this unrest and reflection are not found, or are rarely found, among those nations that have made fundamental contributions to the development of philosophy. They are, so to speak, well installed in the territory of philosophic theory and move within it as in their own dominion. Hispanic Americans, on the other hand, have always, in this regard, felt themselves to be in alien territory, as one who makes furtive and clandestine incursions, for they have had a vivid consciousness of their lack of speculative originality.

6. *There has existed permanently in Hispanic America a great distance between those who practice philosophy and the whole of the community.* There is no way to consider our philosophies as national thought, with a differential seal, as one speaks of a German, French, English, or Greek philosophy. It is also impossible for the community to recognize itself in these philosophies, precisely because we are dealing with transplanted thought, the spiritual products of other men and other cultures, which a refined minority makes an effort to understand and to share. We do not deny that there is a universal factor in philosophy, nor do we think that philosophy has to be popular. However, when an elaborate intellectual creation is genuine, it reflects the conscience of a community finding in it profound resonance especially through its ethical and political derivations.

7. *The same scheme of historic development and the same constellation of traits—although negative—are suitable to the activity unfolded during more than four centuries by the men dedicated to philosophy in a plurality of countries,* often far removed physically and socially from each other as is the case of Hispanic America. Not only does it permit a general judgment of Hispanic American thought—without ignoring the existence of special cases and regional variants resulting from divergent influences within the common framework—it also demonstrates that in order to comprehend the thought of our countries it is necessary to define the basic cultural-historical reality that links them beneath their nearly always artificial confrontations and political separations.

In his *Lectures on the History of Philosophy,* Hegel wrote: "Philosophy is the philosophy of its time, a link in the great chain of universal evolution; from whence it derives that it can only satisfy peculiar interests of its time." In another place, confronted with the existence of systems that pretend to reproduce doctrines of the past, that is, to make a kind of transfer from one mode of thinking to another, he formulated this bitter disqualification:

"These attempts are simple translations, not original creations; and the spirit only finds satisfaction in the knowledge of its own and genuine originality." With this the great master of the history of philosophy underscored a very important fact in the dominion of thought. To wit, philosophy as such expresses the life of the community, but it can fail in this function, and, instead of manfesting its uniqueness, it can detract from it or conceal it. Accordingly, an unauthentic philosophy, or a mystified thought may develop.

To what extent a philosophy can be unauthentic will be made clear in an attempt to specify the purpose and meaning of philosophic thought. As we understand it, a philosophy is many things, but among them it cannot fail to be the manifestation of the rational conscience of a community. It is the conception that expresses the mode in which the community reacts before the whole of reality and the course of existence, and its peculiar manner of illuminating and interpreting the being in which it finds itself installed. Because it comprises the whole of reality, it deals with that which is essential to man, with his vital commitment. In this respect it differs from science which does not commit the whole man. On the other hand, to the extent that philosophy is a rational conscience, an attempt to make the world and life intelligible, it is not confused with religious faith, which operates through feeling and suggestion. Thus, philosophy deals with the total truth of a rationally clarified existence, that appeals to the totality of the personal human being and its full lucidity. The latter are the two means of referring to that which is most unique in each man.

But philosophy can be unauthentic, as we have seen. How does this happen? Man constructs his self-image as an individual and as a social entity; he is, in the words of Ortega, the novelist of himself. But he may be that as an original writer or as a plagiarist; as someone who portrays himself, outlining his genuine idea, or as someone who is self-deluding, "getting ideas" about himself, and takes another's as his own image. And so, thinking that he knows himself, he remains ignorant. A philosophy can be this illusory image of itself, the mystified representation of a community, through which the community "gets ideas"—real ideas—about itself and loses itself as a truthful conscience. This happens when philosophy is constructed as an imitated thought, as a superficial and episodic transference of ideas and principles motivated by the existential projects of other men, by attitudes toward the world that cannot be repeated or shared. At times they may even be contrary to the values of other communities. He who assumes this imitated thought thinks he sees himself expressed in it and in fact makes an effort to live it as his own, but he almost never finds himself in it. The illusion and unauthenticity that prevail in this case are paid for with sterility, and sterility, which betrays a vital defect, is always a risk for collective and individual life.

This anthropological illusion has, nevertheless, a truthful side. The man of mystified conscience expresses through this conscience his own defects and deficiencies. If a community adopts foreign ideas and values, if it cannot give them life and empower them, but instead imitates them in their foreign character, it is because alienating and deficient elements prevail in its being. An illusory self-concept is only possible to the degree that there is no self-fulfillment, at least in certain very important sectors of historical existence. On this point it is, then, inexact—although not false—to deny the veracity of unauthentic philosophies. It is more exact to say that they lie about the being that assumes them, but by lying they reveal their defective existence. They fail in not offering a proper image of reality as it ought to be, but they succeed, unwittingly, as an expression of the lack of a complete and original being.

Because of scientific demands of precision and objectivity, when one speaks of culture in social science, one usually means by the term a unique and neutral concept. Although this use has permitted the empirical manipulation of social life and the generalization of explanations, it is, nevertheless, insufficient. I believe that this science is now in a position to consider as positive data and to elaborate theoretically the facts concerning the unauthenticity and alienation of society and culture. Marxism and psychoanalysis, empirically controlled, can make very valuable suggestions in this respect. I say this because to me it seems impossible to comprehend human life without distinguishing historical deficiencies and plenitudes, the accomplishments and alienations of communities and the individuals that constitute them, all of which obliges us to a diversity of concepts. In this respect, I think that it behooves us to wield a strong and unique concept of *culture* as the organic articulation of the original and differentiating manifestations of a community—susceptible to serving as a guide to contrast the historic work of peoples. We reserve other meanings and other concepts, such as those of mode of working, mode of proceedings, or manner of reacting to other parallel phenomena. These concepts, unlike that of culture, would be applicable to any social group, even if such a group did not achieve cultural originality and maturity in the strict sense of the word. It then is necessary to include in anthropological terminology, at the social and cultural level, the concepts of frustration, alienation, authenticity and mystification, without which the multiple variety of historical existence cannot be comprehended, as we are proving in the case of Hispanic American philosophy.

In Hispanic America a defect of culture may be observed. Hispanic American philosophic thought—and all other thought of similar explanatory purposes—offers that stamp of negativity to which we have been referring in speaking of philosophies as illusory self-conscience. Because of its imitative nature across the centuries, until today it has been an alienated and alienating conscience that has given a superficial image of the world and life to man in our national communities. It has not truly responded to motivations felt by this man, but rather has responded to the goals and vital interests of other men. It has been a plagiarized novel and not the truthful chronicle of our human adventure.

As we have indicated earlier, there is a consensus among the interpreters of Hispanic American thought and culture regarding the existence of a problem that affects its meaning and function. The demonstration of this problematic situation in its applicability to philosophy has suggested various attempts at explanation that should be recalled and examined, even if it is only by way of a very brief résumé.

1. A first reaction is to evaluate Hispanic American thought, such as it is, positively, while disregarding its negative aspects or interpreting them by a kind of sublimation as original forms, different from ordinary philosophic thought, but valuable in themselves as spiritual creations. One may exalt, for example, the universalism of our thought, which is the optimistic reverse of the limitless receptivity that we mentioned earlier, or the disguise that conceals a weakness of theoretical reflection. A kind of autochthonism joins hands here with a conformist conscience in order to see in deficiency or weakness an original mode of philosophizing. It forgets that our thought has proved that it cannot live without external sustenance, and that it is incapable of making its personality felt, for example, by provoking polemic reactions or determining influences that might prolong and enrich it, in the course of world thought.

2. Although close to the preceding, a second attitude has a rather negative cast. Those who adopt it recognize that there is no vigorous and creative philosophy in Hispanic America, and they explain this fact appealing generally to ethnic causes. It is said, for example, that this situation is the effect of our mentality, that our race does not have a philosophic disposition. It is held that philosophy does not harmonize with the genius of our people, which is better endowed for other spiritual creations. The thesis generally presupposes the existence of a vigorous body of values and genuine cultural products different from the philosophic, of which there is, of course, no proof. This opinion cannot long resist the confrontation with well-known facts that demonstrate that deficiencies and unauthenticity reach other very important fields, and even cover the entire gambit of culture.

3. A third explanation appeals to the historical cultural youth of our peoples. It is thought that four hundred years of evolution, without counting the process of previous civilizations, are not sufficient to acclimate philosophy, and that one should reasonably expect a perceptible change in this aspect when the Hispanic American community achieves the maturity that it is lacking today. It is forgotten in this context that other "younger" peoples with a less aged intellectual tradition, as is patently the case with the United States, have indeed managed to create a philosophic thought of their own.

4. Another explanation approaches a position of greater historical real-

ism, although in my opinion it does not touch the most decisive factors. It appeals to the precariousness of institutional conditions and of the necessary social means for the development and advance of genuine theoretical thought. In this case we are considering mainly the coordinated professional and academic organization that encourages the cultivation of philosophy as a university specialty, along with the varied professional activities of Hispanic American thinkers. This allows for the hope of a favorable evolution in view of the fact that in our time a normality has been achieved in the academic status of philosophic studies. At the base of this explanation there is a very limited and partial idea of the conditions in which philosophy prospers. The latter is regarded as a standardized activity and it is taken for granted that the university atmosphere is rather the natural abode of thought. Aside from the fact that such an idea risks confusing creative philosophers with mere professors of philosophy, it passes over the very significant fact that many of the greatest thinkers did not enjoy the facilities mentioned, nor were they—and more than once they did not wish to be— university professors. Take for example Descartes, Locke, Spinoza, Leibniz, Hume, to mention only a few famous names who were dedicated to activities very distinct from that of teaching.

If the explanations that I have reviewed are insufficient or erroneous, as it seems to me that they are, it is necessary to turn to another type of explanatory causes and factors. Broader and more profound, they operate in that sphere of fundamental realities that, in spite of disconnections and separations, lead to a coincidence in their characters and a common evolution of philosophic thought in Hispanic American nations. One must recognize the necessity of seeking in the mode of living of our nations, as social organisms and historical-cultural entities, the causes of the problem that concerns us. A defective and illusory philosophic conscience causes one to suspect the existence of a defective and unauthentic social being, the lack of a culture in the strong and proper sense of the term as previously defined. This is the case in Hispanic America.

Commenting on a book of mine about the history of contemporary ideas in Peru, the young French historian Jean Piel asked, in a paraphrase of Montesquieu's famous sentence, "How can one be Peruvian?" The question is equally applicable to all of Hispanic America, because there is a problem of authenticity in man in this part of the world. Certainly, on the level of simple, natural facts, the question offers no difficulty, and perhaps it is not worth posing. One can be anything from the moment that one is. But when one takes into account all that an historical being as such entails, all that it implies by way of aspirations, plans, norms and values, besides natural realities, then the question acquires full meaning. It is equivalent to asking about the potential and destiny of an unauthentic existence. Because the truth is that Hispanic Americans live beyond a feigned being.

Hence it is that in our communities mystification and fiction prevail. Many institutions have a different design from what they declare, while the majority of ideas acquire a sense that is different from and, as often as not, opposite to the original meaning that they officially possessed. The most varied forms of conduct and inter-personal relationships coincide in functioning and being motivated in a manner contrary to what supposedly corresponds to them. Reflect, for example, on Hispanic American democracy or free enterprise, justice, religion, the University, morality, and it will be seen to what an inversion of being my considerations point. In the last analysis, we live on the conscious level according to models of culture that have no roots in our condition of existence. In the raw material of this historical reality, imitative conduct yields a deformed product which passes itself off as the original model. This model operates as a myth that impedes our recognizing our situation and laying the bases for a genuine building of ourselves. The same kind of mystified awareness leads us, for example, to define ourselves as Westerners, Latins, moderns, democrats or Catholics. We imply in each one of these cases—through the work of the disguising myths that enjoy free rein in our collective conscience—something different from what in truth exists.

This use of foreign and inadequate patterns, ideas and values that do not jibe with reality, and reflect a partial or falsified image of our mode of being is what, in the last analysis, Hispanic American philosophy sanctions. Because of the ambivalence of our existence, it sanctions it in a double sense: (a) as the conscious assumption of concepts and norms without roots in our historical-existential concern; (b) as an imitation of foreign thought, with neither originality nor force. Hispanic American philosophy sanctions unauthenticity in our culture by presenting itself in its ideas and values—whose purpose is to illuminate life—as a product that ignores reality and alienates the spirit.

It is not strange that a community which is disintegrated and lacking in potential, should produce a mystified philosophic awareness. Philosophy, which in an integral culture is the highest form of consciousness, cannot help but be an artificial and insubstantial expression in a defective culture. It cannot help but be a thought alien to the living body of history, foreign and alienating in principle to the destiny of the men in whose community it is nourished.

Where is the cause, the determining complex of this condition of Hispanic America as an entity and also of each of its constituent nations? If we are aware that this condition is not peculiar to Hispanic American countries, but is largely similar to that of other communities and regional groups of nations, belonging to what today is called the Third World, then it is clear that, to explain it, we must utilize the concept of underdevelopment, with the correlative concept of domination. In fact, underdeveloped countries present an aggregate of basically negative characteristics which, one way or the other, are related to dependent bonds with other centers of economic and political power. These centers of power—which direct the activities of the dependent countries according to their own interests—are situated in the developed nations, in the mother countries or in great industrial powers. And these negative characteristics correspond to factors which easily explain the phenomena of a culture like that of Hispanic America. It was not by accident that our countries were first subject to Spanish power and that they evolved from this situation as Spanish political colonies to that of factories and supply centers or markets of the British Empire, subject to their economic control. The United States inherited this empire, with a closer and more effective network of power. As dependents of Spain, England, or the United States, we have been and continue to be underdeveloped—if I may use the expression—*under* these powers, and, consequently, countries with a *culture of domination.*

I am giving here the broader traits of the conditions and global references to the phenomenon of the underdevelopment and domination of Hispanic America. I prefer to remain on this level so as better to call attention to the basic fact of our culture. One could object, no doubt, to the simplicity of the explanation. I believe that it could be shaded considerably without varying the substance of the thesis: but I fear that the trees of the shading might not permit us to see the forest of the basic cause; I fear that the refined pluralism of the explanation might distract us from the original comprehension. Therefore, I insist that the decisive factor in our Hispanic American case is underdevelopment, the dependency and bonds of domination, with the peculiar qualities that allow us to define it as a historical phenomenon.

The socio-cultural effect of this state of things is that misshapen society and defective culture that philosophy reveals. Let us remember that our philosophy was originally a thought imposed by the European conqueror in accord with the interests of the Spanish Crown and Church. It has since been a thought of the upper class or of a refined oligarchical elite, when it has not corresponded openly to waves of foreign economic and political influence. In all these cases underdevelopment and domination are influential. On the other hand, the qualities that we indicated in describing our thought not only fail to contradict this explanation through underdevelopment, but instead harmonize fully with it. The dominated countries live with a view to the outside, depending in their existence upon the decisions of the dominant powers, that cover all fields. This trait is not alien to the receptivity and the imitative character of the philosophy—and not only the philosophy—that is typical of Hispanic America. Likewise, these countries lack vigor and dynamism because of their depressed economy and because of the lack of cohesion in their society that underdevelopment creates. Thus, there is no distinctive cast of thought that could neutralize this receptivity and this tendency toward imitation. Nor can the entirety of spiritual products achieve the necessary vigor to inject themselves as original contributions in the world-wide advance of civilization. The distance between those who practice philosophy and the community at large is in this case—unlike the normal relationship between the specialist and the public—the abyss between the enlightened elite who live according to a foreign model, and the illiterate, poverty-stricken masses, trapped in the framework of remote and sclerotic traditions. And the frustration is rooted in the impossibility of living according to foreign cultural patterns, while experiencing the simultaneous incapacity to make the life of the community fruitful in thought. As we have seen, this situation is common to Hispanic America in the same measure that underdevelopment is common, and with it, dependence and domination.

Our thought is defective and unauthentic owing to our society and our culture. Must it necessarily remain so? Is there no alternative to this prospect? That is to say, is there no way of giving it originality and authenticity? Indeed there is, because man, in certain circumstances rises above his present condition, and transcends in reality toward new forms of life, toward unheard-of manifestations. These will endure or will bear fruit to the degree that the initiated movement can expand and provoke a general dialectic and totalization of development. In the socio-political field this is what constitutes revolutions. This means that that part of man which rises above his circumstances can not do so fruitfully and in a lasting manner unless the movement is capable of articulating itself with the rest of reality and provoking in it an overall change. If this is valid for society and culture in general, it is also true of philosophy, for the latter, being the focus of man's total awareness, could, better than other spiritual creations, be that part of humanity that rises above itself, and overcomes the negativity of the present as it moves toward new and superior forms of reality. But, to achieve this, it must possess certain valences capable of turning theory into live reality. It must operate in such a way that, through an effective and prudent utilization of historical resources, it will produce the most fruitful dialectical reactions in the proper areas of social life. Hegel said that the owl of Minerva took flight at dusk, thus giving philosophy the character of a theory that elucidates the meaning of facts already accomplished. It is not always so. Contrary to what Hegel thought, we feel that philosophy can be, and on more than one historic occasion has had to be, the messenger of the dawn, the beginning of historic change through a radical awareness of existence projected toward the future.

Philosophy in Hispanic America has a possibility of being authentic in the midst of the unauthenticity that surrounds and consumes it, and to convert itself into the lucid awareness of this condition and into the thought capable of unleashing the process to overcome it. It must be a meditation *about* our anthropological status and *from* our own negative status, with a view to its cancellation. Consequently, Hispanic American philosophy has before it—as a possibility of its own recuperation—a destructive task that, in the long run, will be destructive to its current form. It must be an awareness that cancels prejudice, myths, idols; an awareness that will awaken us to our subjection as peoples and our depression as men. In consequence, it must be an awareness that liberates us from the obstacles that impede our anthropological expansion, which is also the anthropological expansion of the world. It must be, in addition, a critical and analytical awareness of the potentialities and demands of our affirmation as humanity. All of which requires a thought that from the beginning will cast aside every deceptive illusion and, delving into the historical substance of our community, will search for the qualities and values that could express it positively. These qualities and values must be precisely those capable of finding resonance in the entirety of Hispanic America, and, along with other convergent forces, unleashing a progressive movement that will eliminate underdevelopment and domination.

I believe it necessary to call attention to the fact that I am not postulating the necessity of *practical, applied* or *sociological* philosophy, as has been proposed more than once as a model of Hispanic American thought. It has been suggested, even by outstanding figures of our culture, that in the distribution of philosophical tasks, theory should belong to Europe and application to Hispanic America. I am convinced also, however, that the strict theoretical character, which is the highest contemplative requirement indispensable to all fruitful philosophy, is merely another way of condemning ourselves to dependency and subjection. In philosophy, as in science, only he who has the key to theory can appropriate the advances and powers of civilization. Our philosophy should be, then, both theory and application, conceived and executed in our own fashion, according to our own standards and qualities. Just as science, which in spite of its declared objectivity, tolerates, particularly in the social disciplines, an ingredient of interpretation and ideology, so too, should philosophy be elaborated by us as theory according to our own standards and applied in accord with our own ends.

Consequently, those who heed the call of reflexive thought in Hispanic America cannot dispense with the acquisition of the techniques developed by philosophy in its long history, nor can they cast aside all those concepts capable of serving as support for a rigorous theory. At the cost of laborious efforts they must appropriate all these products, all the more difficult to acquire without the support of a solid national cultural base. But all the while they must keep in mind their provisional and instrumental character, and not take them as models and contents to be imitated and repeated as if they were absolute. Rather, they must be taken as tools to be utilized as long as there are no others more effective and more adequate to the discovery and expression of our anthropological essence.

This is the task that we have ahead of us. In some cases it would be impossible to fulfill its goals completely, but we must aim toward them with the awareness that the difficulty increases daily through the dynamics of world history. In the great field of international competition, the differences between the underdeveloped and developed countries, the proletarian and industrialized countries, are ever more pronounced. The subjection of the former to the latter is, therefore, increasingly stronger and more permanent. Likewise, the alienation of being becomes more serious in the dominated nations, among which the Hispanic American countries must be counted. But there is still the possibility of liberation. While this is so, we are obligated to choose a line of action that will materialize this possibility. Philosophy also has this option.

Arturo Andrés Roig
(b. 1922)

Roig was born in Mendoza, Argentina. Having graduated from the National University of Cuyo (1949), he did postgraduate work in the history of ancient philosophy, under the direction of Pierre-Maxime Schuhl, at the Sorbonne (France) between 1953 and 1954. Before his politically motivated discharge from the post he held at the National University of Cuyo in 1974, he had taught there for thirty years. In 1984 he was allowed to return to his former position, which he now holds. In addition he has had visiting appointments in France, Mexico, and Ecuador. Presently he is also director of the Center for Latin American Studies of the Pontifical Catholic University of Ecuador and researcher of the Latin American Faculty of Social Sciences in Quito.

He has published numerous articles in professional journals in Latin America, Europe, and the United States. Among his books the following should be noted: *La filosofía de las luces en la ciudad agrícola* (1968), *Los krausistas argentinos* (1969), *Platón o la filosofía como libertad y expectativa* (1972), *El espiritualismo argentino entre 1850 y 1900* (1972), *Esquemas para una historia de la filosofía ecuatoriana* (1977 and 1982), *Filosofía, universidad y filósofos en América Latina* (1981), *El humanismo ecuatoriano de la segunda mitad del siglo XVIII* (1984), *El pensamiento social de Juan Montalvo* (1984), and *Bolivarismo y filosofía latinoamericana* (1984).

Roig has specialized in the study of classical Greek as well as Latin American thought. In addition he has attempted to develop a philosophical position that could be characterized as a "historical empiricism." It is founded in an ontology based on the description of the human being. This philosophy, which is also described as a "philosophy of liberation," aims to supersede the various dichotomies, such as those between subject and object, soul and body, and signified and signifying, that according to Roig characterize Western thought. In this context, philosophy must be in the last analysis an effort to place man in society's bosom, while keeping in mind that man is a being capable of making and begetting himself.

J. G.

The Actual Function of Philosophy in Latin America*

[A PHILOSOPHY OF LIBERATION]

Our present time is characterized by an attitude of commitment that is strongly felt by great nuclei of intellectuals throughout our continent. We could say that that commitment has a twofold aspect: on the one hand it is a commitment to knowledge itself in a strict sense, and on the other it is clearly a commitment to knowledge *qua* social function.

The second aspect is possibly the one that more strongly characterizes our human attitude. Its existence presupposes a form of positioning with respect to the very concrete reality of our peoples. If we had to identify the most obvious feature of that taking of a position we would say that it is connoted by the conviction that social structures, considered in themselves, are unjust insofar as they are based on the dominating-dominated relationship—a fact that becomes more acute because of our dependent cultural state. From this origin, the task that arises from this commitment has been characterized throughout the continent as a *social and national* liberation, and insofar as the liberating action required a cojoined realization of all the social groups who suffered dependency, it has been postulated with the character of *integration* as well.

Within this framework philosophy keeps alive some of the principles that guide contemporary European idealism, but most assuredly with a new sense of direction. We demand that philosophical thought move "toward things-in-themselves" and we also demand that the knowledge of those things be a "knowledge without presuppositions"; but between this idealism of the essences and us has intervened the existential crisis that has the virtue of rendering bankrupt every form of Platonism, in the pejorative sense of that term, and has opened us toward the search for an ontology in whose field

*From Arturo Andrés Roig, "Función de la filosofía en América Latina," in *La filosofía actual en América Latina* (Mexico: Grijalbo, 1976), 135-54.

the foundation of our thinking is today disputed. At bottom, we live the bankruptcy of every philosophy of conscience on whose foundation Western rationalism has been founded during the nineteenth and twentieth centuries. The philosophies of what we might call denunciation, among which are principally Marxism and Freudianism, have provided the bases of assumptions, elements without which that commitment to knowledge *qua* social function would again run the risk of remaining behind the masked attitudes that would, finally, reduce the task of the philosopher to what it generally was among our "founders."

It is obvious, moreover, that the social function of knowledge and, parallel to it, the philosopher's mission, have for us a new meaning. The social, national, and continental liberation, as well as the integration of the Latin American peoples, is not the exclusive work of the intelligentsia, even if the latter may propose a change in mental attitude. Philosophy must become conscious of its task within the framework of the system of connections of its times, and it must be discussed whether if, within it, it will be added to those processes that move toward what is historically new or if, in the maturity of times, it will play a mere role of justification. This issue necessarily takes us to the reformulation of ontological knowledge within which the theme of the historicity of the [Latin] American man is fundamental, as it also takes us to a reformulation of our history of philosophy.

From the postulation of the forms and modes of *integration,* understood as condition of *liberation,* depends likewise the whole of philosophy. Every philosophy begins with the assumption that it is a mode of universal knowledge and because of that integrating, but the history of that claim has demonstrated and still demonstrates how integration has implied and still implies forms of rupture and marginalization. This fact, presented succinctly, takes them to the issue of the value, as much of conscience, as of the concept *qua* proper instrument of philosophical thought. It is appropriate that we ask ourselves how the philosophy of liberation must be organized in order not to fall into a new philosophy of dependence. Without exception, all of our "founders" spoke of "freedom" and their philosophy could be characterized for the whole continent as a "theory of freedom." Korn, Deústua, and Caso posit freedom as a basic category of their thought, but this message has turned out to be ambiguous and, if at some point present Latin American philosophy must supersede all ambiguity, it is purely in this regard. Integration requires, then, the elaboration of a doctrine that may provide us with adequate conceptual tools with which thinking man could, without treason, join the cause that is the cause of the people.

We know the epistemological difficulties that control our present-day philosophy in Latin America. Rationalism imposed the requirement of arriving at a strict philosophy from the point of departure of immediate and apodictic evidence. Our modern impulse for philosophizing is also immediate, but assertoric; it has to do with factual, not necessary truths that are inscribed in existence itself. Could we say that our beginning is given by *facticity?* We necessarily have to say it, but only as long as we do not understand by it a brute fact or a pure facticity, for there is no facticity except insofar as it is inscribed in an understanding and evaluation. Perhaps it might be necessary to say that it has to do with an enveloping facticity within which are given simultaneously the thinking subject and the object of thought. In other words, it has to do with an existential situation grasped with what we could call, along with Michel Foucault, a certain *historical a priori,* in spite of the risks it implies, and while pointing out that for us that concept ought to be redefined insofar as what is *a priori* is not so with regard to what is historical, as something that determines what is temporal from the outside, but that it is likewise historical. It is a determinate and determining historical structure in which social conscience plays, in our judgment, a preponderant causality and where *a priori*-ness is posited in a nonnecessary way beginning in experience and is, for that reason, also an *a posteriori*-ness in respect to its origin in the moments of formation of an epoch or of a generation. From what has been said, moreover, the *historical a priori* is not only constituted by intellectual categories, but also by states of mind that give sense as much to the discourse in which knowledge is expressed as it does to the conduct of those who develop that knowledge in relation to the medium in which they perform.

Neither does philosophy as we understand it fit in with the old classical category of contemplative and disinterested knowledge, or with the notion of objectivity that accompanied it and pretends to fulfill a social function from a critical consciousness with a new direction. At the same time, this philosophy claims to develop its discourse rigorously, but the requirement of rigor departs as well from the modalities with which it was understood within the vast ranges of modern and contemporary rationalism.

The "founders" also started off from a certain *historical a priori* from which they gave their own philosophical answers to their own facticity. The theory of objects and the theory of values—common themes to almost all of them—constitute an answer to a certain unconscious order proper to a cultural state on the basis of which they developed the classifications and on which experiences were judged. From that *a priori* that functions in them as a condition of the possibility of the hierarchical forms of entities and values, they were placed in a discourse from which they understood that they ful-filled, in their own fashion, the double requirement of rigorous knowledge and commitment. This fact permits the consideration of the "normalization" of the philosophical task in Latin America that began precisely with them, from the ideological point of view. The typically conservative discourse with which that task was begun caused the Brazilian philosopher Luis Washing-ton Vita to denounce as reactionary the philosophy of Bergsonian inspiration with which it expressed itself. The ideology of "normalization," inherited in our time by ontologists, phenomenologists, logical positivists, and structuralists, undoubtedly constituted a very special way of understanding the requirement of philosophical rigor.

Hence, that notion of "philosophy as such" has acquired for us a new meaning—for Risieri Frondizi it meant to do philosophy and immunize it against nonphilosophical activities (and politics in particular), since, as this author tells us, European thought had lost philosophical character in Latin America. Philosophy, Leopoldo Zea has said, does not only have to pay attention to "how it is done," but also to "for what it is done"; in other words, it must be something more than rigorous science, i.e., it must certainly also be consciously adopted ideology.

"Philosophy as such" cannot avoid substance and take refuge, as happens in some cases, in the mere sign or in mere structures, developing a formalist discourse that ignores the historical process. The strong influence of linguistic doctrines has precisely cut through the philosophical task and fractured it down to its very core. The requirement of rigor proper to "normalization" has dangerously led the way within the field of structuralist epistemology to an attempt at the analysis of the pure form of philosophical discourse, emptying it of its contents while earlier having eliminated the referential function of language, which is what ties it to the historically concrete. Having emptied the discourse of its substantial content, and therefore the human project it embraces, it has degenerated into a totalization of concepts through which the will to power is easily developed. In this way the rigor of academic philosophy has not only been content in some cases with the reduction of philosophical subject matter to essences, based on the teachings of Husserl, but by advancing further toward that requirement it has ended up altogether avoiding consciousness as a subject.

We have stated that "philosophy as such" cannot avoid substance, but neither can it lapse into another form of evasion of thought, the same one into which ontologism lapses. The assertion that being as well as the tendency to inquiry about being is lived or livable within the immediate experience of consciousness, is the essential characteristic of ontologism in our opinion. Consciousness ends up being understood as the place where what is real is revealed, whether as a result of eidetic intuition or as the fruit of the existential frame of mind that found an opening to being, and parallel to it, the task of man is to give himself to an alienating inquiry urged by the need to give an explanation to 'entity', breaks asunder every dignity and ends up by nullifying man as the builder of his own world. As Agoglia has appropriately stated with regard to existentialism, its proposed substitution of the question of entity for the question of being is an evasion of philosophy at the ontological level, for what gives philosophical authenticity to the question concerning being is not an assumed or implied relation of being to man, but rather an inquiry about being in terms of man. Ontologism asserts, moreover, on the basis of the foundation of the claimed revelatory power of immediate consciousness, a permanent distinction between *doxa* and *episteme* from which it would be possible only to arrive at rigorous knowledge. [This is the dilemma into] which one falls with the condemnation of thought *qua* thought of the world, understanding [by] this the infinite web of entities and entitative relationships within which we move and have our being, such as is assumed in the realism of the common man and expressed in everyday speech. The need to erect the foundations of an ontology that does not fall into ontologism, therefore, implies the acknowledgement that consciousness is object before it is subject; that it is a social entity before it is an individual reality; that there is no transparent consciousness, which, for this reason, not every *episteme* need be developed on the basis of a criticism alone, but necessarily also on the basis of a self-criticism; that intuition does not take the place of the concept and that this concept is a representation; that the preeminence of being and of man as such is the inescapable point of departure and the terminus of every question about being; and, finally, that an ontology is also necessarily an anthropology.

Formalism and ontologism in all their diverse forms overlook two aspects that have significant importance if we give heed to the attitude of commitment that we referred to at the outset: the historicity of man and the relationship of man to technology. At bottom one sees in many instances the position evident within the aestheticism of our "founders," which was a predominant characteristic of nearly all of them, that in addition it included an ontologism and on its foundations an axiology in which what is economic, confused with what is crudely utilitarian, was presented as a pseudo-value. The case of Alejandro Deústua is typical in that sense. The line that proceeds from Bergsonian influence to Heideggerianism, as philosophy of consciousness and as intuition, has been a prime example of the uprooting and the alienation in Latin American thought denounced so vehemently by Augusto Salazar Bondy.

This fact is even more serious in our own time given the ignorance of the American man's historicity hidden beneath a profusion of investigation of that same historicity. The concrete case [of this profuse investigation] is found in the philosophy of "existential disposition" and in particular in one of its formulations developed by the Venezuelan philosopher Mayz Vallenilla, for whom the "disposition" that characterizes the Latin American man would be "expectation," which, as such, is subjected "to the most absolute contingency in relation to the content of what comes near and is convenient." This would be the reason why technology appears to us as something alien and as coming from the outside. It is in this manner that our dependency comes to be justified ontologically at the same time that the possibility of our man making himself in the act of his labor is denied.

We have already pointed to the close relationship that exists between the aestheticism of our "founders" and the ontologism of the present. But there is yet another fact that cuts negatively through to the historicity of our man: the continuation of a certain kind of ethicism expounded by Alejandro Korn and Antonio Caso. Undoubtedly, this ethicism is watered down nowadays and in some cases even apparently lost completely beneath the development of formalist philosophy; it is not for that reason less present. Ethicism is a consubstantial attitude with the mental structure imposed by liberalism on the whole continent, and it can only be explained within the framework of the "order" that arises out of the *historical a priori* within the scope we have assigned to this concept—this *a priori* serves as a substratum for all of our intellectuals, and makes their thought an expression of a determinate social class. Ethicism is a response that tries to maintain the *integrating* formula imposed by an age on a given society, resorting to a hierarchy of values that is above doubt, but is reinforced and even ontologically founded insofar as every social problem is reducible, on this view, to a moral program. Also, in its own way, ethicism reinforces the a-historical view of our man insofar as the moral formulae of integration assert the roles of dominating and dominated groups, preventing in this way the rise of proper historicity, of the proper self-making that man, as such, deserves since it proposes no change of social structures and with them no new integrating formulae.

We face, in addition, the problem concerning the discourse in which we ought to locate ourselves, in other words, in what way ought we to act with respect to that *a priori* from which every discourse tends to develop. The single fact of denouncing its existence presupposes for Latin American philosophy a new and innovative attitude and leads, among other things, to the need to analyze its structure in those that preceded us. Thus arises once more the need to reexamine the thought of our "founders" from our present perspective and with our current methodological principles.

It is appropriate that we ask ourselves about the meaning of the fact in which they placed themselves with an almost generational sense within the framework of Bergsonian discourse and would continue to elaborate Rodó's discourse again. The symbol of Ariel and philosophy of the spirit appropriate to immediate consciousness were not incompatible. But we could say, moreover, that Arielism continued and was reinforced under the generalized influence of Bergsonian thought in that stage after the 1900s, and Ariel continued being the symbol of a task that those intellectuals from whom we are descended imposed upon themselves. To these influences must be added, without any doubt, the authority exerted by Ortguian philosophy, also a thought of enlightened elites. Though Rodó's spiritualism developed as an answer to the question concerning what our thought *qua* Hispanic-American should be, and as a consequence of Ortega y Gasset's circumstantialism, there was an attempt to adopt the facticity that we spoke of at the beginning. With these tools our "founders" undoubtedly gave an answer to the pressing problem of cultural dependency, and they forcefully pointed out—and particularly in the case of Rodó—the presence of imperialism as one of the negative factors that integrated the facticity from which they, and we, begin. This was possible to the degree that the discourse of the "founders"—especially some of them such as José Vasconcelos—continued being, in spite of its ambiguity, a response to the problems of liberation and integration and for that very reason had not become emptied of content.

But this message requires that it be taken from a new beginning of our philosophy and the symbols in which it felt itself to be incarnated required a decodification, and to the degree that the symbol has an inner force that goes beyond a mere intellectual posturing of what is symbolized, our age needs, as Abelardo Villegas has indicated while commenting on Roberto Fernández Retamar, a new symbolism for Latin American culture. Let us not forget that "the old and reserved teacher, who was usually called Prospero, in reference to the wise teacher of Shakespeare's *The Tempest*," according to the initial words of Ariel, ends up in Roberto Arlt's short story by hanging himself in an outhouse. This hard and cruel image represents the end of the presuppositions from which those very elites developed their philosophical discourse.

The categories with which spiritualism tried to fulfill an integrating function undoubtedly find themselves in a crisis. Caliban, who is not an abject being, is our most direct symbol in the same way that we stopped believing in the "Civilization" that the liberal bourgeoisie in the nineteenth century placed in oppositon to the "barbarism," which is the name Caliban is given in Sarmiento's framework. And in the same way we have lost our horror of the "masses," the sociological pseudoconcept with which Ortega y Gasset crippled his own circumstantialism and with which he in turn pointed out the presence of Caliban.

The mission of current Latin American philosophy essentially lies, then, in the search for new integrating concepts, whether or not they are expressed in new symbols. And because of that we feel the need of an ontology that may separate us from every formalism and may not fall, in turn, into a new ontologism: In other words, [we require] an ontology that insures the preeminence of the object with respect to consciousness, that may not flow into new forms of Platonism, and that may lay bare the historicity of man as a given reality in everyday experience, but beginning not with a singular and unique experience understood under a pretense as revealing the historicity of the privileged consciousness of the philosopher.

Philosophy is concerned with entity and being, but whether it is erected as an ontology of entity or an ontology of being, in the sense that it is beyond entity, or as an attempt at the dialectical integration of both, the inescapable point of departure is always given in entity. Man has no other access to being except through the way it is given to us *qua* entity, and it is realized in our own ontic nature. For this reason we may say with Miguel Angel Virasoro, that for us being does not speak with its own voice nor does it have its own sense and that its sense is built in entities so that being for man is primarily a pure availability that threshes itself out in the infinite world of entities and their relations. Now, although in any way that we may construe philosophy, there is always the risk of its being developed as a system of the oppression of life as exercised from the objective totality of the concept and orchestrated by the will to power, in other words, of falling into a Platonism such as the one Nietzsche denounced in his own times, something that appears to us unquestionable is only beginning from a strong preeminence of entity, captured in its otherness and in its novelty, we will be able to develop an open dialectical thought.

The fact that what is truly in an act is given for men in entity and for entity opens up to us the sense of his own historicity and his task as creator and transformer of his world. The struggle for the unmasking of the objective, oppressive totalities and the elaboration of the integrating categories that may not detract from his historical presence, but rather allow him to reintegrate himself with himself, is undoubtedly the principal undertaking of a philosophy of liberation. And every eschatological answer to the problem of being, that ignores this real and crude insertion of man within entity, cannot be but negative.

That facticity from which we begin is not, as we had said, a pure facticity without signification, for when man is found placed within his world he receives a "from where" and a "to where" that prescribe his destiny and from which he does not escape by denouncing everydayness as a form of alienation and by trying to separate himself from it by a singular and unique abstract experience, but rather it is within that very everydayness and in terms of it that he must assume his origin and his destiny.

In that same sense it is undoubtedly highly valuable to point out the affective relation to the world, conditioned by our social consciousness and on whose foundation we are disposed with respect to entities. An analysis of the *historical a priori* undoubtedly cannot avoid the existence of those states of mind that do not constitute a mythical opening with respect to an ontological reality, but a very concrete way that directs our evaluating activities in our relational life and is later projected in philosophical discourse.

If we had to mention the state of mind from which many of our intellectuals have opened up to their world, we would venture to say that it is one of fear. This affective attitude is the one that most obviously regulates and conditions behavior in a society in which the figures of master and slave, oppressor and oppressed, continue to exist. Dread runs through our continent in the face of the "revolt of the masses," "social revolution," "loss of order and hierarchies," "social decomposition," "changes of structures," "doctrines foreign to national interest," or "forgetfulness of our most treasured traditions." Oppressive political discourse offers, in this sense, a clear reading and a state of mind that conditions and has conditioned the theories of even those who believed themselves saved from the very facticity in which they began, and on which they confer an inevitably ideological content.

The "theory of freedom" that fills the discourse of our "founders" must, no doubt, be replaced by the "theory of liberation" that should have as its fundamental task the elaboration of new integrating categories beginning with a redemption of the historical sense of man. History, the occurrence, Carlos Astrada has stated, has to derive its meaning from existing man, whose fundamental ontological structure is already historicity. Meaning is not to be extracted from history as if man were an a-historical subject that depends on it, as integrating categorical foundation alien to him, as hypostatic reality. History is history of man's realization in accordance with a historical repertoire of ends. The assuming of one's own ends presupposes a self-making, a self-happening, as act of freedom. As Oward Ferrari has said, "Finality means an ongoing task of man, it implies a *Geschehen,* a self-begetting, a self-making, because of which the thought of man's will leads directly to the *Geschichtlichkeit.*"

Because of that, history is an ontological vocation of man that is to be fulfilled and is fulfilled completely when the improper modes of self-making or self-begetting are denounced, modes that generally claim to make of history a tautology, a repetition of the same. In this was the self-making or the self-begetting that in history is developed theoretically over a justifying dialectic, that closes the doors to the rushing in of the other or that at least ignores it. But that self-begetting or self-making presupposes, as a constitutive note of man's being, an other-ness that, by its single presence, breaks the successive dialectic totalities with which the attempt was made to put a brake on the historical process of man's liberation.

The oppressed, the man who suffers pain, poverty, hunger, torture, persecution, and death, is the one who presents himself to us as the "other" with respect to our "self-ness" and of the integrating categories with which we attempt to support that self-ness, and it is the one that takes charge of the humanizing mission of imposing otherness as an essential condition of man. Undoubtedly, Caliban is the symbol of the latent or explicit force that begets what is new within the historical process. It is the Indian, the black, the mestizo face-to-face with the white, the humble man from the fields and the proletariat from the cities face-to-face with the oligarchies and diverse power groups; the old gaucho and the contemporary black head, in short, the man who came to be called anonymous and whose anonymity was consummated from the claimed integrating categories called "Civilization" or "Spirit" or "Christian Western World" and so many other similar types.

In relation to the self-begetting and self-making, an answer to the problem of technology must be given. Without a doubt our contemporary world has led to a loss of man that has given form to the vast theme of alienation. But technology, leaving aside whether man can attain or lose happiness through it, cannot be thought of as something alien to human nature, since it constitutes a fundamental part of self-begetting and self-making, which is precisely where freedom is gambled. For that reason, the problem of technology will find its adequate answer when the relation between man and production is formulated correctly, in other words, when labor is a function in which and through which man is able to make his humanity by himself.

Labor and technology, then, are two issues that must be understood on the basis of an ontology that affirms in a conclusive way the historicity on the basis of which is developed the self-realization or the self-destruction of man. It is certainly necessary to be on guard in order not to fall into ontologism insofar as this is a risk incurred in every type of answer. Abelardo Villegas has shown how it is present in the economic formulation of alienation, which in some cases would repeat, with modifications, the doctrine of the "natural state" to which we would have to return in order to be saved from the alienating situation. This supposedly natural man that originally was to be one with the products of his activity, turns out to be in this way an a-historical being. Faced with this formulation one cannot but assert, as Villegas does, that there is no original ontological structure undone later by events that would turn out to be foreign to it, but that man is a developing being, immersed in social and historical conditions within which *ab initio* his possibilities of realization or frustration have been given.

The need that man reach his own humanity in his own self-making, through nonalienated labor, undoubtedly displaces the metaphysical need to inquire after being, and above all inhibits that inquiry to the degree that through it one runs the risk of deteriorating the liberating imperative. The problem of transcendence must be recognized from the perspective of that imperative. In that sense, the assumption of the "death of God" within theological thought, and particularly within our Latin American liberation theology, is an answer to the problem of the determination of new integrating categories, and has the heavy burden of finding the way to assume, for the believing man, the historicity of the self-making and the self-begetting, joining with this the vast liberating movement of peoples.

The great revolution of our age consists in the discovery of historicity, which is the fundamental key to every task concerned with decoding oppressive discourse. This one, we knew, has been essentially characterized by having interpreted as natural the relations among men, that is to say, as foreign to self-happening and self-making and the force with which dialectical totalities have been imposed over this base is directly related to fear and the will to power. In this sense the history of philosophies and the history of ideologies can be subjected to the same type of question and are not, in fact, two histories, but one: the history of thought and its multiple expressions. Undoubtedly, our times are not satisfied with a history of philosophy concerned exclusively with academic knowledge or knowledge expressed formally as philosophical discourse, but rather to the degree that that discourse has an epistemological status in terms of which we can declare it to be within the category of the particular discourse of the social sciences, or simply the spontaneous political discourse declared by the common man.

On the basis of everything that has been said there is no doubt that the function to be fulfilled by the historian of thought in Latin America requires him to redirect his task in a new orientation. The discovery that between a "philosophical discourse" and a "political discourse" it is possible to determine a common epistemological structure through which both can be understood as oppressive or liberating discourses—in other words, that it is possible to analyze them from common ideological points of view in close relationship to the *historical a priori* from which both arise—opens the door for an extension of the field of research. Methodologically what we propose is simply to accept a truth that has been enunciated many times, but that has not always been possible to incorporate into the historian's task, which is to assert the necessary relation that there is between philosophical discourse and the system of connections of a given age. If philosophy is the expression of a determined culture it is because it is integrated in it and what has to be looked for is how in its very root that relation is given. One of the unfocusings has been perhaps to think that within that system of connections "philosophical discourse" played a directing role from a level claimed to be purely theoretical, and the presence of factors that place that discourse at the same level as others has been neglected, causing the philosopher's metalanguage, once its presuppositions have been indicated to have ontologically neither more nor less value than the language of the common man. This is then part of the task: to reduce in that sense the metalanguages of language. For the construction of a philosophy of liberation there is nothing more important than to recognize that many times what is new, what truly shows man's historicity and his struggle to make his otherness explicit in its context, is not to be found in academic philosophies, but in the "political discourse" of marginal and exploited elements and that through it proceeds precisely a thought that would have had to have been adopted in the formally philosophical task. Thus we are far from the historiographic categories that were imposed as a consequence of the requirement of "normalization" and of "rigor" that have ruled to this day. Our "rigor" has as a goal to discover truly if a "philosophical discourse" is properly philosophy, above all, if we still harbor the belief that philosophical knowledge points to truth and in that sense to an unconcealment to the degree that we exercise the function of hiding, consciously or unconsciously, from a bad conscience. Certainly we do not wish with this to reduce philosophical historiography to the investigation of ideological presuppositions, for we know that philosophy, although containing what is ideological, also transcends it. There is a reason why philosophy claims to establish itself as critical and self-critical knowledge, located not beyond what is ideological, but rather adopting it openly and within the categories of a liberating thought. Because of what we have been saying, a historiography of Latin American philosophy could not be accomplished without undertaking the study of the development and the modes of social consciousness with all the thematic ramifications involved in this problem.

In order to finish, we should say a few words concerning the so-called "ontologies of the national being" and also something about what is utopian within the liberating discourse.

The horizon from which we intend to give an answer to the ontological question claims to consider the problems of the historicity of man *qua* man. This is to say that, properly speaking, there is neither an "ontology of the [Latin] American man" nor an "ontology of the national being" as it has been postulated, in some cases resulting in the bankruptcy of both rationality and universality. Precisely this requirement is among those listed by Leopoldo Zea in his meditation concerning our philosophy of history.

In that sense we do not accept the presupposition in which "populism" is founded, to the degree that within this doctrine the integrating categories of "people" and of "national being" deny, in our case, otherness, or deform it when they interpret it as an absolute cultural specificity. The notion of "people" is used to hide a real heterogeneity, on the basis of a claimed homogeneity, unreal, within which is disguised the class struggle, and social liberation is postponed with the pretext that it must be preceded by national liberation. The notion of "national being," in turn, is thus founded on an unreal heterogeneity. And that unreal heterogeneity, in its turn, hides a real homogeneity, that is to say, where national differences are emphasized until irrationality is reached. In this way "people" and "national being" appear as typical categories of "integration" proper to contemporary oppressing discourse. An ontology that claims to serve as basis for a philosophy of liberation should then neither ignore the presence of the diverse modes of otherness, nor deform it obscuring entity's rationality, something that makes impossible its understanding in relation to other beings before which it is "other." Without a doubt, "populism" has Caliban as its symbol, but it is a Caliban newly shackled and bound.

The problem of utopia is the problem of the regulating power of ideas. The issue concerns the question as to which is its function within the liberating discourse and whether its presence as a creative force is to be rejected. We understand that what is utopian is a natural ingredient of this discourse, just as the antiutopian attitude is proper to oppressive discourse, above all if we do not understand by utopian the return to the past, but to be open to the future as the place for what is new. This last is and will always be an answer given as a result of the preeminence of entity, without whose acknowledgement a philosophy of liberation is not possible. Our own discourse in which we have decided to situate ourselves cannot ignore the risks and benefits of what is utopian. A praxis that does not belong to the philosopher, but upon which philosophy must be developed, is giving the superseding formulae of the dialectical road that moves between the will to reality and reality itself.

Select Bibliography

Abbagnano, Nicola. *Diccionario de filosofía.* Translated by Alfredo N. Galleti. 2nd ed. in Spanish. Mexico: Fondo de Cultura Económica, 1966.

Abellán, José Luis. *Filosofía española en América, 1936-66.* Madrid: Guadarrama, 1967.

Actas. Primer Congreso de Filosofía y Filosofía de la Educación convocado por la Facultad de Filosofía, Letras, y Ciencias de la Educación de la Universidad Central. Quito: Cultura Ecuatoriana, 1954.

Actas. Segundo Congreso Extraordinario Interamericano de Filosofía. San José: Nacional, 1962.

Alvarez de Miranda, Angel. *Perfil cultural de Hispanoamérica.* Madrid: Cultura Hispánica, 1950.

Antología del pensamiento social y político de América Latina. Introduction by Leopoldo Zea. Selection and notes by Abelardo Villegas. Washington, D.C.: Unión Panamericana, 1984.

Arciniegas, Germán. *Latin America: A Cultural History.* Translated by Joan MacLean. New York: Alfred A. Knopf, 1967.

Ardao, Arturo. "Assimilation and Transformation of Positivism in Latin America." *Journal of the History of Ideas* 24 (1963): 515-22.

———. *Filosofía de lengua española.* Montevideo: Editorial Alfa, 1963.

Armstrong, A. M. "Contemporary Latin American Philosophy." *The Philosophical Quarterly* 3 (1953): 167-74.

Berndston, Arthur. "Latin American Philosophy." In *The Encyclopedia of Philosophy,* edited by Paul Edwards, 4:396-400. New York: Macmillan, 1967.

Berndtson, C. Arthur E. *Readings in Latin-American Philosophy.* Columbia, Mo.: University of Missouri, 1949.

Bibliografía filosófica del siglo XX. Catálogo de la Exposición Bibliográfica Internacional de la Filosofía del Siglo XX. Buenos Aires: Peuser, 1952.

Brightman, Edgard S. "Personalism in Latin America." *The Personalist* 24 (1943): 147-62.

Bruning, Walther. "La antropología filosófica actual en Iberoamérica." *Revista de la Universidad Nacional de Córdoba* 40 (1953): 935-65.

Cannabrava, Euryalo. "Present Tendencies in Latin American Philosophy." *Journal of Philosophy* 46 (1949): 113-19.

Carrillo Narvaez, Alfredo. *La trayectoria del pensamiento filosófico en Latinoamérica.* Quito: Casa de la Cultura Ecuatoriana, 1959.

Caturla Brú, Victoria de. *¿Cuáles son los grandes temas de la filosofía latinoamericana?* Mexico: Novaro-México, 1959.

Clissold, Stephen. *Latin America. A Cultural Outline.* New York: Harper and Row, 1966.

Conversaciones filosóficas interamericanas (homenaje de centenario al Apóstol José Martí). La Habana: Comisión Nacional del Centenario de Martí, 1955.

Crawford, William Rex. *A Century of Latin-American Thought.* Cambridge, Mass.: Harvard University, 1944; 2d rev. ed., 1961; 3rd ed., New York: Praeger U-606, 1966.

Cursos y Conferencias 48 (1956); issue dedicated to Latin American philosophy.

Davis, Harold Eugene. *Latin American Thought: A Historical Introduction.* Baton Rouge: Louisiana State University Press, 1972; 2d ed., New York: The Free Press, 1974.

————. *Latin American Social Thought.* Washington, D.C.: The University Press of Washington, 1963.

————. *Social Science Trends in Latin America.* Washington, D.C.: American University Press, 1950.

————. "Social and Political Thought in Latin America." In *Twentieth Century Political Thought,* edited by Joseph E. Roucek. New York: Philosophical Library, 1946.

Donoso, Antón, "Philosophy in Latin America: A Bibliographical Introduction to Works in English." *Philosophy Today* 17 (1973): 220-31.

Dussel, Enrique D. *América Latina: dependencia y liberación*. Buenos Aires: Fernando García Cambeiro, 1973.

———. *Caminos de liberación latinoamericana*. Buenos Aires: Latinoamérica Libros, 1973.

Echevarría, José. *La enseñanza de la filosofía en la universidad hispanoamericana*. Washington, D.C.: Unión Panamericana, 1965.

Ferrater Mora, José. *Diccionario de filosofía*. Mexico: Atlante, 1941; several subsequent enlarged editions.

La filosofía en América. Vol. 1, Actas del IX Congreso Interamericano de Filosofía. Caracas: Sociedad Venezolana de Filosofía, 1979.

Filosofía y Letras 38 (1950); articles on Latin American philosophy by Ferrater Mora, Frondizi, Zea, and others.

"First Inter-American Conference of Philosophy, Papers and Discussions." *Philosophy and Phenomenological Research* 4 (1943-44): 127-235.

Frank, Waldo. *América Hispana: A Portrait and a Prospect*. New York and London: Scribner's, 1931.

Frankl, Víctor E. *Espíritu y camino de Hispanoamérica. La cultura hispanoamericana y la filosofía europea*. Bogotá: Biblioteca de Autores Colombianos, 1953.

Fránquiz, José A. "The Concept of Freedom in Latin American Philosophical Thought." *Proceedings of the Fourteenth International Congress of Philosophy*, 1: 193-200. Vienna: Herder, 1968.

Frondizi, Risieri, y Jorge J. E. Gracia. *El hombre y los valores en la filosofía latinoamericana, del siglo XX*. Mexico: Fondo de Cultura Económica, 1975, 1980.

Frondizi, Risieri. *La universidad en un mundo de tensiones. Misión de las universidades en América Latina*. Buenos Aires: Editorial Paidós, 1971.

———. "On the Unity of the Philosophies of the Two Americas." *Review of Metaphysics* 4 (1951): 617-22. Translated from "Tipos de unidad y diferencia entre el filosofar en Latinoamérica y en Norteamérica." *Filosofía y Letras* 19 (1950): 373-77.

———. "Is There an Ibero-American Philosophy?" *Philosophy and Phenomenological Research* 9 (1948-49): 345-55.

———. "Tendencies in Contemporary Latin American Philosophy." In *Inter-American Intellectual Interchange*, 35-48. Austin: Institute of Latin American Studies of the University of Texas, 1943.

Frondizi, Risieri. "A Selective Guide to the Material Published in 1939 on Latin American Philosophy." *Handbook of Latin American Studies* 5 (1939): 418-27.

Fuentes de la filosofía latinoamericana. Serie de Bibliografías Básicas 4. Washington, D.C.: Unión Panamericana, 1967.

Los "fundadores" en la filosofía de América Latina. Serie de Bibliografías Básicas 7. Washington, D.C.: Unión Panamericana, 1970.

Gaos, José. *Antología del pensamiento de lengua española en la edad contemporánea.* Mexico: Séneca, 1945.

———. *Pensamiento de lengua española.* Mexico: Stylo, 1945.

———. *El pensamiento hispanoamericano.* Mexico: El Colegio de México, 1944.

García Astrada, Arturo. *América y las ideologías.* Buenos Aires: Universidad Nacional, 1971.

Gómez Martínez, J. L. "Pensamiento hispanoamericano: una aproximación bibliográfica." *Cuadernos Salmantinos de Filosofía* 8 (1981): 287-400.

Gracia, Jorge J. E. "Panorama actual de la filosofía en América Latina." In *Actas. La filosofía hoy en Alemania en América Latina.* Cordoba: Instituto Goethe. 1985.

———. "Philosophical Analysis in Latin America." *History of Philosophy Quarterly* 1 (1984): 111-22.

———. "Importance of the History of Ideas in Latin America." *Journal of the History of Ideas* 36 (1975): 177-84.

———. "Antropología positivista en América Latina." *Cuadernos Americanos* 33 (1974): 93-106.

———, ed. *Risieri Frondizi. Ensayos filosóficos.* Mexico: Fondo de Cultura Económica, 1986.

Gracia, Jorge J. E., Eduardo Rabossi, Enrique Villanueva, y Marcelo Dascal, eds. *El analisis filosófico en America Latina.* Mexico: Fondo de Cultura Económica, 1985.

———, eds. *Philosophical Analysis in Latin America.* Dordrecht: Reidel, 1984.

Gracia, Jorge J. E., and Iván Jaksić. "The Problem of Philosophical Identity in Latin America." *InterAmerican Review of Bibliography* 34 (1984): 53-71.

Handbook of Latin American Studies. Washington, D.C.: Hispanic Foundation, 1936-; since 1939 a separate section on Latin American philosophy has been added. Prepared by R. Frondizi, A. Sánchez Reulet, and more recently by Carlos Torchia Estrada.

Hershey, John. "Recent Latin-American Philosophy." *Philosophy and Phenomenological Research* 13 (1952-53): 128-31.

Höllhuber, Ivo. *Geschichte der Philosophie im spanischen Kulturbereich.* Munich: E. Reinhardt Verlag, 1967.

Index to Latin American Periodical Literature (1929-60). 8 vols. Washington, D.C.: Unión Panamericana, 1962.

Indice general de publicaciones periódicas latinoamericanas; humanidades y ciencias sociales. Metuchen, N.J.: Scarecrow, 1961-.

Insúa Rodríguez, Ramón. *Historia de la filosofía en Hispanoamérica.* Guayaquil: Universidad de Guayaquil, 1945; 2d ed., 1949.

Inter-American Intellectual Interchange. Austin, Tex.: University of Texas, 1943.

Jacobini, H. B., *A Study of the Philosophy of International Law as Seen in Works of Latin American Writers.* The Hague: Martinus Nijhoff, 1954.

Jornadas Universitarias de Humanidades Vol. 2. Mendoza: Universidad Nacional de Cuyo, 1964.

Jorrín, Miguel, y John D. Martz. *Latin American Political Thought and Ideology.* Chapel Hill: The University of North Carolina Press, 1970.

Kempff Mercado, Manfredo. *Historia de la filosofía en Latinoamérica.* Santiago: Zig Zag, 1958.

Kilgore, William J. "The Development of Positivism in Latin America." *Revista Interamericana de Bibliografía* 19 (1969): 133-45.

Kunz, Josef L. *Latin American Philosophy of Law in the Twentieth Century.* New York: Inter-American Law Institute, 1950.

Larroyo, Francisco, y Edmundo Escobar. *Historia de las doctrinas filosóficas en Latinoamérica.* Mexico: Porrúa, 1968.

Larroyo, Francisco. *Tipos históricos de filosofar en América.* Mexico: Universidad Nacional Autónoma de México, 1959.

———. *La filosofía americana: su razón y su sinrazón de ser.* Mexico: Universidad Nacional Autónoma de México, 1958.

Lasalle, Edmundo. *Philosophic Thought in Latin America; A Partial Bibliography.* Washington, D.C.: Pan American Union, 1941.

Latin American Legal Philosophy. Cambridge, Mass.: Harvard University, 1948; contains translations of the following: L. Recaséns Siches, *Vida humana, sociedad y derecho,* 7-341; Carlos Cossio, *Fenomenología de la decisión,* 345-400; J. Llambías de Azevedo, *Eidética y aporética del derecho,* 403-58; E. García Máynez, *El problema filosófico-jurídico de la validez del derecho,* 461-512; *La libertad como derecho y como poder,* 515-47.

Liebman, Seymour B. *Exploring the Latin American Mind.* Chicago: Nelson-Hall, 1976.

Liss, Sheldon B., and Peggy K. Liss, eds. *Man, State and Society in Latin American History.* New York: Praeger Publishers, 1972.

Martí, Oscar. "Is There a Latin American Philosophy?" *Metaphilosophy* 14 (1983): 46-52.

Mayz Vallenilla, Ernesto. *Latinoamérica en la encrucijada de la técnica.* Caracas: Universidad Simón Bolívar, 1976.

———. *El problema de América.* Caracas: Universidad Central, 1959; 2d ed., 1969.

Miliani, Domingo. "Utopian Socialism, Transitional Thread from Romanticism to Positivism in Latin America." *Journal of the History of Ideas* 24 (1963): 523-38.

Miró Quesada, Francisco. *El problema de la filosofía latinoamericana.* Mexico: Fondo de Cultura Económica, 1976.

———. *Despertar y proyecto del filosofar latinoamericano.* Mexico: Fondo de Cultura Económica, 1974.

———. "The Impact of Metaphysics on Latin American Ideology." *Journal of the History of Ideas* 29 (1963): 539-52.

Nicol, Eduardo. *El problema de la filosofía hispánica.* Madrid: Editorial Tecnos, 1961.

Pérez Marchand, Monelisa. "A Critical Study of Some Currents of Contemporary Philosophical Thought in Latin America." Unpublished M.A. thesis, Johns Hopkins University, 1940.

Primer symposium iberoamericano de filosofía. Edited by Ernesto Cinchilla Aguilar, Vincente Díaz Samayoa, and Virgilio Rodríguez Beteta. Guatemala: Editorial del Ministerio de Educación Publica, 1961.

Recaséns Siches, Luis. "Juridical Axiology in Ibero-America." *Natural Law Forum* 3, no. 1: 35-169.

Revista Portuguesa de Filosofia 17 (1961); issue dedicated to Latin American philosophy.

Redmond, Walter B. *Bibliography of the Philosophy in the Iberian Colonies of America.* The Hague: Nijhoff, 1972.

Ripoll, Carlos. *Conciencia intelectual de América. Antología del ensayo hispanoamericano.* New York: Eliseo Torres, 1974.

Roig, Arturo Andrés. *Filosofía, universidad y filósofos de América Latina.* Mexico: Universidad Nacional Autónoma de México, 1981.

———. *Teoría y crítica del pensamiento latinoamericano.* Mexico: Fondo de Cultura Económica, 1981.

———. *Sobre el tratamiento de filosofar e ideologías dentro de una historia del pensamiento latinoamericano.* Santa Fe: Centro de Divulgación "Colegio Mayor Santa Fe," 1973.

Romero, Francisco. *Sobre la filosofía en América.* Buenos Aires: Raigal, 1952.

———. "Tendencias contemporáneas en el pensamiento hispanoamericano." *Philosophy and Phenomenological Research* 4 (1943): 127-34.

Salazar Bondy, Augusto. *¿Existe una filosofía de nuestra América?* Mexico: Siglo XX, 1968.

Sambarino, Mario. *Identidad, tradición, autenticidad: tres problemas de América Latina.* Caracas: Centro de Estudios Latinoamericanos Rómulo Gallegos, 1980.

Sánchez Reulet, Aníbal, ed. *Contemporary Latin American Philosophy; A Selection.* Albuquerque, N.M.: University of New Mexico Press, 1954. Translated by W. R. Trask from *La filosofía latinoamericana contemporánea.* Washington, D.C.: Pan American Union, 1949.

Sarti, Sergio. *Panorama della filosofia ispanoamericana contemporanea.* Milano: Cisalpino-Golliardica, 1976.

Schwartzmann, Félix. *El sentimiento de la humano en América.* 2 vols. Santiago de Chile: Editorial Universitaria, 1950.

Second Inter-American Congress of Philosophy, (Dec., 1947, Columbia University), in *Philosophy and Phenomenological Research* 9 (1949): 345-626. Most papers are in English. There are essays by Vasconcelos, Fatone, Romero, Zea, Frondizi, and others.

Seventh Inter-American Congress of Philosophy. Quebec: Université Laval, 1967.

Soler, Ricaurte. *Estudios sobre la historia de las ideas en América.* Panamá: Imprenta Nacional, 1961.

Stabb, Martin S. *In Quest of Identity: Patterns in the Spanish-American Essay of Ideas, 1860-1960.* Chapel Hill: University of North Carolina Press, 1967.

Symposium Iberamericano de Filosofía. Vol. 1. Guatemala: Ministerio de Educación Publíca, 1961.

Valle, Rafael Heliodoro. *Historia de las ideas contemporáneas en Centroamérica.* Mexico: Fondo de Cultura Económica, 1960.

Villegas, Abelardo. *Antología del pensamiento social y político de América Latina.* Washington, D.C.: Unión Panamericana, 1964.

———. *Panorama de la filosofía iberoamericana actual.* Buenos Aires: EUDEBA, 1963.

Wagley, Charles. *The Latin American Tradition: Essays on the Unity and Diversity of Latin American Culture.* New York: Columbia University Press, 1968.

Wagner de Reyna, Alberto. *La filosofía en Iberoamérica.* Lima: Sta. María, 1949.

Williams, Edward J. *Latin American Political Thought: A Developmental Perspective.* Tucson: The University of Arizona Press, 1974.

Zea, Leopoldo. *El pensamiento latinoamericano.* Barcelona: Ariel, 1976.

———. *Filosofía y cultura latinoamericanas.* Caracas: Centro de Estudios Latinoamericanos Rómulo Gallegos, 1976.

———. *La filosofía americana como filosofía sin más.* Mexico: Siglo XXI, 1969.

———. *Antología de la filosofía americana contemporánea.* Mexico: Costa Amic, 1968.

———. *The Latin American Mind.* Norman, Okla.: University of Oklahoma, 1963. Translated by J. H. Abbot and L. Dunham from *Dos etapas del pensamiento en Hispanoamérica: del romanticismo al positivismo.* Mexico: Colegio de México, 1949.

———. "History of Ideas in Latin America: Recent Works." *Journal of the History of Ideas* 20 (1959): 596-600.

Zea, Leopoldo. "Contemporary Latin American Philosophy." In *Philosophy in the Mid-Century,* edited by R. Klibansky, 4:218-23. Firenze: La Nuova Italia, 1959.

———. *América en la historia.* Madrid: Revista de Occidente, 1957, 1970.

———. *Esquema para una historia de las ideas en Iberoamérica.* Mexico: Universidad Nacional Autónoma de México, 1956.

———. *América como conciencia.* Mexico: Cuadernos Americanos, 1953.

———. "The Interpretation of the Ibero-American and North American Cultures." *Philosophy and Phenomenological Research* 9 (1948-49): 538-44.